THE DERRYDALE PRESS
TREASURY
OF FOXHUNTING

EDITED BY NORMAN FINE

For Jody and Barbara,
With sincere thanks for your
friendship, your hospitality, and the gift
of a wonderful day with your hounds.
Warmest regards,
Norm Fine

THE DERRYDALE PRESS
Lanham and New York

THE DERRYDALE PRESS

Published in the United States of America
by The Derrydale Press
An imprint of The Rowman & Littlefield Publishing Group
4501 Forbes Boulevard, Suite 200, Lanham, Maryland 20706

Distributed by NATIONAL BOOK NETWORK, INC.

British Library Cataloguing in Publication Information Available

Library of Congress Cataloging-in-Publication Data

The Derrydale Press treasury of foxhunting / [compiled by] Norman Fine.
    p. cm.
Includes bibliographical references (p.).
  ISBN 1-58667-100-6 (hardcover : alk. paper)
  1. Fox hunting. 2. Fox hunting—Fiction. I. Fine, Norman M. II.
Title.
  SK285.D45 2003
  799.2'59775—dc21

2003009938

∞™ The paper used in this publication meets the minimum requirements of
American National Standard for Information Sciences—Permanence of
Paper for Printed Library Materials, ANSI/NISO Z39.48-1992.
Manufactured in the United States of America.

CONTENTS

ACKNOWLEDGMENTS

A great measure of appreciation is due the friendly and helpful staff of the National Sporting Library in Middleburg, Virginia. Special thanks to Rob Weber, the librarian, who directed me to the many hiding places of the old Derrydales; who, on many occasions, had the needed books stacked and ready before I arrived; and who cheerfully photocopied many of the selections for me from the fragile and valuable old volumes. Lisa Campbell refreshed my memory on what's where in the library stacks, and allowed me access in the rare book room. Walta Warren inducted me into the mysteries of the library's computerized author/title catalog and always had an encouraging smile of welcome. And a special thanks to my dear friend, the late Alexander Mackay-Smith, for conceiving this splendid resource.

I also want to thank my publisher, Jed Lyons, president of the Rowman and Littlefield Publishing Group of which The Derrydale Press is one imprint. Jed brought the respected but moribund Derrydale Press back to life not because it was a wise business decision (it wasn't), but because he's a foxhunter and a sportsman and he believes in the enduring value of the printed word.

Finally, I thank my wife, Joan, the editor's editor, for her ever ready and cheerful willingness to help me in my projects.

INTRODUCTION

This *Treasury* includes many personal long-time favorites, and also many with which I was unfamiliar until commencing the pleasant task of exploring the old Derrydale mines for gold. The result is, I hope, a balanced offering of fiction, fact, intriguing histories, humor, and pathos. I guarantee there is something here for every sportsman or woman whose heart has ever been moved by the depth of devotion of a special hound, the generosity of an extraordinary horse, the gameness of a straight-necked fox.

In considering sources for this *Treasury*, I decided to limit my selections to the early Derrydales, published by the Press's founder, Eugene V. Connett, III (1891–1969). While I am immensely proud of the contemporary work we have published over the past four years under the umbrella of The Derrydale Press Foxhunters' Library, I felt that the collection in this volume should hark back to the original sources of classic, rare, and mostly out-of-print works that established The Derrydale Press as the preeminent sporting publisher of the first half of the twentieth century.

It is my strong belief that a vigorous body of literature is as important to an enduring sporting culture as is the very practice of the sport. It is the literature that records foxhunting's history; captures for all time the genius of the great breeders and huntsmen; and carries on, for all to absorb, the unbroken thread of sportsmanship and tradition, without which foxhunting would be so much the poorer. It was Connett's Derrydale Press that nurtured and provided an outlet for the talents of the premier writers and artists of its time.

For these reasons, foxhunting owes a major debt of gratitude to Eugene Connett, who, in 1927, founded The Derrydale Press. For the next fourteen years, Connett and his press single-handedly created the first American body of literature on field sports—shooting, angling, riding, and foxhunting. Nor were Connett's publishing activities limited to literature. He also promoted the talents and reputations of the best American sporting artists of the period by publishing limited editions of their paintings in hand-colored aquatints and employing their services to illustrate his books.

Included in this *Treasury* are works that must be considered classics today by any definition of the term. Readers will feast on examples of the best of David Gray, Somerville and Ross, Gordon Grand, Joseph B. Thomas, J. Blan van Urk, and others. Also reproduced are many of the wonderful illustrations by Paul Brown, Eleanor Iselin Mason, Edith Somerville, J. Alden Twachtman, and other distinguished artists.

Part I of this *Treasury* is devoted to the three animals that form the triumvirate of organized foxhunting—fox, hound, and horse. In "Dedication," from *Hounds and Hunting Through the Ages*, Joseph B. Thomas offers a lesson in living to his son by examining the virtues and vices of the foxhound—honesty, sagacity, determination, drive, skirting, babbling and dwelling—and relating those traits to the human character. Thomas's book, first published in 1928, was the first comprehensive book on hunting with hounds written by an American. It proved to be one of Derrydale's best-selling titles.

Boston-born Joseph B. Thomas followed a career in architecture in New York and became M.F.H. of the Piedmont Fox Hounds in 1915. Four years later, in a controversy with Dan Sands, M.F.H. of the Middleburg Hunt, Thomas resigned from the Piedmont and established his own pack, Mr. Thomas's Hounds in nearby Ashby Gap in the Blue Ridge Mountains. There he began a program of hound breeding on a prodigious scale and was able to provide entire packs of entered hounds to newly formed hunts. His influence on the American foxhound was enormous, and his bloodlines still thrive in the Piedmont pack and in many of the American and Crossbred packs across the country.

The selection titled "No Fleas on this Fox" from J. Blan van Urk's *The Story of American Foxhunting* should forever define "cleverness" as relates to that most respected woodland creature. Also included in Part I is van Urk's treatment of Mountain and Muse, the famous but unruly Irish foxhounds brought to Maryland in 1814. The prepotent bloodlines of Mountain and Muse are present today in most of the principal American foxhound strains—July, Henry, Birdsong, Trigg, Bywaters, and Walker.

"Martha Doyle" from Richard E. Danielson's book by the same name is a true and heartwarming horse story. From the other end of the spectrum comes "Legend of the Hounds." Fair warning: don't read this tale of horror before bedtime!

Three selections are offered in **Part II: Hunting Humor**. Each is brilliantly written and unusual. *The Epping Hunt* by Thomas Hood, Esq. is a fun-filled epic poem as rhythmic as the footfalls of a bold horse's walk. It was originally published in London in 1829 and relates the hunting adventure of the stolid tradesman, John Huggins, retailer of dairy and sausage products. Could John Huggins have been the inspiration for Surtees's John Jorrocks? I think it likely. The following stanza—

> For all the live-long day before,
> And all the night in bed,
> Like Beckford, he had nourish'd "Thoughts
> On Hunting" in his head.

—struck me upon realizing that it was written no more than twenty years after Beckford's death. To us, Beckford has always been a figure from ancient foxhunting history. To Thomas Hood, Beckford was practically a contemporary, commanding the same respect and recognition then as now.

When it comes to David Gray's "Mr. Carteret and His Fellow Americans Abroad," if I read it once I have surely read it a half dozen times; yet even when I know what's coming the hilarious images conjured up by Gray cause me to burst out uncontrollably. The story takes place just before the turn of the twentieth century. Mr. Carteret is on a hunting visit to England. The conversation turns to the Wild West show in London and the riding abilities of the Indians on their ponies:

> Major Hammerslea [author of *Schooling and Riding British Hunters*] reached toward the tea table for another muffin and hemmed. "It is one thing, my dear Madame, to ride a stunted, half-starved pony, as you say, 'bareback,' and another thing to ride a conditioned British hunter (he pronounced it huntaw) without a saddle. I must say that the latter is an impossibility."

Lord Frederic, "an enthusiastic, simple-minded fellow," is unconvinced. He has a "topping idea":
"Let's have them down and take them hunting!"
I don't believe there is a funnier story in all of foxhunting literature.

I hope my selections from *Young Entry*, the third and last in the Hunting Humor category, will convey at least some inkling of Gordon Grand's rollicking narrative, written in a series of letters—progress reports, really—from Eddie Walsh, the groom, to his employer, John Weatherford, M.F.H. of the Millbeck Hounds in New York state. Walsh has been sent with three ponies to Weatherford's unmarried sister's house in Dorchester, Massachusetts, to teach their three young wards, the orphaned children of their younger brother, to ride and to hunt. Weatherford knows that these important aspects of the children's education would be ignored by his sister. Finding no hounds in Miss Weatherford's country, Walsh, a hunting man through and through, has an inspiration. With three terriers as the pack, he organizes the children into forming the South Dorchester Rat Hounds. Events and adventures progress rapidly from there.

Part III: Stories will appeal to fiction lovers. Here are examples of some of the best foxhunting fiction written in the first half of the twentieth century: David Gray, Somerville and Ross, Gordon Grand, and the others. From the second book in David Gray's trilogy—*Gallops I*, *Gallops II*, and *Mr. Carteret*—"Ting-a-Ling" is the bittersweet story of a horse that is rescued from the shafts of an overburdened horse-drawn streetcar in New England for a new career as a field hunter and timber horse in the Genesee Valley of New York. Although the story is fiction, Ting-a-Ling *was* a real horse actually rescued from streetcar service by the legendary Harry Worcester Smith.

I have included two selections from Somerville and Ross, whose books my wife, Joan, and I were introduced to more than thirty years ago by our Irish hunting hostess, the late Lady Mollie Cusack-Smith. When Lady Mollie discovered our ignorance of the works of her countrywomen, she immediately telephoned her bookseller in Dublin and ordered them to put Somerville and Ross's two Irish R.M. (Resident Magistrate) books on the first train to Galway for us.

In 1927, Derrydale's first year, Connett republished *Some Experiences of an Irish R.M.* and *Further Experiences of an Irish R.M.* as a single volume, along with five other Somerville and Ross books. Without those two books, later made the subject of a special British television series broadcast here by PBS, I know my total foxhunting experience would be sorely wanting.

"Philippa's Fox-Hunt" takes place shortly after her arrival in Ireland from England as the newly-married Mrs. Sinclair Yeates. Philippa's husband, Major Yeates, a stuffy but likeable Englishman, after accepting his appointment as the new Resident Magistrate for Skebawn, precedes her to Ireland to take up his duties and to find an appropriate house to lease.

> Finding a house had been easy enough. I had my choice of several, each with some hundreds of acres of shooting, thoroughly poached, and a considerable portion of the roof intact.

And later:

> My landlord was there on horseback, and with him was a man standing at the head of a stout grey animal. I recognised with despair that I was about to be compelled to buy a horse.

Handily manipulated by the residents of Skebawn, Major Yeates leases a house that conceals, as he eventually discovers, his landlord's cousins living in its furthest hidden recesses. Adding insult to injury, he discovers the squatters in possession of a case of his favorite Scotch whisky.

Somerville and Ross were highly unusual women for their period, feminists in fact. Because their mothers insisted that well brought up young ladies could not consider writing for publication and, heaven forbid, money, the two women sent their manuscripts off under the pen-names, "E.Œ. Somerville and Martin Ross." The former was Edith Œnone Somerville, who had the distinction to become the first woman M.F.H. in Ireland; the latter was Edith's second cousin, Violet Martin of Ross. The pair met in their late twenties, began collaborating on their first novel, *An Irish Cousin* (published 1889), very soon thereafter, and became true soul mates for life. A total of twenty-nine books were published under their names.

Gordon Grand is probably the best-known American writer of foxhunting fiction. For him, writing was a part-time activity, however. In real life, Grand was a lawyer who later became president of a New York utility. He wrote his first hunting story to pass the time while on a trans-Atlantic voyage. It was published by *The Sportsman* magazine, the editor of which was Richard Danielson, author of "Martha Doyle," included in Part I of this *Treasury*. Connett took notice of Grand's work and persuaded him to write stories for a book. Grand's first book was *The Silver Horn*, published in 1932. The wonderful story from which the book took its title is included in this *Treasury*.

Gordon Grand hunted with the Millbrook Hunt in New York state, hence the Millbeck Hunt in his stories. Some believe that Grand's main character, the crusty but fair-minded consummate gentleman, Colonel Weatherford, is a composite of Frederic H. Bontecou and Dr. Howard Collins, joint-M.F.H.s of Millbrook at the time.

Finally, in **Part IV** are reproduced a variety of interesting and unusual historical selections from J. Blan van Urk's monumental two-volume history, *The Story of American Foxhunting*. These include some American firsts: "The First M.F.H."; "The First Organized Hunt"; "The First Foxhound Studbook."

Van Urk's and Connett's original plan was to publish *The Story of American Foxhunting* in one volume. However, according to Connett's "Publisher Notes" in Volume I, it was soon apparent that two volumes would be necessary due to the "unsuspected abundance of material" uncovered. Then the estimate was increased to four volumes! Volume I, published in 1940, covers the period 1650 to 1861. Volume II, published in 1941, covers the period 1865 to 1906.

Volume II grew to the extent that almost four hundred pages of manuscript notes and drafts of hunt histories intended for inclusion into that volume had to be held over for the planned, but never published, Volume III. What a pity that Connett closed down Derrydale in 1941, and the series was not completed. This tale has an encouraging ending, however.

While it was feared that, after van Urk's death in 1998, those manuscript notes and drafts were destroyed, they did surface in the possession of James Cummins, the New York antiquarian bookseller. They were purchased, then donated to the National Sporting Library in Middleburg, Virginia. Today, van Urk's notes and drafts are in the literate hands of James L. Young, M.F.H. of the Orange County Hunt, who is in the process of completing the mammoth undertaking and bringing *The Story of American Foxhunting* up to the twenty-first century. When Young's work is finished, Derrydale will be able to complete, finally, its publication of the now 350-year history of American foxhunting.

PART I
FOXES, HOUNDS, AND HORSES

ONE

DEDICATION

Joseph B. Thomas, M.F.H.

My dear Boy:

When you were a tiny baby, Mary, your old nurse, most often lulled you to sleep by singing in a minor key the old Irish hunting-song:

> *Hark Tally Ho! Hark Tally Ho!*
> *Hark Tally Ho! We'll chase him*
> *Hark Tally Ho! before we go*
> *We'll surely kill or earth him.*
>
> *Hark! Fifer, Fiddler, Jonah,*
> *Giggler, Dido, Fanny, Farmer,*
> *Spanker, Spoker, Tanker, Joker,*
> *Gaylass, Miller, Ranger.*

This song together with the hunting scenes painted on your crib and the walls of your room by your mother had you well "entered" to hunting atmosphere before you could toddle. Later, you were wont to see your mother and daddy go a-hunting, sometimes on foot with beagles, more often ahorse with foxhounds. The poignant smell of the saddle room with its shining steel, the furious scourings of cleaning rooms, the "doing" of scarlet coats, the glint of top hats as they passed the vigilant eye of Albert Alabaster, the arts of horse and hound management as practiced by James Stuart and Charlie Carver, not forgetting the admonitions of Frank Stuart in the hunting of "Banker," your first beagle; in short, the entire machinery of the chase has been an open book to you from infancy. Regarding riding whips, do you remember when I took a whip to school and asked Mr. Manders to use it on you if you were not as keen at your lessons as you were at shouting, "Gone away!" A puppy that does not stick to the line, or runs riot, is not much use, is he?

Sometimes, you must wonder why your forebears and so many of their friends apparently have gone mad about hunting; so, my boy, I shall try to tell you all I can about it, that you may profit just a little from what the "old man" has gleaned during the ups and downs of his hunting experience, and then apply or correct the observations.

Many hunt, but few have knowledge of hounds,—the reason for this, the history of that; hence without such knowledge, they lose much pleasure. If you really study all phases of hunting in its historical background, the game, the hounds, the horses, you will attain a life-long mental resource, and will thus enhance your knowledge of literature, art, and history.

In hunting, there is much more than mere beauty to enchant the eye or promote the physical exhilaration of perfect enjoyment. There is, above all, the lesson to be learned from qualities so necessary in the first-class hound, qualities which are also so essential in the first-class man:

Honesty—Sagacity—Determination—Drive.

Adversely, there are certain hound vices from which you should take warning, to wit,—

Skirting (philandering)—Babbling—Dwelling (dawdling).

Astute observation of hunting technique should tend to form a firm foundation to help you face your personal as well as the more serious problems of the modern industrial world with its chaotic struggle.

Men, especially in America, are prone to imagine that machinery, invention, efficiency systems, are about to free them from all drudgery and care, and make it possible for them to conquer the earth and all it has to offer. There is, perhaps, a danger that without proper counter spiritual influence, such as the love of the beautiful in nature derived from contact with God's green fields and woods, each new invention, instead of making man more free, is in reality enslaving him by mechanizing his very soul.

Individuality today is, perhaps, in a measure becoming atrophied by stereotyped enjoyments. In the maelstrom of so-called progress, many men play the part of submissive individuals. A human being wholly under the influence of modern industry is in danger of losing qualities of initiative, judgment, certain fundamental instincts of moral and physical courage, and the capacity for appreciation of much that is delightful in life. The hunting field should help maintain the proper balance between man and machine, between business routine and the physical freedom of primitive living.

The general technique of the chase, and the human qualities necessary for its successful pursuit, have changed little during the ages. It still demands the same courage, horsemanship, and a proper understanding of nature and animals as it did when practiced by our remote ancestors. The thrill today of a mounted pageant flashing across a delightful country, the cry of hounds ahead, a blue sky above, is the same thrill that made the great Charlemagne, over a thousand years ago, alternate the governing of an immense empire with weeks in the hunting field.

Dear Boy, I hope a clear understanding and love of the chase may always be a source of increasing interest and a refuge to you, as it has been to me.

Your affectionate,
FATHER.

TWO

NO FLEAS ON THIS FOX

J. Blan van Urk

To indicate the fox's native intelligence and ability to figure things out for himself, we need only cite his approach to a few personal problems. For example, the method he adopts to get rid of fleas:

Taking in his mouth a tuft of wool or a piece of wood, a fox will slowly sink himself, tail first, into a pond and thus gradually drive the fleas forward until the last refuge is the wool or wood on the surface of the water. The fox then sets this adrift teeming with the parasites, and keeping clear of it lands on the bank and makes off.

This bit of scientific knowledge comes from no less an authority than Reginald Innes Pocock, *F.L.S., F.Z.S., F.R.A.I., F.R.S.*, Natural History Editor of *The Field* and assistant of the Zoological Department of the British Museum.

For additional proof we have accounts[1] of eyewitnesses in this country, who have come forth to tell what they have seen:

While in the woods recently, I came to an old sawmill dam. I heard a rustling in the leaves, and keeping quite still, I saw a Red-fox come up to the water with a piece of pine bark in his mouth. He waded into the water, so I could see only his nose, or the piece of bark sticking out. He stayed that way for about five minutes, then dropped the bark in the water, scampered out and ran back into the woods. I examined the bark and found it covered with fleas.[2]

Another interesting report states:

Some weeks ago, while fishing in the State of Pennsylvania, a Red-fox came out from the edge of the woods into a cornfield. He put his front feet up on the side of a shock of corn and looked as though he was eating corn, but a little closer watching showed he was pulling out cornsilk from the end of the ears. After he got a mouthful of this cornsilk about the size of a man's fist, he started for the stream and, stepping very carefully to the edge of a nice, placid pool, he started to back into the water with his tail first, going very slowly until only his nose and cornsilk appeared above the surface. He then ducked his head under the water and let the cornsilk float. He came up, swam to the other shore, climbed up on the bank, shook the water off and started off in a fox-trot for parts unknown. In getting the floating corn-silk with a long stick to examine it, I found it full of lice, and could see it was a plain case of the lice keeping just ahead of the water, running up his back, then from his nose into the cornsilk to escape getting wet. A friend and I experimented with some Dogs a few days after. The Dogs had fleas, and we used cotton and tubs of water, and, by dipping the Dogs in very slowly, the fleas would run up their backs and jump into the cotton held at the tip of the Dog's nose. Surely the Fox has intelligence.[3]

And how right this gentleman is! How many animals, domestic or otherwise, can match this display of acumen and wisdom? Surely man's slave and companion, the house pet, with all its understanding and adaptability, does nothing comparable.

Notes

1. One account of this flea-ridding trick appears in *The American Field,* June 6, 1896, p. 533.
2. *Recreation,* June 1898, p. 476.
3. *Field and Stream,* March 1921, pp. 1004, 1030.

THREE

THE HUNTERS

Samuel J. Henry

The hoot of an owl and a fox drinking at the water's edge, twittering birds in the willows and a burnt-orange sun sinking beyond the hill. The Red One had just come out of his den on Moccasin Creek that flows in to the Upper Rappahannock, when I came upon him. Sounds of my approach evidently had not reached him, and I stood frozen like setter on quail for fear I might disturb him. The observation of wild creatures in their native environment has ever been a source of pleasure and amazement, and the close proximity of the crafty creature gave me an exceptional thrill.

Nature's fox, the Red One—lean and knowing. His fluffy brush appeared out of proportion to his thin body which, high off the ground, was supported by supple, if spindly, legs. Fortunately only a riffle of wind stirred; the man taint did not assail his sensitive nose, and when he had satisfied his thirst he leaped on a moss-covered log, where tilting his muzzle skyward he sniffed the frosty air.

Overhead in the trees that lined the creek, restless birds settling down for the night eyed the Red One nervously, but he paid no attention to them, and jumping from the log, slowly walked off, his figure as he topped the ridge forming an unforgettable silhouette against the reddened sky. In an adjacent wood an owl hooted.

For men the day was done. But for Reynard there was work ahead—the interminable search for food. I knew that in this questing he would trace an eccentric pattern through the countryside, and if game happened to be scarce or wary in the neighborhood, his hunger would take him to distant parts before returning to his sanctuary.

Query: What becomes of all the earth which the fox excavates from his den? That which is strewn about the entrance being obviously only a portion, where is the remainder? Hunters have pondered the mystery and are without a satisfactory solution.

just out of den

crows

Paul Brown '30   *now or never*

"Now or Never," Paul Brown

November nights settle down early, and in the thickening gloom the Red One gets his first whiff of the whereabouts of game. As he pauses to orient its location he hears the faintest whir of wings, feels a delicate caress of air followed by sounds of a scuffle, and then only a few yards distant an enormous owl rises clutching a struggling rabbit. The feathery raider alights on a stout limb and fixing the still conscious body of his victim firmly between his powerful talons, proceeds to feast greedily on chunks of bloody flesh.

Well, it's just one of those things, this losing a meal. Being a philosopher, the disappointed fox knows that Nature is neither for nor against him—only indifferent—and if he does not eat today he will feast tomorrow, that everything comes to him who hunts—food for the bold and heaven for the virtuous.

The night air carries a multitude of odors—skunks, weasels, muskrats—their vileness offends the Red One. Where there is food there is game, and where there is game there are killers. Without reward the fox stalks the Lilliputian runways whereon raiding field mice transport garnered grain. He crouches patiently at the entrance to their underground snuggeries hoping to catch them going or coming, but cunning as any fox, they have provided multiple doorways. Is not a mouse with one hole soon caught?

The fox crosses trails of coon and possum; the former is more than his match, while the latter only appears on the menu of hunter *africanus* and, when roasted, is the equivalent of the succulent shoat.

Midnight comes and still nothing to eat. A half-moon hangs low over the eastern horizon, stars appear startlingly near, and the dipper displays its unvarying form while the pale northern beacon—"unshaked of motion"—holds its fixed position.

Stealthily the old red creeps through patches of dry broom sage. He is disappointed in not scenting quail. Bunched together they slumber hereabouts on the ground, tail to tail, all primed for a quick getaway. Frog and crawfish, cricket and grasshopper are no longer abroad—frost has seen to that.

Thirst assails the fox, for he has put forth continuous exertion and covered many miles. He laps daintily, but not in the waters of Moccasin Creek.

Dawn comes and the sun that saw him fourteen hours ago leave his den keen but hungry, now finds him leg weary and famished. Yet foxes must eat, and so far as he is concerned he is going to eat. Squirrels peep from their lofty nests and, proceeding head down on treesides, begin the search for nuts and acorns, not being averse to rifling cornshocks. Scanning earth and sky for furry or feathery victim, a piratical hawk sweeps through the woods. Hungry, like the fox, several crows appear and set up a fearful clamor. The sable birds, finding an intruder on their feeding grounds, order him to move on. They wish to alight and, tossing aside layers of forest moss, feed on juicy worms and grubs.

The Red One craves quiet. He slinks into a thicket and lies down on the dry leaves, feigning a sleep which an iron will forbids. Foxes are anathema to crows and more noisy than ever, they complain bitterly. Reynard, however, remains concealed. He wears the crows out and eventually they take wing, not to land within a mile.

With eyes, ears and nose as allies of an aching stomach, the hunter emerges from his retreat. Now comes an odor which he has sought the entire night. It is so intriguing that he begins to drool and drops of saliva fall from his tongue. Soon his spotless white chest is wringing wet. Without disturbing a twig, the Red One creeps off, not in the direction from whence the scent emanates, but wide to the left. He knows from the nature of the effluvia that the game are on the ground, and judging by the conflicting sources, there are many of them.

The fox ignores a rabbit which springs up in front of him—he is not interested in second-rate food. Ordinarily, however, he could not see a hare without going after it.

The hungry hunter, well-concealed, circles round and round before he decides to have a look. What he beholds constitutes a heavenly view. Quite unconscious of danger, a covey of quail are feeding on the tasty and satisfying fruit of weed and bush. Some with seed-filled craws bask in the warmth of an Indian summer's sun; if only the earth were a bit softer a dust bath would be in order. Many are last summer's chicks which while now full grown, have much to learn—fox raids and shotguns, setters and hawks are unknown to them. A year hence, if surviving, they will be vastly more suspicious.

As the Red One gazes on his victims covetously he notes a significant maneuver—a few birds are restlessly retiring beneath the scrubby trees that skirt the clearing. While the fox sees or hears nothing to disturb them, he instinctively feels that the time has arrived to strike. The owl-hare episode recurs to him. Almost melted into the ground, and showing only one-fourth of his body, he creeps forward. Suddenly a shadow flashes across the earth, whereupon the covey exhibit the wildest alarm. Some, paralyzed, crouch close to the ground, camouflaged except to penetrating eyes, others run to cover, but the *whir-r-r* of flight is not heard. Striking with lightning speed, the hawk swoops down, clutches a cowering bird in his talons, and disappears. If there had been a dozen hawks, they would have found awaiting them as many victims helpless with fear.

The Red One, realizing it is now or never, dashes forward and, grasping a pair of the luscious beauties, retreats to his erstwhile shelter where, a cosmopolitan *bon vivant,* he once more reclines on the sweet-smelling leaves, this time to feast generously and sleep dreamlessly with no crows to pester him, no yesterdays and no tomorrows.

FOUR

THE HOUNDS

Frederick Watson

Modern hunting people are rather prejudiced against the hounds because they are so apt to get under horses' feet when they are jumping fences or in full gallop over wheat. But tradition is tradition, and every pack of any standing maintains a few hounds for Peterborough, and the Puppy Show, and to go about with the huntsman when he passes the village inns. Always remember hounds are counted in couple. It is important to mention this as sometimes you hear it said the huntsman must have had a couple. That refers to his duties.

In the good old days before huntsmen knew so much and rode so fast the hounds were expected to find their fox and hunt him too. As no one knew the exact spot where a fox might be it was customary while the hounds were busied about their duties for the Hunt staff and the members of the Field to combat the inclement weather within a tavern. Now it is quite obvious, when the hounds push up their fox that unless they let the huntsman know, there would be disappointment all around. So it was absolutely essential that every hound possessed a resonant, carrying, long distance call. A secondary but by no means unworthy ambition of every Master was that the music of a pack should harmonize. There might be small hounds with penetrating sopranos or huge hounds with reverberating basses or medium hounds with throaty tenors. But harmonize they must. So in old records you may still see if you can find any (which we must admit we have failed to do) Master thanking Providence that he can trace back his eminent mezzocontralto Plaintive to that great basso-profoundo Quorn Caroller.

Only in Wales today does this reverence for hound music survive. Why is that? This is the first time the truth has been revealed. It is entirely due to the national weakness for local eistoddfods which are competitions in voice endurance either alone or in parties of resolute friends. In many a lonely cottage all through the winter months grandfather and grandmother, parents, Auntie Rebecca from Bwlch-y-gwlch, and the man who feeds the calves—all of them inflamed with high tea and indigestion—sing without cessation for eight hours by the old kitchen clock that passionate summons "Awake Beloved" to the fine old tune of Aberystwyth. Consequently hound puppies who have been walked in such melodious homes acquire a range of tongue which is never heard with the Bicester. Indeed its practical object has in these modern times quite disappeared. For one thing everyone (even the huntsman) knows just where a fox will be found and in which direction he is bound to run. In fact only very athletic and carefully dieted foxes can hope to keep much ahead of members who are trying out blood horses with an idea of Cheltenham or Aintree. For another in these hard times, when the influence of the City must be scrupulously observed, a mute hound does not make such an infernal rumpus when a large subscriber lands on his stern over a post and rails.

Now about the puppies. A whelp is the innocent with the trustful gaze who is walked by those simple persons who hope they will win the silver cup for the parlor window. A puppy does not become a hound until he has eaten all the hens and killed all the cats at the farm where he is walked, taken his place in the Puppy Show and met the huntsman.

Every Hunt must have a Puppy Show because that is how a Master has his young entry kept and fed and taught incurable habits for nothing. Puppies enter to fox in the cubbing season. As they have hitherto entered to everything else it is quite a new thrill for them. The Puppy Show is held in order that the simpletons who have walked a puppy, or even a couple, may put on their Sunday clothes and realise how much better their puppy looks than the other people's.

Puppies are destructive, expensive, homicidal, and full of sorrow. Fortunately they never live. It is rumoured that some busybody has invented a vaccine which will preserve them from distemper. That is, we suppose, what short-sighted people call progress. Do we speak too strongly? Without a surplus of puppies there will be no puppy walkers and without puppy walkers no Puppy Show. Don't forget that a fifty-to-one chance for a prize, a dish of tea and the Master's speech is about all the farmer's wife gets out of the Hunt. And if the farmer's wife loses interest what then? What indeed! Where's your precious vaccine now?

It is customary at a Puppy Show for the Master to invite two or even three fellow Masters to come over and judge his puppies. With derisive smiles these Masters accept. They arrive and put on kennel coats and have little books and look very knowing indeed. In a ring where all the walkers can see their puppies dragged and propelled about the ring the judging goes on for hours and hours. The only other function comparable to it in length of time, solemnity, and absence of all spiritual or physical compensations is the pibroch playing at a Highland gathering.

After the judging is over the whole party with hosts of members, strangers, farmers, and all their friends troop towards the tea-tent. Here the Master, whose smile has never fluctuated throughout the day, is surrounded by fellow Masters of all kinds—even of beagles and otter hounds—so broken down are social distinctions on that great day.

After tea—with which cold beef and ham may be eaten if the Master can run to it—the prizes are presented. Then come the speeches. These are always given by the same people at every Hunt because it is absolutely essential that the right thing is said every year. After the most coherent visiting Master has congratulated the Hunt on such a fine show of puppies, old Mr. Dumbleday gets up. There is one of his sort in every Hunt. He has retired long enough to forget what farming is really like, or possibly he has lived so long he goes back before the bad times; in any case he has spent an hour with the Hunt Secretary, who writes all the speeches anyhow, for fear they don't stop. Mr. Cracklethorpe, the Field Master's gamekeeper (who either has a fox in the home coverts or makes out his own advertisement for *The Field*) then deprecates the notions of some keepers who blame the fox for their own lack of knowledge. He recalls instances of vixens adopting pheasant poults who had lost their mother (he doesn't say how). There is then a steady old subscriber to express the feelings of the gathering towards the Master. Finally the Master rises and consulting his notes from time to time makes the Master's famous speech.

What now about the hounds?

Well there are hounds and Welsh hounds. The English hound is a depressed looking replica of another English hound. The Welsh hound looks like no other hound nor like a hound at all. It prefers its hair on end, is voracious, and usually lurks in a butcher's shop. But it can kill foxes. In fact it can kill anything. On hunting days in Wales, Secretaries advise farmers to shut up all stock smaller than a Hereford cow. Welsh hounds, through what advanced French scholars call "joie de vivre," will hunt any line from the postman reading the morning mail to the widow's only nanny goat, and they will speak with authority and all together to anything from a weasel to the vicar's Angora rabbits. The Welsh hound is also useful for sheep dog trails in the summer because it keeps him in practice for the riot later on and may even earn a bit in between.

There are harriers and beagles, but no real gentleman knows much about these. The harrier chases a hare in small circles so that members can pull one rein and still maintain the usual grip on the saddle. When the hare crosses the same field for the seventh time, how the farmer cheers and waves his hat. The beagle is smaller and therefore eats less. It is followed quite a long way off by persons of maturity acting under medical advice.

To establish a pack is child's play. The proper procedure is to write a nice boyish letter to some Master—anyone will do—and put yourself in his hands. Explain that you have money but no practical knowledge (because he will reply more quickly then), and that you feel it is cheaper in the end to pay a good figure for really good hounds which will hunt all day and kill foxes all the time and be steady and not eat the sandwiches at the Meets. Don't lose your head if he puts through a long distance call.

The Master will invite you down to his kennels either for the night or for luncheon. (No-one ever sees kennels before a hearty meal.) When he has explained that he has the best pack and huntsman in England you will know your luck is in. But be prepared for a rather trying scene. It happens when the Master tells the huntsman he has decided to part with old Chorister. The huntsman will start back and in a strangled voice exclaim *"Not old Chorister, Sir!"* proving beyond cavil what a one old Chorister must be. Himself considerably moved, the Master will explain. He will say that you are a beginner going to hunt hounds yourself and that Masters must cling together.

You will be surprised when you see old Chorister. He will strike your inexperienced eye as very old, very tired, and extremely deaf. But you will know by his price you must be mistaken. Dreadnought, Captain, Hornet, and Champion will also be yours. As they are all sixth season hounds they have nothing to learn and will in fact teach you far more than you might suspect.

If you pay half a dozen calls like that you will have your pack, and very soon you will know where you are. You will also know where they are. Some will have kennel lameness, and some will only hunt now and again. The rest will follow you about in covert with dog-like devotion or tarry with the Field. Never mind. Console yourself with the thought that *some day you will get a letter too.*

FIVE

SOME THINGS ARE TOO SERIOUS FOR JOKING: POTATOES IS ONE

J. Blan van Urk

The American foxhound attained a high degree of hunting perfection by 1900, but attention had not been, for the most part, directed to conformation. The combination of hunting ability and well-planned and efficient structural qualities was to develop later. For a long time American Masters and foxhunters took a good-natured ribbing from English hound advocates because the native American type lacked in physical appearance the "glamour" of their English cousins. The great English poet, William Somerville, set the pace in describing his impressions of these latter when he wrote:

> On shoulders clean, upright and firm he stands;
> His round cat-foot, straight hams, and wide-spread thighs,
> And his low-dropping chest, confess his speed,
> His strength, his wind, or on the steepy hill,
> Or far-extended plain.

And some 250 years later an American foxhunter paid this tribute to English hound breeders, "There is no animal in the world, not even the horse, that has had such attention paid to its breeding as the foxhound has had in England."[1] But when the American hound needed defending in the not so distant past, students of the native breed usually said something like this, "Yes, the English hound is more standard as to size, symmetry, conformation and beauty of form and style, but the price of all this is nose, speed, endurance and fox sense."[2]

The late Redmond C. Stewart, Esq., beloved Maryland sportsman and Master of the Green Spring Valley Hunt who experimented with cross-breds (English-American), listed four weaknesses which, in his opinion, were likely to be found in imported hounds[3]—particularly those hunted in heavily wooded, hilly, dry and much ploughed American country:

1. A lacking in that far-reaching, bell-like note which constitutes the music so necessary in a heavily-wooded country.
2. The nose, whilst by no means deficient in accuracy, does not possess sufficient "softness" to enable to carry the scent over the plough and thick woodlands.
3. The vital energy and hunting powers are by no means so inherent in the fashionably bred hounds as in those which have been bred for sport alone irrespective of any question of the Show benches.
4. The bone, size and weight of the standard hound are too great for obtaining the maximum amount of work with the minimum amount of wear and tear over such a rough, hilly country.[4]

It took time for even the most conscientious observer to appreciate the importance and value of both the English and American foxhound types, and to be able to differentiate between the requirements, objectives and desires of their respective breeders. This is understandable in view of our human frailty of seldom looking beyond the surface of the things around us to which we are accustomed. I am reminded, along this line, of Dr. Edith Œnone Somerville's delightful glance at THE STATES THROUGH IRISH EYES. While in Virginia she was present at a meet of a famous pack and wrote, in describing the various events:

> But the hounds—?
> I suppose if, stamped on the retina, to reign there, apart, unspotted from the world, there is a definite and well-marked ideal, it is impossible to bring an unbiased mind to a wholly different type of anything. And this applies, supremely, to hounds. So I will offer no opinion on these—to me—so strange and unfamiliar red and yellow creatures, beyond a diffident suggestion that if a red Irish setter were neatly shaved, and the permanent wave obliterated, he might—but, perhaps, it is better to remember the saying that "There are some things too serious for joking, and one of them's potatoes." So it is also with hounds.[5]

But joking apart, occasionally an imported hound looked so similar to the "native" American that he was thought to be a home-bred. Some years ago a prominent present-day M.F.H. purchased a tan (café au lait) hound purported to be an excellent example of a well-known American strain. The hound, known as J.Y., was sold in good faith, and the new owner thought he was getting a specific type of American hound blood. And although this specimen had a scar inside one ear, it looked like the result of torn tissue and was passed over as unimportant until the M.F.H. visited a certain section of Wales. There he saw Fell hounds, and they were almost identical to the hound he had thought American—some of even the same color[6]—and they all had the identifying scar, a uniform tattoo mark, inside their ears.

Incidentally, these Fell hounds are an interesting type of foxhound—standing about twenty-two and a half inches in height, light of bone and frame, with sloping shoulders, oblique pasterns and harefeet, they are fleet and self-reliant. The country they hunt is a most difficult one, containing precipitous crags, rocks, boulders, very high walls, scree-beds, heather and blaeberry, where riding to hounds is out of the question. And because packs are followed by people afoot, hounds must have good nose and tongue—"The matter of cry is important, for the Fell hounds often get out of sight of their followers [and Huntsman], the field then being guided by the distant music."

Bred as they have been since early times for suitability in rough countries, the Fells have never been influenced by English show standard of points. Any student of American foxhounds should take serious note of Fell hounds. There is enough similarity between them to lead to the conclusion that somewhere along the line they played a part, however small, in the development of the American hound.

Notes

1. Cross Country with Horse and Hound, Frank Sherman Peer; Charles Scribner's Sons, 1902, p. 157.

2. As expressed by Roger D. Williams in 1905.

3. This referred especially to the fashionable blood from the Shires.

4. "The English Foxhound in America," editorial notes and comments on a letter from Mr. Redmond C. Stewart, Master of the Green Spring Valley Hounds, U.S.A., in The Foxhound, April 1912, p. 324.

5. The States Through Irish Eyes, E. E. Somerville; Houghton Mifflin Co., Boston and New York, 1930, p. 81.

6. The predominant Fell hound color is white, with variations of black, "badger pie, hare pie," black and tan, black, lemon and white, white and tan added. Also there is the all tan color.

SIX

THE IRISH HOUNDS: MOUNTAIN AND MUSE

J. Blan van Urk

Around 1814, it is determined, Bolton Jackson, Esq., arrived in Maryland with the two Irish foxhounds, *Mountain* and *Muse.* These had been given to Mr. Jackson by the Duke of Leeds, who married a member of the Charles Carroll family of Carrollton, Maryland. The placing of this event by modern authors as late as 1830 is erroneous, for we have the word of one writer in 1832 who, when treating the subject of hound breeding, had this to say:

As to the various *breeds* of hounds in this country, so little attention has been paid to the stock from which they have been bred, that no description can be given. There has been no *system*—consequently nothing can be distinctly affirmed in regard to them. The most remarkable and distinct family of hounds, recollected in Maryland, sprang from two that were brought *some twenty odd years since* from Ireland, by *Bolton Jackson, Esq.* They fell into the hands of *Col. Sterett Ridgely,* at the time one of the most gallant horsemen, as well as one of the most ardent and hospitable sportsmen in the state.

They were remarkable, as are their descendants, according to their degree of the original blood, for great speed and perseverance, extreme ardour, and for *casting ahead* at a loss; and in this, and their shrill chopping unmusical notes, they were distinguished from the old stock of that day; which when they came to a loss, would *go back,* and *dwelling,* take it along, inch by inch, until they got fairly off again, whilst these Irish dogs would cast widely and by making their hit *ahead,* would keep their game at the top of his speed, and break him down in the first half hour.[1]

From Colonel Ridgely, the hounds *Mountain* and *Muse* went to Maryland's Governor Samuel Ogle. "The blood of these Irish dogs is in unmixed purity in Mr. Ogle's pack," wrote a visitor to the Governor's kennel—presumably in Belle Air where he also maintained a racing stable.

Sophy was the noted result of Governor Ogle's breeding program—so outstanding and esteemed that a portrait of her hung in his library.

The next call on the visiting list of this celebrated pair of Irish hounds was Homewood, the estate of Mr. Charles Carroll, Jr. The couple became separated when Dr. James Buchanan, who lived near Sharpsburg (Maryland), came into possession of *Mountain*.

Later, Patrick Henry's grandson Dr. Thomas J. Henry, of Virginia, obtained two hounds, *Captain* and *Jim*, from Dr. Buchanan; and the hound *Captain* became the greatest stallion of his day.[2] It is said about him that he had no equal when it came to speed and endurance. When ordered south for his health, Dr. Henry took his pack from Virginia to Florida. Thence they were taken to Georgia; and Mr. G. L. F. Birdsong of Thomaston, Georgia, who had come into the Doctor's life, became the proud owner of the, by then, famous *Henry pack*.

The results of this acquaintanceship and acquisition are the Birdsong or July hounds of Georgia (*July* having been the name of a hound belonging to Nimrod Gosnell, a Maryland farmer). The well-known Trigg hounds of Kentucky also descended from the Henry, Irish hounds.

One of the most expert and thoroughly posted hound men of present-day America, Joseph B. Thomas, Esq., ex-M.F.H., refers to this line in his book *Hounds and Hunting through the Ages*:

> Probably the true Virginia foxhounds of the present time are descended in part from this blood, although the exact records are unobtainable on account of the upheaval caused by the Civil War. At least, the hounds bred

Muse (bitch)　　　　　　　　　**Mountain (dog)**
**The Irish foxhounds, Mountain and Muse, were imported to Maryland in 1814.
These sketches were drawn from life by their second Maryland owner, Benjamin
Ogle, Jr. (1775–1844). Unruly and troublesome, they passed through the hands of
several foxhound breeders. They were hard hunting hounds, highly prepotent, and
are progenitors of virtually every important strain of American foxhound.**
Courtesy of the Museum of Hounds and Hunting, Leesburg, Virginia

by Dr. Henry tally in description with the Virginia foxhounds, the best blood of which I have assembled and breed to-day, with the hope that it may be preserved for the use of the future sportsmen of this country.

Mr. Thomas comments further that he is convinced the most efficient pack hound in the world to hunt a fox is the old Virginia foxhound:

> Anyone can become foolishly sentimental over a breed of animals; however, I have continued to breed this strain of hounds not on account of sentiment or romance, but because, after searching throughout Europe and America to discover hounds excelling them for pack hunting under difficult conditions of scenting and rough country, I have failed to do so.
>
> Such hounds may be considered deficient if they cannot regularly hunt hard at least three days a week, or more than this if required. They must have sufficient determination and stamina never to stop trying as long as their fox remains above ground or there is a vestige of a line left. A pack of such hounds must be able to account for foxes in the roughest woodland and hill country in July heat (as my pack is required to do), sound of foot, and sufficiently agile to negotiate the steepest of rocky cliffs in the North, as well as have enough nose and drive to kill red foxes in sandy Carolina. This pack must hunt with dash and style, carrying great head, negotiating burnt-over tracts, and pressing tirelessly for hours, if necessary, through briers, cane, half-frozen swamp water, as if there were nothing to stop them, and, gallantly killing their fox, come home with their sterns up, a pack in fact as well as in name. In a grass country, these hounds must be able to outpace, under good conditions, the best of thoroughbred horses.
>
> To summarize: such hounds have ability based on the following essentials,—
>
> *Nose*—that the hound may follow the line of a fox and show sport under almost any difficult American conditions.
>
> *Maximum cry*—by which a pack may be heard in undulating American country of large woodlands.
>
> *Drive, stamina,* and *determination* to get forward and stay at it.
>
> *Mentality*—that adapts itself to pack hunting and control by a huntsman.[3]

Although many a good hound man favors a different type of foxhound and can present arguments showing why he has such leanings, no one can gainsay Mr. Thomas's opinions and observations—they are studied, experienced, sincere and authoritative.

So the Irish once more started something, and this time with two M's—*Mountain* and *Muse;* the Marylanders aided and abetted, and Virginia streamlined what have come to be known as state-named (Virginia) hounds.

Notes

1. *American Turf Register,* February 1832, p. 286.

2. *Captain*—by *Traveler* out of *Sophy* (both by *Mountain* out of *Muse).*

3. Hounds and Hunting through the Ages, Joseph B. Thomas, M.F.H.; Derrydale Press, 1928.

SEVEN

ATTRIBUTES OF A GOOD HOUND

Joseph B. Thomas, M.F.H.

In America, in general, hounds have been bred for their ability to meet local hunting conditions and perhaps too little for other characteristics. These local conditions, varied and difficult to overcome, have, however, led to the development of remarkable hounds—remarkable not for looks but in achievement.

In certain sections,—notably Virginia, Kentucky, and Tennessee,—where the custom of racing hounds for love or lucre obtains, the selection of the fittest during many generations has fostered and developed the best hound, probably, in the world, in its ability to find, work a cold line, hunt at speed, and account for foxes. Under the difficult local conditions of scent and going, such hounds are able, if necessary, to "stay" for hours, negotiating the roughest possible terrain, often including rocky cliffs, burned forests, sandy wastes, ploughed fields, brush and briers; fording brooks, swimming rivers; and able to follow scent in hot September and snowy January, in dusty roads and frozen fields, with speed and drive. This may seem fine romance to some people, nevertheless those who have hunted in America can testify to the accuracy of the contention that these conditions are not exceptional but are the general rule.

The type of hound that can do all this carries as little superfluous weight as the high-class thoroughbred or trotting horse, yet has sufficient bone on which to hang ample muscle. Such hounds have strength and substance without lumber—they are well moulded and knit to stand wear and tear. In no sense are they weedy, nor yet so large, over-boned or clumsy as to be unable to negotiate timber or woven wire fences, or walk the top of rails and stone walls. The natural foxlike feet of such hounds, similar in their strength and spring to those of the greyhound, are singularly able to withstand lameness. As in the thoroughbred horse, the outward quality seems to denote the nervous energy within.

Mr. Thomas' *Flier,* '26. "A hound that carries as little superfluous weight as the thoroughbred horse, yet has sufficient bone on which to hang ample muscle." In tale male through eighteen generations, this hound traces to *Mountain,* imported from Ireland in 1814. *From an etching by Bert Cobb, 1928.*

Mr. Thomas' *Frantic,* '20. "Such hounds have strength and substance without lumber—they are well moulded and knit to stand wear and tear, nor yet so large or over-boned as to be unable to negotiate timber, woven wire fences, or walk by the top of rails. The outward energy seems to denote the nervous energy, within," *From an etching by Bert Cobb, 1928.*

* * *

[V]ery few young hounds enter my "old" pack until they are eighteen months to two years old. Assuming that it takes two years before a young hound begins to show precise indications of its abilities, there must be two years of waiting for proof of the breeder's wisdom, in the case of each hound. Therefore, theoretically speaking, only five generations of line-breeding can be produced in ten years. In actual practice, one produces much less: in other words, it takes at least a decade to satisfactorily prove any theory of breeding.

Is it wise to imagine that one can arbitrarily produce any theoretically ideal hound in a generation or two by crossing X and Y? Would it not be better to decide what requirements are needed in the pack, and then attempt to ascertain what existing strain of hounds *already* possesses the maximum of such qualities and can most consistently reproduce the same? Possibly, in time, such hounds may eventually be improved toward the end in view. Two or three years spent in really ardent investigation of the merits of various strains and their power to uniformly reproduce specific requirements, will save time and money, provided it is carried on analytically, dispassionately, and from a world-wide point of view. Empiric experimentation, on the other hand, affords but little guarantee of ultimate success.

To further complicate the matter, breeding is not an exact science, for there are so many unknown and fluctuating factors with which to contend. As a matter of fact, circumstances beyond the control of any one man, especially in volatile America, usually make breeding experiments of little avail, for the reason that so few exact proofs of results are quickly obtainable.

It is suggested, if nose, determination, and cry are desired in a pack, one should select a definite strain of hounds known positively to possess a maximum of such qualities and the ability to reproduce them. This done, assuming that one can reproduce a large number of young hounds per annum equal or superior in ability to their parents, and still have more hounds than are needed, then, and then only, draft for color and other non-essential points to suit the fancy. Do not think, if you desire first, last, and all the time certain qualities,—say A, B, and C,—that there can be produced something else in addition (say, Y) by magic or by crossing with some strain that has mediocre ABC qualities, but maximum Y qualities. It is mathematically obvious that the only way to retain the ABC qualities, and still add the Y quality is by judicious mating *within* the give strain, and perhaps occasional diluted-out crosses having the Y quality as well as the ABC qualities. It should be remembered that untold patience is all-essential to insure results.

Because it has cost me endless time and effort to learn what has just been written, the suggestion is humbly offered that the above deductions cannot be overemphasized.

To sum up, it can hardly be repeated too often that one must have in mind a standard of perfection. It is also essential that one should select breeding hounds *known* to have been proved by comparison to such a standard, and *know* that their progenitors have a like dependable history. These points should be seriously recognized and remembered.

In breeding, one should never, absolutely never, breed a hound *only* because he or she is a good individual; one should be cognizant of *all the characteristics of the ancestry.* A pedigree a mile long is useless if it cannot be translated; one must be able to definitely and accurately interpret the quality of the ancestors. If the breeder, or someone in whose opinion absolute confidence may be placed, does not know and highly approve from every angle the working ability of a hound's progenitors, he should not breed the brute, but "let George do it," if he so wishes. The one who knows will win.

> *Oh, worthiness of nature, breed of greatness,*
> *Cowards father cowards, and base things sire the base.*
> Cymbeline.

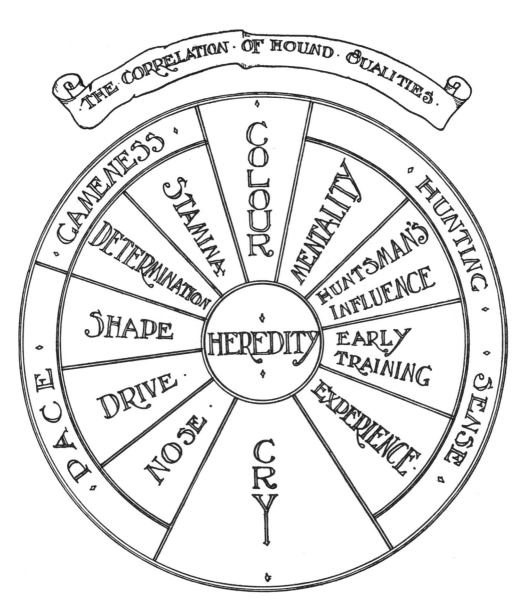

THE CORRELATION · OF HOUND · QUALITIES ·

THIS DIAGRAM IN THE SEMBLANCE OF A WHEEL SHOULD BE STUDIED
WITH THE THOUGHT THAT HEREDITY (THE HUB) CARRIES QUALITIES
(THE SPOKES), AND THAT CERTAIN QUALITIES COLLECTIVELY (E.G., NOSE,
DRIVE AND SHAPE) SUSTAIN THEIR SEGMENT OF THE RIM (PACE).

EIGHT

LEGEND OF THE HOUNDS

J. Blan van Urk

At this point in that which is "unsuspected and unique," I should like to call attention to "The Legend of the Hounds"—a most amazing and remarkable poem written, in 1867, by George Henry Boker of Philadelphia. This poem was based upon a story told to Mr. Boker by a man from Pennsylvania's Lebanon Valley, and it recounted the tale of an M.F.H. of a private pack—a wealthy owner of a local smelting furnace—"who capped the climax of a long course of dissolute deeds" by having his whole pack of foxhounds cast into a flaming furnace because he was disgusted with their work in the field while visitors were present. And in a fit of anger he topped this horrible deed by himself flinging to her cremation "his one remaining friend, *Flora,* the noble foxhound who led his pack."

To disguise the so-called foxhunting squire and M.F.H. and also the locale of the story, the poet placed the setting in Cornwall, England—among the tin mines; and of course he did not name the man in the poem. Descendants of this bestial fiend are reputed to have bought up all available copies of KONIGSMARK AND OTHER POEMS and had them burned. But on June 17, 1904, a Paper read before the Lebanon County Historical Society by Henry C. Grittinger, on the subject of "The Iron Industries of Lebanon County," included a reference to "The Legend of the Hounds"; and when Mr. Grittinger's Paper was published by the Society (Volume III, Number I), the poem was "appended," with the following notation:

> This Legend, referred to in Mr. Grittinger's Paper—a tale grim and fateful—it was thought proper to give here in its entirety, for its value along the line of legendary lore as one of the many legends pertaining to the early period of Lebanon County, the collection and preservation of which is also one of the objects of its Historical Society.

This Paper with its strange combination of industry and foxhunting is one of the most curious and interesting documents to be found within the classification of sporting literature. As for the poem, quoted here in part—it is of exceptional classical beauty, entitled to everlasting immortality.

> . . . one rare hound,
> The wonder of the country round—
> *Flora,* the leader of his pack . . .
>
> ---
>
> No hound, however great of pride,
> Had ever reached her milk-white side;
> Unchallenged in the flying front,
> She shone, a star, to all the hunt.
>
> ---
>
> For all his boasts, the Squire's fine pack
> Sulked at the outset, and held back,
> With drooping tail and humble head,
> And deprecating eyes that said,
> Almost as tongues, this morning's sport
> Finds us with spirits slack and short.
> The Huntsman and the angry Whips,
> With curses hissing through their lips,
> Drove the reluctant dogs along,
> A sullen and rebellious throng.
> *Flora* herself had lost her pride,
> And strayed, with vacant eyes, mouth wide
> And lolling tongue, behind them all,
> Deaf to her duty's urgent call.
> In wrath the Squire exclaimed, "Why, zounds!
> Matthew, what ails these cursed hounds?"
> "I know not, sir," replied the Whip,
> "Unless some scoundrel chose to slip
> A drug into their feed last night,
> To do your promises a spite.
> These city chaps—" "Pshaw! drive along!
> And—damn your mercy—use the thong!"
> "No good in that. We'd best turn back.
> You'll get no run, Squire, from the pack.
> And see yon cockney's tallow face;
> He's grinning at our hounds' disgrace!"
> "I'll show these town bred gentlemen,
> If my dogs cannot hunt so well
> On earth, another hunt in hell!"

Bawled the mad Squire; and all the beast
In his base nature so increased
That he could crown the deed he sought
With laughter brutal as the thought.

—————————————

Into the flames with howl and yell,
Hurled by the rugged firemen, fell
That pack of forty. Better hounds,
Fuller of music, of the sounds
That fire the hunter, drawing near
His furry prey with whoop and cheer—
The dogs all bursting in full cry,
Crashing through brush and timber high—
Never could Cornwall boast; and still
The silent lands lament their ill,
And the mysterious spell that lay
Upon them on that fatal day.
For now the bubbling liquid fire
Swallowed them all. Beside the Squire,
Flora alone stood desolate,
Sole relique of the general fate.
A hundred times had *Flora* dashed,
As some poor comrade yelling plashed
Into the sparkling molten lake,
With cries that any heart might shake—
A hundred times had *Flora* sprung,
Half frantic, moaning, giving tongue,
Up to the very furnace-brim,
Then slowly backward crawled to him,
Her lord, her idol, with her eyes
Speaking her piteous surprise
"What, you vile wanton, are you there?
In with the bitch!" "But, Squire—" "I swear
I'll brain the fool that wags a lip!"
Up rose his heavy hunting-whip:
Another word had sent it full
Upon the talker's naked skull.
"In with her! She's the last and worst:
Mere justice should have sent her first!"
Towards her approached the loathful gang;
But *Flora* bared her ivory fang,
And snarled a warning. Every hair
That bristled on her said—"Beware!"
As crouching low, her dangerous eye

Fixed on the ruffians drawing nigh,
She fairly awed them, till they stood
Quailing before her lion mood.
"You shrinking cowards!' foamed the Squire,
Now with redoubled rage afire,
"Is't for your pretty skins you fear
To venture? *Flora!*—here, dog, here!"
At once the look of wrath was gone;
A trusting, tender, loving dawn
Rose in her eyes; her talking tail
Quivered with joy; a low, soft wail
Broke from her, as the iron hand
Of the stout Squire from off her stand
Swung her; and striding towards the ledge
With his pleased burden, on the edge
Oh, awful death—oh, foul disgrace!—
She turned and licked his purple face.
Sheer out he flung her. As she fell,
Up from the palpitating hell
Came three shrill cries, and then a roll
Of thunder. Every pallid soul
Shrank from the pit; and ghastly white,
As was the snow one winter night,
The Squire reeled backward. Long he gazed
From face to face; then asked, amazed,
"Was it a fancy? If you heard,
Answer! What's was it?—that last word
Which *Flora* flung me?" Answer came,
As though one mouth pronounced the name,
And smote the asker as a rod;
"The word she said was—'God, God, God'!"

The Squire's last hour is drawing near . . .
Through the wide sash he fixed his eyes;
Then strained, and rose, full half his length,
Upon his mattress, by main strength,
Shouting, so all the house might hear,
Aghast with more than mortal fear,—
"Here they all come, the hellish pack,
Pouring from Colebrook Furnace, back
Into the world! Oh, see, see, see!
They snuff, to get the wind of me!
They've found it! *Flora* heads the whole,—
Whiter than any snows that roll

O'er Cornwall's hills, and bury deep
The wanderer in blissful sleep.
Ho! mark them! We shall have a run
Before this ghastly meet is done!
Now they give tongue! They've found their prey!
Here they come crashing—all this way—
And all afire! And it is I—
Weak as I am, and like to die—
Who must be hunted!" With a bound
He reached the floor, and fled around;
Once, twice, thrice, round the room he fled,
Then in the nurse's arms fell dead.

If any foxhunter on reading the above extraction fails to shudder, or lacks the impulse to rush to the nearest kennels to assure himself that hounds are resting easy, and are well and happy, I should say his case is a most sad one. The only cure is for him to phone his M.F.H., without mentioning the ice-water in his veins, and offer to *walk* a few hounds.

NINE

MARTHA DOYLE

Richard E. Danielson

Permit me, Muse, to sing the praises of *Martha Doyle*, a great lady in her own right and the noblest hunter I have ever seen or known. If I ever did see a better, I would not admit it, for that would be disloyalty to *Martha's* memory and I am the High Priest of her cult. Many admired her, a certain few revered her greatness, but I adored her. She had my heart and perhaps, in a grudging, spinsterish, slightly contemptuous way, I had hers. You give your heart, I believe, to only one woman, one countryside, one horse and one dog. Mr. Kipling who, though no scientist, was an accurate observer, once wrote—about a countryside:

> "Parsons in pulpits, taxpayers in pews,
> Kings on your throne, you know as well as me,
> We've only one virginity to lose,
> And where we lost it, there our hearts will be."

I may have philandered with hundreds of horses, gone—as it were—from blonde to brunette and back again, but if the Mayo Brothers were to open my heart tomorrow, they would see graved—in the horse section of it—the words, *"Martha Doyle."* However prodigal in his emotions, however wastrel in his amours, every horseman has one separate and holy place where stands, with candles burning constantly before it, the shrine of the one horse that he loved.

The sons and daughters and grandchildren of *Man O' War* might win more races and more money than their famous progenitor, but they could never replace him in the heart of Mr. Riddle. When he was leading in *War Admiral* after winning the 1937 Belmont, following his victories in the Kentucky Derby and the Preakness, someone congratulated Mr. Riddle on his great horse. It is reported that he answered sadly—"Yes, but he's not as great

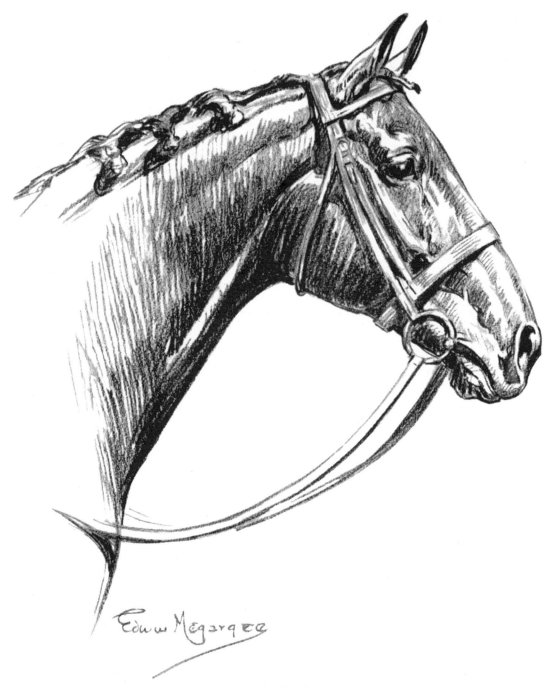

Martha Doyle

a horse as *Man O' War*." He couldn't be, to Mr. Riddle. In my much humbler sphere, I too have measured all the hunters I ever rode or saw by one standard—were they or were they not the equal of *Martha Doyle*? And none of them, to me, ever was.

She was a brown mare, about sixteen-two, with a white streak on her face and two white stockings behind. A Canadian filly, she was sired by a thoroughbred named *Martin Doyle* of whose antecedents or performance I am entirely ignorant. I never even knew the name of her dam and, although frequently assured that *Martha* was "in the book," no papers were shown to prove it. I do not believe that she was clean bred, but the "nick" which produced *Martha Doyle* from the mating of a little-known sire and an unknown dam is one of those mysteries which make horse breeding and racing so fascinating.

Peter Roche, of Leominster, Massachusetts, picked her out and bought her, a shaggy, rough young thing hardly halter-broken. She had a deceptive mouth, and even so superlative a horseman as Peter rated her a three-year-old when, as we afterwards discovered, she was just two. Peter clipped her and cleaned her up, bitted and backed her in his big stable and indoor ring at Leominster, schooled her once or twice, and then entered her in the show at Worcester. This was in the days just after the War when the Worcester show brought out some excellent competition, particularly in the hunter division. I cannot remember what, if anything, she did in other classes, but I do know that she won the high jump at six-feet-four with a wild, "sprangling" jump, landing all abroad, but triumphant on the ground. My wife was so impressed with the gallantry and the looks of the young mare that she promptly bought her and brought her home to Groton. I must have shown by the yearning in my eyes that I coveted my wife's horse, for on my next birthday morning I found, under my pillow, a sheet of note paper with the two words on it: "*Martha Doyle*"; and a nobler gift or a more unselfish giver I have never known.

As a three-year-old we hunted her in the drags at the Norfolk Hunt Club, thinking her a year older. Both of us tried to ride her, with only a very qualified success. The sight of hounds filled her with a fine careless rapture. Hunting was her destiny and her delight. All she wanted on earth was to be—not up with hounds—but up with the leading hound, or a trifle ahead of him. Consequently our performance in the field was an alternation of riding on the heels of the Master and Whippers-In and, when the opportunity served, of turning her in a great circle which gave us another chance to ride from the tail to the head of the hunt. In narrow places or wood roads our exploits were particularly noteworthy, and soon *Martha Doyle* with either Mr. or Mrs. Danielson up became just about as popular at Norfolk as a first-rate case of

Asiatic cholera. We cut down her oats, worked her hard, and tried every bit known to the ferocity of man. It was possible to turn her in a big field, but short of breaking her jaw I knew of no way to stop her when hounds were running. The head groom at the Club stables, an optimistic man, submitted that he had the skill and the equipment to control any puller and begged to be allowed to hunt her. I consented graciously. He appeared at the meet but I did not see him again for several hours. He turned up very wet and fatigued with a broken curb chain and a strange tale of how the mare had run away with him and had not stopped until she ran into a lake where, he said, "she swam around with me, like a seal." It is reasonable to suppose that on that day he had "no pleasure in the strength of an horse."

Mind you, there was no vice in her, only an unconquerable determination to "be first in the rush and come home with the brush." Keenness is a fine quality but, of course, it can be exaggerated. In fact, the case looked almost hopeless until I thought of Peter Roche, and asked Mr. Henry Vaughan, the Master of Norfolk, if he would permit him to ride my mare in one of the Norfolk drags. He consented and Peter turned up in due season. He rode *Martha* in a plain snaffle and he rated her up and down the hunt, in front, in the middle, or with the stragglers. She was completely docile and apparently did not pull an ounce. I asked this great horseman how he did it. He laughed in the embarrassed way one laughs at a foolish question: "I dunno, Mr. Danielson," he said. "I just tell 'em they got to do what they're told." Apparently it's just as simple and easy as that. The trouble is that I've never been able to tell them anything.

That lesson taught *Martha Doyle*, to a certain extent, the sweet virtues of obedience and, with the help of a gag snaffle we were able to restrain her natural exuberance. The gag was discarded the next season, and from then to her retirement the only bit we used with her was a simple pelham, and she never needed a martingale. I do not mean to imply that she exactly wanted to lag behind. On the contrary. In fact, one of my reasons for starting the Groton Hunt was that *Martha* had to be in front and I had to ride *Martha*, and the only way I could really be in front and thus ride *Martha* was to hunt my own hounds. But, until she was an old maid with "some relish of the saltness of time" and a mouth hardened by years and years of my rough, unskillful hands, she was never really a puller—so long as she was in her appointed place, out in front. In her last few seasons I developed muscles like iron bands and a "back," trying to keep *Martha* from trampling on the drag boy or catching foxes with her teeth. But that was my fault.

Martha was a success in every department except that of mother in Israel. When her honorable infirmities forced her to retire from the hunting field she was mated for three successive seasons to one of General Peabody's good stallions and, although in each instance her figure became distinctly matronly, her children were brain children only and not flesh and blood.

I couldn't begin to recount her exploits or tell you her virtues. Hunting folk will understand when I say that I hunted her, roughly, twice a week, for eleven years, with only two falls, neither of which was in any sense her fault. The first was in a drag at Norfolk. She was going very strong and eager but, for a wonder, halfway back in the ruck. Some one ahead of me knocked a large, round stone off a wall and it was still rolling when *Martha* landed on it and turned a somersault. *Le bon Dieu* so willed that, when she rolled over me, only her neck and shoulders touched me and I was quite unhurt. I held on to the bridle, which broke, and she galloped on after the hounds, finally bogging down in a dismal swamp. She was extricated by the entire population of Dover, Medfield, South Natick and Natick, all of whom were quite willing to accept a reward for their services. Altogether it made up into quite an expensive afternoon's sport.

Incidentally, among the spectators who saw our fall was the late Percy Haughton, then coaching the Harvard football team. I met him at tea after the run and he asked me how I felt. I told him that I was perfectly well and hadn't even a bruise. He said, "Tomorrow you will be the lamest man in Massachusetts." And I was, bent double, tied up in knots, unable to walk without a cane—although in any specific sense entirely uninjured. I have often wondered at his prescience.

The other fall was entirely my fault. I got the mare so completely wrong into a trappy post-and-rails that any other horse would have refused and walked home in disgust. *Martha*, however, tried to make the hopeless effort and we crashed. I could number her refusals on one hand or one and a half. As a matter of fact, I only recall three. I have re-read my hunting diary and only find one instance of a refusal in the field, which is not conclusive evidence. That particular incident I remember very well because it involved an optical illusion. The diary reads—"Swung to the right in Miss Minnie Coburn's field, down a slope to a drop jump with a stiffish in-and-out at the foot of the hill. This was a bad-looking but perfectly practicable place—it must have looked bad to the riders and to the horses as well."

The reason it looked so evil was that the angle of descent made the two stone walls of the lane look like one enormous wall or, at best, two walls with only a few feet between them. I have never seen a more deceptive obstacle.

"*Martha* surprised me by swerving at the in—as did every succeeding horse. *Cracksman* gave Fred Armstrong (my huntsman) a sharp refusal, shooting him high overhead so that he fell heavily on his back on the wall. He staggered across the lane, apparently badly hurt and I was convinced that he had broken a majority of his ribs. I called to him to stay put and that I would send help, and went on with only Mrs. Lindsay and Mrs. Timmins. Most of the field got into the lane and milled about there for some time.

"I had hardly gathered hounds together at the check when Fred on *Cracksman* galloped up and the courageous fellow told me that only his wind had been knocked out and that no bones were broken. I was greatly relieved."

Martha's greatness was not in the fact that she was a natural jumper, nor that she had foot enough to stay with any hounds in the world, but that she had a heart as big as the biggest barn. She never asked what was on the landing side. I think if you had headed her at a house and given her "the office," she would have tried to crash the second-story windows and bull her way through the other side. I rode her with complete and utter confidence, knowing that, barring accidents, she would carry me anywhere.

We understood one another almost too well. Once at a meet she felt peevish and kicked at a hound. I was shocked and surprised. *"Martha!"* I said. "Shame, shame on you!" She lowered her head, began quivering, and for the five or ten minutes before we moved off, she stood perfectly still with no motion at all except the trembling which was her act of contrition. Finally I slapped her shoulder and said, "All right, *Martha*, let's go!" and she came to life and moved off with hounds, with that strong, pushing, purposeful stride—impossible to describe, but which means that a hunter is going to do its duty and more than its duty that day.

I have always felt a sense of guilt that I didn't do right by *Martha*. Instead of being a local phenomenon, she could have been made into a national figure. She was a show hunter of indefinite potentialities. It so happens that I dislike horse shows and the showing of horses—a boring business in my opinion. Consequently I never took *Martha* to any but local shows when we wanted entries for our own—on the principle of "you scratch my back and I'll scratch yours." In the show ring *Martha* was an actress. Not only did she perform with an almost faultless precision, but she pranced and curveted and put on all those acts which are so appealing in the case of a lovely mare and so very annoying when performed by a Roman-nosed gelding. She knew quite definitely the color of her ribbons and if, as sometimes happened, she was awarded the red, her disgust was manifest. Mostly she won with monotonous regularity, being Champion Hunter at such shows as Worcester, Norfolk, Millwood, and several times at Groton. I should have trained her and shown her at Bryn Mawr and Devon and the National. I should have turned her over to the Army as a candidate for the Olympic team. But I didn't. I hoarded her as my priceless possession, more precious than rubies. I think she knew that I had kept her from the fame that was her due, hence her sense of disappointment and frustration. I felt it.

In her later days she gave me to understand by baleful glances and gestures of impatience that she knew perfectly that she was entitled to see her name in electric lights on Broadway and that I, for selfish reasons, had kept her out of the Big Time. She was right, and I am ashamed. This is my apology to her memory.

The end? If she could have broken her neck in the hunting field, I would not mourn, as I do, the sad anticlimax of disease and disabilities which made it seem humane and proper to bestow oblivion. I do not know, for I have never asked, at whose hand or just when she was sent down "that short, dark passage to a future state."

I do not know if we shall ever meet again or if in the Elysian Fields her ears will prick forward once more to the cry of hounds. I know she is buried in the horse cemetery in our place in Groton on the banks of the Nashua River. On her gravestone are the two words *Martha Doyle*, just that—as they were on the note paper under my birthday pillow. I couldn't inscribe that gallantry, that personality, that beauty on stone. What more could I say? What more could I say?

PART II
HUNTING HUMOR

"And like a bird was singing out, While sitting on a thorn."
From an engraving after the design of George Cruikshank.

TEN

THE EPPING HUNT

Thomas Hood, Esq.

Here are selections from The Epping Hunt, Thomas Hood's humorous 1829 epic poem about shopkeeper John Huggins, who goes hunting one day astride a horse that he shares with his neighbor, Fig.

John Huggins is introduced . . .
> JOHN HUGGINS was as bold a man
>   As trade did ever know,
> A warehouse good he had, that stood
>   Hard by the church of Bow.

A stolid man of business was John Huggins . . .
> Six days a week beheld him stand,
>   His business next his heart,
> At *counter* with his apron tied
>   About his *counter-part.*

With a sporting core . . .
> For all the live-long day before,
>   And all the night in bed,
> Like Beckford, he had nourish'd "Thoughts
>   On Hunting" in his head.

Our poet, Thomas Hood, loved to play with (and on) words . . .
> Of horn and morn, and hark and bark,
>   And echo's answering sounds,
> All poets' wit hath every writ
>   In *dog*-rel verse of *hounds.*

And again, describing the horses on the way to the meet . . .
> Somelong-ear'd jacks, some knacker's hacks,
>   (However odd it sounds,)
> Let out that day to *hunt*, instead
>   *Of going to the hounds!*

A canny, savvy old hunting man was John Huggins, like John Jorrocks who followed later in the century . . .
> Now when they saw John Huggins go
>   At such a sober pace;
> "Hallo!" cried they; "come, trot away,
>   You'll never see the chase!"

> But John, as grave as any judge
>   Made answers quite as blunt;
> "It will be time enough to trot,
>   When I begin to hunt!"

A sociable man was John Huggins, who didn't mind taking a drop . . .
> And so he paced to Woodford Wells,
>   Where many a horseman met,
> And letting go the *reins,* of course,
>   Prepared for *heavy wet.*

Playing on words again, speaking of all the tradesmen out hunting . . .
> 'Twas strange to think what difference
>   A single creature made;
> A single stag had caused a whole
>   *Stag*nation in their trade.

The stag was off, but so, apparently, were many riders . . .
> Some lost their stirrups, some their whips,
>   Some had no caps to show;
> But few, like Charles at Charing Cross,
>   Rode on in *Statue* quo.

Those that kept their seats were amused . . .
> And hunters good, that understood,
>   Their laughter knew no bounds,
> To see the horses "throwing off,"
>   So long before the hounds.

The carted stag quickly realized the peril of his freedom . . .
> Away, away! he scudded like
>> A ship before the gale;
> Now flew to "hills we know not of,"
>> Now, nun-like, took the vale.

Flying to the front . . .
> But who was he with flying skirts,
>> A hunter did endorse,
> And like a poet seem'd to ride
>> Upon a winged horse,

The tradesmen follow . . .
> Some gave a shout, some roll'd about,
>> And antick'd as they rode,
> And butchers whistled on their curs,
>> And milkmen *tally-ho'd!*

The race takes its toll . . .
> But even those that galloped on,
>> Were fewer every minute,—
> The field kept getting more select,
>> Each thicket served to thin it.

> For some pulled up, and left the hunt,
>> Some fell in miry bogs,
> And vainly rose and "ran a muck,"
>> To overtake the dogs.

John Huggins is still in the race, but . . .
> No means he had, by timely check,
>> The gallop to remit,
> For firm and fast, between his teeth,
>> The biter held the bit.

> Trees raced along, all Essex fled
>> Beneath him as he sate,—
> He never saw a county go
>> At such a county rate!

Our hero finally parts company with his nag . . .
> Yet worse than all the prickly points
>> That enter'd in his skin,
> His nag was running off the while
>> The thorns were running in!

One farmer runs out of horse and takes advantage . . .
> Now seeing Huggins' nag adrift,
> > This farmer, shrewd and sage,
> Resolv'd, by changing horses here,
> > To hunt another stage!

> Tho' felony, yet who would let
> > Another's horse alone,
> Whose neck is placed in jeopardy
> > By riding on his own?

Our poet explains how horses are able to jump . . .
> And here of Nature's kindly care
> > Behold a curious proof,
> As nags are meant to leap, she puts
> > A frog in every hoof!

Muddy and horseless, John Huggins drenches his sorrows in Wells. Our poet concludes with a moral . . .

> *Moral*
> Thus Pleasure oft eludes our grasp,
> > Just when we think to grip her;
> And hunting after Happiness,
> > We only hunt a slipper.

THE END

ELEVEN

MR. CARTERET AND HIS FELLOW AMERICANS ABROAD

David Gray

"It must have been highly interesting," observed Mrs. Archie Brawle; "so much pleasanter than a concert."

"Rather!" replied Lord Frederic. "It was ripping!"

Mrs. Ascott-Smith turned to Mr. Carteret. She had been listening to Lord Frederic Westcote, who had just come down from town where he had seen the Wild West show. "Is it so?" she asked. "Have you ever seen them?" By "them" she meant the Indians.

Mr. Carteret nodded.

"It seems so odd," continued Mrs. Archie Brawle, "that they should ride without saddles. Is it a pose?"

"No, I fancy not," replied Lord Frederic.

"They must get very tired without stirrups," insisted Mrs. Archie. "But perhaps they never ride very long at a time."

"That is possible," said Lord Frederic doubtfully. "They are only on about twenty minutes in the show."

Mr. Pringle, the curate, who had happened in to pay his monthly call upon Mrs. Ascott-Smith, took advantage of the pause. "Of course, I am no horseman," he began apprehensively, "and I have never seen the red Indians, either in their native wilds or in a show, but I have read not a little about them, and I have gathered that they almost live on horseback."

Major Hammerslea reached toward the tea table for another muffin and hemmed. "It is a very different thing," he said with heavy impressiveness. "It is a very different thing."

The curate looked expectant, as if believing that his remarks were going to be noticed. But nothing was farther from the Major's mind.

"What is so very different?" inquired Mrs. Ascott-Smith, after a pause had made it clear that the Major had ignored Pringle.

"A little more in the middle"

"It is one thing, my dear Madame, to ride a stunted, half-starved pony, as you say 'bareback,' and another thing to ride a conditioned British hunter (he pronounced it huntaw) without a saddle. I must say that the latter is an impossibility." The oracle came to an end and the material Major began on the muffin.

There was an approving murmur of assent. The Major was the author of "Schooling and Riding British Hunters"; however, it was not only his authority which swayed the company, but individual conviction. Of the dozen people in the room, excepting Pringle, all rode to hounds with more or less enthusiasm, and no one had ever seen any one hunting without a saddle and no one ever experienced any desire to try the experiment. Obviously it was an absurdity.

"Nevertheless," observed Lord Frederic, "I must say their riding was very creditable—quite as good as one sees on any polo field in England."

Major Hammerslea looked at him severely, as if his youth were not wholly an excuse. "It is, as I said," he observed. "It is one thing to ride an American pony and another to ride a British hunter. One requires horsemanship, the other does not. And horsemanship," he continued "which properly is the guiding of a horse across country, requires years of study and experience."

Lord Frederic looked somewhat unconvinced but he said nothing.

"Of course the dear Major (she called it deah Majaw) is unquestionably right," said Mrs. Ascott-Smith.

"Undoubtedly," said Mr. Carteret. "I suppose that he has often seen Indians ride?"

"Have you often seen these Indians ride?" inquired Mrs. Ascott-Smith of the Major.

"Do you mean Indians or the Red Man of North America?" replied the Major. "And do you mean upon ponies in a show or upon British hunters?"

"Which do you mean?" asked Mrs. Ascott-Smith.

"I suppose that I mean American Indians," said Mr. Carteret, "and either upon ponies or upon British hunters."

"No," said the Major, "I have not. Have you?"

"Not upon British hunters," said Mr. Carteret.

"But do you think that they could?" inquired Lord Frederic.

"It would be foolish of me to express an opinion," replied Mr. Carteret, "because, in the first place, I have never seen them ride British hunters over fences—"

"They would come off at the first obstacle," observed the Major, more in sorrow than anger.

"And in the second place," continued Mr. Carteret, "I am perhaps naturally prejudiced in behalf of my fellow countrymen."

Mrs. Ascott-Smith looked at him anxiously. His sister had married a British peer. "But you Americans are quite distinct from the red Indians," she said. "We quite understand that nowadays. To be sure, my dear Aunt—" She stopped.

"Rather!" said Mrs. Archie Brawle. "You don't even intermarry with them, do you?"

"That is a matter of personal taste," said Mr. Carteret. "There is no law against it."

"But nobody that one knows—" began Mrs. Ascott-Smith.

"There was John Rolfe," said Mr. Carteret; "he was a very well known chap."

"Do you know him?" asked Mrs. Brawle.

The curate sniggered. His hour of triumph had come. "Rolfe is dead," he said.

"Really!" said Mrs. Brawle, coldly. "It had quite slipped my mind. You see I never read the papers during the hunting. But is his wife received?"

"I believe that she was," said Mr. Carteret.

The curate was still sniggering and Mrs. Brawle put her glass in her eye and looked at him. Then she turned to Mr. Carteret. "But all this," she said, "of course, has nothing to do with the question. Do you think that these red Indians could ride bareback across our country?"

"As I said before," replied Mr. Carteret, "it would be silly of me to express an opinion, but I should be interested in seeing them try it."

"I have a topping idea!" cried Lord Frederic. He was an enthusiastic, simple-minded fellow.

"You must tell us," exclaimed Mrs. Ascott-Smith.

"Let us have them down, and take them hunting!"

"How exciting!" exclaimed Mrs. Ascott-Smith. "What sport!"

The Major looked at her reprovingly. "It would be as I said," he observed.

"But it would be rather interesting," said Mrs. Brawle.

"It might," said the Major, "it might be interesting."

"It would be ripping!" said Lord Frederic. "But how can we manage it?"

"I'll mount them," said the Major with a grim smile. "My word! They shall have the pick of my stable though I have to spend a month rebreaking horses that have run away."

"But it isn't the difficulty of mounting them," said Lord Frederic. "You see I've never met any of these chaps." He turned to Mr. Carteret with a sudden inspiration. "Are any of them friends of yours?" he asked.

Mrs. Ascott-Smith looked anxiously at Mr. Carteret, as if she feared that it would develop that some of the people in the show were his cousins.

"No," he replied, "I don't think so, although I may have met some of them in crossing the reservations. But I once went shooting with Grady, one of the managers of the show."

"Better yet!" said Lord Frederic. "Do you think that he would come and bring some of them down?" he asked.

"I think he would," said Mr. Carteret. He knew that the showman was strong in Grady—as well as the sportsman.

The Major rose to go to the billiard room. "I have one piece of advice to give you," he said. "This prank is harmless enough, but establish a definite understanding with this fellow that you are not to be liable in damages for personal injuries which his Indians my receive. Explain to him that it is not child's play and have him put it in writing."

"You mean to have him execute a kind of release?" said Mr. Carteret.

"Precisely that," said the Major. "I was once sued for twenty pounds by a groom that fell off my best horse and let him run away, and damme, the fellow recovered." He bowed to the ladies and left the room.

"Of course we can fix all that up," said Lord Frederic. "The old chap is a bit overcautious nowadays, but how can we get hold of this fellow Grady?"

"I'll wire him at once, if you wish," said Mr. Carteret, and he went to the writing table. "When do you want him to come down?" he asked, as he began to write.

"We might take them out with the Quorn on Saturday," said Lord Frederic, "but the meet is rather far for us. Perhaps it would be better to have them on Thursday with Charley Ploversdale's hounds."

Mr. Carteret hesitated a moment. "Wouldn't Ploversdale be apt to be fussy about experiments? He's rather conservative, you know, about the way people are turned out. I saw him send a man home one day who was out without a hat. It was an American who was afraid that hats made his hair come out."

"Pish," said Lord Frederic, "Charley Ploversdale is mild as a dove."

"Suit yourself," said Mr. Carteret. "I'll make it Thursday. One more question," he added. "How many shall I ask him to bring down?" At this moment the Major came into the room again. He had mislaid his eyeglasses.

"I should think that a dozen would be about the right number," said Lord Frederic, replying to Mr. Carteret. "It would be very imposing."

"Too many!" said the Major. "We must mount them on good horses and I don't want my entire stable ruined by men who have never lepped a fence."

"I think the Major is right about the matter of numbers," said Mr. Carteret. "How would three do?"

"Make it three," said the Major.

Before dinner was over a reply came from Grady saying that he and three bucks would be pleased to arrive Thursday morning prepared for a hunting party.

This took place on Monday, and at various times during Tuesday and Wednesday Mr. Carteret gave the subject thought. By Thursday morning his views had ripened. He ordered his tea and eggs to be served in his room and came down a little past ten dressed in knickerbockers and an old shooting coat. He wandered into the dining-room and found Mrs. Ascott-Smith sitting by the fire entertaining Lord Frederic, as he went to and from the sideboard in search of things to eat.

"Good morning," said Mr. Carteret, hoarsely.

Lord Frederic looked around and as he noticed Mr. Carteret's clothes his face showed surprise.

"Hello!" he said, "you had better hurry and change, or you will be late. We have to start in half an hour to meet Grady."

Mr. Carteret coughed. "I don't think that I can go out to-day. It is a great disappointment."

"Not going hunting?" exclaimed Mrs. Ascott-Smith. "What is the matter?"

"I have a bad cold," said Mr. Carteret miserably.

"But, my dear fellow," exclaimed Lord Frederic, "it will do your cold a world of good!"

"Not a cold like mine," said Mr. Carteret.

"But this is the day, don't you know?" said Lord Frederic. "How am I going to manage things without you?"

"All that you have to do is to meet them at the station and take them to the meet," said Mr. Carteret. "Everything has been arranged."

"But I'm awfully disappointed," said Lord Frederic. "I had counted on you to help, don't you see, and introduce them to Ploversdale. It would be more graceful for an American to do it than for me. You understand?"

"Yes," said Mr. Carteret, "I understand. It's a great disappointment, but I must bear it philosophically."

Mrs. Ascott-Smith looked at him sympathetically, and he coughed twice. "You are suffering," she said. "Freddy, you really must not urge him to expose himself. Have you a pain here?" she inquired, touching herself in the region of the pleura.

"Yes," said Mr. Carteret, "it is just there, but I daresay that it will soon be better."

"I am afraid not," said his hostess. "This is the way pneumonia begins. You must take a medicine that I have. They say that it is quite wonderful for inflammatory colds. I'll send Hodgson for it," and she touched the bell.

"Please, please don't take that trouble," entreated Mr. Carteret.

"But you must take it," said Mrs. Ascott-Smith. "They call it Broncholine. You pour it in a tin and inhale it or swallow it, I forget which, but it's very efficacious. They used it on Teddy's pony when it was sick. The little creature died, but that was because they gave it too much, or not enough, I forget which."

Hodgson appeared and Mrs. Ascott-Smith gave directions about the Broncholine.

"I thank you very much," said Mr. Carteret humbly. "I'll go to my room and try it at once."

"That's a good chap!" said Lord Frederic, "perhaps you will feel so much better that you can join us."

"Perhaps," said Mr. Carteret gloomily, "or it may work as it did on the pony." And he left the room.

After Hodgson had departed from his chamber leaving explicit directions as to how and how not to use the excellent Broncholine, Mr. Carteret poured a quantity of it from the bottle and threw it out of the window, resolving to be on the safe side. Then he looked at his boots and his pink coat and white leathers, which were laid out upon the bed. "I don't think there can be any danger," he thought, "if I turn up after they have started. I loathe stopping in all day." He dressed leisurely, ordered his second horse to be sent on, and some time after the rest of the household had gone to the meet he sallied forth. As he knew the country and the coverts which Lord Ploversdale would draw, he counted on joining the tail of the hunt, thus keeping out of sight. He inquired of a rustic if he had seen hounds pass and receiving "no" for an answer, he jogged on at a faster trot, fearing that the hunt might have gone away in some other direction.

As he came around a bend in the road, he saw four women riding toward him, and as they drew near, he saw that they were Lady Violet Weatherbone and her three daughters. These young ladies were known as the Three Guardsmen, a sobriquet not wholly inappropriate; for, as Lord Frederic described them, they were "big-boned, upstanding fillies," between twenty-five and thirty and very hard goers across any country, and always together.

"Good morning," said Mr. Carteret, bowing. "I suppose the hounds are close by?" It was a natural assumption, as Lady Violet on hunting days was never very far from the hounds.

"I do not know," she responded, and her tone further implied that she did not care.

Mr. Carteret hesitated a moment. "Is anything the matter?" he asked. "Has anything happened?"

"Yes," said Lady Violet frankly, "something has happened." Here the daughters modestly turned their horses away.

"Some one," continued Lady Violet, "brought savages to the meet." She paused impressively.

"Not really!" said Mr. Carteret. It was all that he could think of to say.

"Yes," said Lady Violet, "and while it would have mattered little to me, it was impossible—" She motioned with her head toward the three maidens, and paused.

"Forgive me," said Mr. Carteret, "but do I quite understand?'"

"At the first I thought," said Lady Violet, "that they were attired in painted fleshings, but upon using my glass, it was clear that I was mistaken. Otherwise, I should have brought them away at the first moment."

"I see," said Mr. Carteret. "It is most unfortunate!"

"It is, indeed!" said Lady Violet; "but the matter will not be allowed to drop. They were brought to the meet by that young profligate, Lord Frederic Westcote."

"You amaze me," said Mr. Carteret. He bowed, started his horse, and jogged along for five minutes, then he turned to the right upon a crossroad and suddenly found himself with hounds. They were feathering excitedly about the mouth of a tile drain into which the fox had evidently gone. No master, huntsmen or whips were in sight, but sitting wet and mud-daubed upon horses dripping with muddy water were Grady dressed in cowboy costume and three naked Indians. Mr. Carteret glanced about over the country and understood. They had swum the brook at the place where it ran between steep clay banks and the rest of the field had gone around to the bridge. As he looked toward the south, he saw Lord Ploversdale riding furiously toward him followed by Smith, the huntsman. Grady had not recognized Mr. Carteret turned out in pink as he was, and for the moment the latter decided to remain incognito.

Before Lord Ploversdale, Master of Fox-hounds, reached the road, he began waving his whip. He appeared excited. "What do you mean by riding upon my hounds?" he shouted. He said this in several ways with various accompanying phrases, but neither the Indians nor Grady seemed to notice him. It occurred to Mr. Carteret that, although Lord Ploversdale's power of expression was wonderful for England, it nevertheless fell short of Arizona standards. Then, however, he noticed that Grady was absorbed in adjusting a Kodak camera, with which he was evidently about to take a picture of the Indians alone with the hounds. He drew back in order both to avoid being in the field of the picture and to avoid too close proximity with Lord Ploversdale as he came over the fence into the road.

"What do you mean, sir!" shouted the enraged Master of Fox-hounds, as he pulled up his horse.

"A little more in the middle," replied Grady, still absorbed in taking the picture.

Lord Ploversdale hesitated. He was speechless with surprise for the moment.

Grady pressed the button and began putting up the machine.

"What do you mean by riding on my hounds, you and these persons?" demanded Lord Ploversdale.

"We didn't," said Grady amicably, "but if your bunch of dogs don't know enough to keep out of the way of a horse, they ought to learn."

Lord Ploversdale looked aghast and Smith, the huntsman, pinched himself to make sure that he was not dreaming.

"Many thanks for your advice," said Lord Ploversdale. "May I inquire who you and your friends may be?"

"I'm James Grady," said that gentleman. "This," he said, pointing to the Indian nearest, "is Chief Hole-in-the-Ground of the Ogallala Sioux. Him in the middle is Mr. Jim Snake, and the one beyond is Chief Skytail, a Pawnee."

"Thank you, that is very interesting," said Lord Ploversdale, with polite irony. "Now will you kindly take them home?"

"See here," said Grady, strapping the camera to his saddle, "I was invited to this hunt, regular, and if you hand me out any more hostile talk—" He paused.

"Who invited you?" inquired Lord Ploversdale.

"One of your own bunch," said Grady, "Lord Frederic Westcote. I'm no butter-in."

"Your language is difficult to understand," said Lord Ploversdale. "Where is Lord Frederic Westcote?"

Mr. Carteret had watched the field approaching as fast as whip and spur could drive them, and in the first flight he noticed Lord Frederic and the Major. For this reason he still hesitated about thrusting himself into the discussion. It seemed that the interference of a third party could only complicate matters, inasmuch as Lord Frederic would so soon be upon the spot.

Lord Ploversdale looked across the field impatiently. "I've no doubt, my good fellows, that Lord Frederic Westcote brought you here and I'll see him about it, but kindly take these fellows home. They'll kill all my hounds."

"Now you're beginning to talk reasonable," said Grady. "I'll discuss with you."

The words were hardly out of his mouth before hounds gave tongue riotously and went off. The fox had slipped out of the other end of the drain and old Archer had found the line.

As if shot out of a gun the three Indians dashed at the stake-and-bound fence on the farther side of the road, joyously using their heavy quirts on the Major's thoroughbreds. Skytail's horse being hurried too much, blundered his take-off, hit above the knees and rolled over on the Chief who was sitting tight. There was a stifled grunt and then the Pawnee word "Go-dam!"

Hole-in-the-Ground looked back and laughed one of the few laughs of his life. It was a joke which he could understand. Then he used the quirt again to make the most of his advantage.

"That one is finished," said Lord Ploversale gratefully. But as the words were in his mouth, Skytail rose with his horse, vaulted up and was away.

The M.F.H. followed over the fence shouting at Smith to whip off the hounds. But the hounds were going too fast. They had got a view of the fox and three whooping horsemen were behind them driving them on.

The first flight of the field followed the M.F.H. out of the road and so did Mr. Carteret, and presently he found himself riding between Lord Frederic and the Major. They were both a bit winded and had evidently come fast.

"I say," exclaimed Lord Frederic, "where did you come from?"

"I was cured by the Broncholine," said Mr. Carteret, "amazing stuff!"

"Is your horse fresh?" asked Lord Frederic.

"Yes," replied Mr. Carteret, "I happened upon them at the road."

"Then go after that man Grady," said Lord Frederic, "and implore him to take those beggars home. They have been riding on hounds for twenty minutes."

"Were they able," asked Mr. Carteret, "to stay with their horses at the fences?"

"Stay with their horses!" puffed the Major.

"Go on like a good chap," said Lord Frederic, "stop that fellow or I shall be expelled from the hunt; perhaps put in jail. Was Ploversdale vexed?" he added.

"I should judge by his language," said Mr. Carteret, "that he was vexed."

"Hurry on," said Lord Frederic. "Put your spurs in."

Mr. Carteret gave his horse its head and he shot to the front, but Grady was nearly a field in the lead and it promised to be a long chase as he was on the Major's black thoroughbred. The cowboy rode along with a loose rein and an easy balance seat. At his fences he swung his hat and cheered. He seemed to be enjoying himself and Mr. Carteret was anxious lest he might begin to shoot for pure delight. Such a demonstration would have been misconstrued. Nearly two hundred yards ahead at the heels of the pack galloped the Indians, and in the middle distance between them and Grady rode Lord Ploversdale and Smith vainly trying to overtake the hounds and whip them off. Behind and trailing over a mile or more came the field and the rest of the hunt servants in little groups, all awestruck at what had happened. It was unspeakable that Lord Ploversdale's hounds which had been hunted by his father and his grandfather should be so scandalized.

Mr. Carteret finally got within a length of Grady and hailed him.

"Hello, Carty," said Grady, "glad to see you. I thought you were sick. What can I do? They've stampeded. But it's a great ad for the show, isn't it? I've got four reporters in a hack on the road."

"Forget about the show," said Mr. Carteret. "This isn't any laughing matter. Ploversdale's hounds are one of the smartest packs in England. You don't understand."

"It will make all the better story in the papers." said Grady.

"No it won't," said Mr. Carteret. "They won't print it. It's like a blasphemy upon the Church."

"Whoop!" yelled Grady, as they tore through a bullfinch.

"Call them off," said Mr. Carteret, straightening his hat.

"But I can't catch 'em," said Grady, and that was the truth.

Lord Ploversdale, however, had been gaining on the Indians, and by the way in which he clubbed his heavy crop, loaded at the butt, it was apparent that he meant to put an end to the proceedings if he could.

Just then hounds swept over the crest of a green hill and as they went down the other side, they viewed the fox in the field beyond. He was in distress, and it looked as if the pack would kill in the open. They were running wonderfully together, the traditional blanket would have covered them, and in the natural glow of pride which came over the M.F.H., he loosened his grip upon the crop. But as the hounds viewed the fox so did the three sons of the wilderness who were following close behind. From the hilltop fifty of the hardest going men in England saw Hole-in-the-Ground flogging his horse with the heavy quirt which hung from his wrist. The outraged British hunter shot forward scattering hounds to right and left, flew a ditch and hedge and was close on the fox who had stopped to make a last stand. Without drawing rein, the astonished onlookers saw the lean Indian suddenly disappear under the neck of his horse and almost instantly swing back into his seat waving a brown thing above his head. *Hole-in-the-Ground had caught the fox!*

"Most unprecedented!" Mr. Carteret hear the Major exclaim. He pulled up his horse, as the field did theirs, and waited apprehensively. He saw Hole-in-the-Ground circle around, jerk the Major's five hundred guinea hunter to a standstill close to Lord Ploversdale and address him. He was speaking in his own language.

As the Chief went on, he saw Grady smile.

"He says," said Grady translating, "that the white chief can eat the fox if he wants him. He's proud himself bein' packed with store grub."

The English onlookers heard and beheld with blank faces. It was beyond them.

The M.F.H. bowed stiffly as Hole-in-the-Ground's offer was made known to him. He regarded them a moment in thought. A vague light was breaking in upon him. "Aw, thank you," he said, "thanks awfully. Smith, take the fox. Good afternoon!"

Then he wheeled his horse, called the hounds in with his horn and trotted out to the road that led to the kennels. Lord Ploversdale, though he had never been out of England, was cast in a large mold.

The three Indians sat on their panting horses, motionless, stolidly facing the curious gaze of the crowd; or rather they looked through the crowd, as the lion with the high breeding of the desert looks through and beyond the faces that stare and gape before the bars of his cage.

"Most amazing! Most amazing!" muttered the Major.

"It is," said Mr. Carteret, "if you have never been away from this." He made a sweeping gesture over the restricted English scenery, pampered and brought up by hand.

"Been away from this?" repeated the Major. "I don't understand."

Mr. Carteret turned to him. How could he explain it?

"With us," he began, laying an emphasis on the "us." Then he stopped. "Look into their eyes," he said hopelessly.

The Major looked at him blankly. How could he, Major Hammerslea of "The Blues," tell what those inexplicable dark eyes saw beyond the fenced tillage! What did he know of the brown, bare, illimitable range under the noonday sun, the evening light on far, silent mountains, the starlit desert!

TWELVE

YOUNG ENTRY

(SELECTIONS)

Gordon Grand

To

His Honor Colonel Weatherford, M.F.H.

Sir:

Seems like what I got to do most is to fix things so Miss Aleece and the young gentlemen take to this riding and like it and want to do it.

Please sir, maybe your honor would remember when Callahan O'Shea was brought up to Millbeck by Mr. Monford to learn Mr. Monford's children to ride and to go out huntin' with 'em. He were a fine rider, that Callahan O'Shea, and a nice boy—good with the horses and tries hard to do good by the children, but the children don't ever learn to ride and don't want to ride or go huntin' but only play tennis and swim and all like that.

Well, I been thinkin' a lot about that Callahan O'Shea and those Monford children and don't want to get in no such fix as that. Maybe I would have to ask your honor what must I do if my children don't take to ridin' like they should.

'Course what made the trouble with those Monford children was Mr. Monford, 'cause he tells that Callahan O'Shea to take 'em out every day for two hours and tells the children what was only little children, that they must go out. Lots o' times it was hot, and lots o' times the flies were bad and it were dusty and they out there in the sun pokin' along the roads. And when they get home it were lunch time and they can't have a swim. 'Course while they be ridin', other children be playin' games or swimmin'. It don't be good fun for little children just followin' one after the other jigglin' along on a horse for two hours every day.

I see as how I must work it different from what that Callahan O'Shea worked it. First place I don't lay to say to the children that they must go ridin', so hurry up and get ready. I says to myself I'm goin' to wait till they start pesterin' me can they ride. The ponies and me get here about four o'clock and the children come runnin' out and want to know can they ride but I tell 'em the ponies need to rest. Then the next day when they get home from school they come to the stable again and want to get on the ponies but I tell 'em I had 'em all out once but maybe we can go ridin' tomorrow. We go out the next day for only fifteen minutes 'cause I say as how we must start conditionin' the ponies slow and get 'em in good, hard huntin' shape and put lots of muscle on 'em but not take the flesh off too quick.

When the children come down to the stable I tell 'em stories about fox huntin' at Millbeck and race meets and horse shows and children gettin' the brush out huntin' and jumpin' big fences. Please sir, they be turrable excited about everything and want to know when can they learn to jump and how old would they be afore they could go huntin' and would I think your honor would take 'em to Millbeck when they learned to ride good.

It don't look like I was goin' to have the trouble that Callahan O'Shea had but I'm not goin' to let 'em ride only two days a week till they bother me to ride more. I'm goin' to keep 'em wantin' it, if I can, 'cause it seems like the more they want to ride why the quicker they're goin' to learn. Today when Master John gets off his pony he says to me, "Eddie, how long will it be afore I can ride again?" "Two days," I tell him. He picks up two little pieces of gravel and says, "If I throw that one away tonight when I go to bed and this one the next night, then when I get up it will be the day I can ride. Is that right, Eddie?" "Yes, Master John," I says.

Resp.

EDDIE

To

HIS HONOR COLONEL WEATHERFORD, M.F.H.

SIR:

I reported last week about bein' upside down about all this pretendin' business the children were doin' and how I figured I had to make up some real sport for 'em.

Your honor wouldn't know, not by no manner o' means, all the kind of sport I thought about and then had to give up 'cause I couldn't see how we would do 'em. Then to a sudden I get the wonderfulest idea what ever was at any time.

Now this is how the idea come to me. Yesterday I figured to run the clipper over Clark Gable's mane so I get the twitch what I have to use on that pony.

"Me and the children be goin' to do some rat huntin'." By Paul Brown

Well sir, it's a grand mornin' and I'm feelin' a little extra top and as your honor would know, a twitch handle, made out of a Irish stable broom, feels like it would be nice to do something with—tap somethin' or somebody.

I go down to Clark Gable's box, open it, and if a rat don't run out right between my feet, and set as bold a line as ever I see straight for the pump house. I let out a tally-ho, give the twitch handle a twirl and was on his line. He whizzes 'round the pump house right handed, but I lifts myself off the line, ducks around the other side thinkin' to run into him and give him a grand tap but he's takin' a new line. He's a stout rat. He's boilin' along wide open for the corner of the green house. There I be, sir, runnin' him from view, tally-hoin', whoopin', twirlin' the twitch handle and gainin' on him every foot. Then the idea comes. It comes when I'm still kinda in mid-air, and I says to myself, right up there in the air "Me and the children be goin' to do some rat huntin'."

I stand like I was froze, watchin' the rat duck under the green house, and please sir, maybe you wouldn't think I be reportin' the truth but I go to hopin' he's got a nice safe place and that no cat or nothin' be goin' to hurt him.

I walk back to the tack room, sit down and think about my idea and it gets growin' bigger and then a lot bigger than that, and if I don't forget to go up to the house for lunch, what I never did afore in my life. That were yesterday, and this mornin', why, I walked clean into a wheel-barrow all on account of havin' a picture goin' in my mind of me and the children and some terriers runnin' a rat.

Please sir, I know I can learn the children a lot about fox huntin' and all other kinds of huntin' just by huntin' rats.

I lay to get me some perticeler nice rats, build a rat covert, find a few terriers, and work hard on this business just like we were fox huntin', and do everything smart and proper. I will report to your honor regelar how every thing goes.

Resp.

EDDIE

To

HIS HONOR COLONEL WEATHERFORD, M.F.H.

SIR:

Thank you for that $25. I bought the three old terriers I writ about and another one what the man says can catch a rat in the air same as a bird grabs onto a bug. There be $5 left what I have to spend for collars and leashes.

Resp.

EDDIE

An S. P.

There now be five of the beautifulest rat coverts what ever was. We have 'em all over Miss Weatherford's orchard and meadow and please sir they look extra perticeler nice.

The children keep wantin' me to talk to 'em about huntin' in Millbeck and like it when I tell 'em about some of the grand runs what the Millbeck hounds have. Well, sir, 'course when I'm tellin' about a run I got to tell what covert the fox was found and where hounds run and all, so the children now know the names of all the Millbeck country. When we finished buildin' our rats coverts why they give 'em names, and now we have Miss Molly Crawford's Covert, the Stick Heap, Pugsley Hill, Three Spires Upland and Squire Oakleigh's Covert.

Master Cabot goes off extra hard on his back. *By Paul Brown*

Miss Aleece made a map showin' our huntin' country and says I'm to send it to you, what I do by puttin' it in this envelope with my report. It is a grand map altogether, only I wouldn't want your honor to think I built Miss Molly Crawford's covert leanin' over so much. Then the rat comin' out of Stick Heap, what is the beautifulest covert, looks like he were too big for it.

Resp. again

EDDIE

To

HIS HONOR COLONEL WEATHERFORD, M.F.H.

SIR:

The three velvet caps what your honor sent, for the rat huntin', and the horn for Master Cabot came today and I tell the children they must write quick and thank you, and they're goin' to do it. The caps fit good.

The governess fixed things so I could speak to Miss Weatherford; I tell Miss Weatherford the children should have some huntin' clothes what they don't use no other time but only rat huntin' and got to keep neat, and Miss Weatherford wants to know what kind. "Well," I say, "please Mam, some grey shorts (short pants) and grey shirts and grey sweaters and grey socks." Miss Weatherford tells Miss Thornton, what's the governess, that it's all right to get these things and new brown shoes. We have everything now. I wish your honor could see the children all dressed up so perticeler proper.

The children come to the tack room and I talk to 'em good about it not matterin' none how bad they look fishin' or shootin' or playin' or nothin', only that huntin' be different and that no body nowhere ever hunts that don't do 'emselves right—horses, tack, clothes, boots, hats, gloves and everything. I tell 'em about Albert turnin' your honor out on a huntin' mornin', silk hat, afore you was Master, all steamed and beautiful ironed, boots boned, and I show 'em a bone and how it's used, and show 'em pictures of the Prince of Wales with the Pytchley and all the ladies and gentlemen turned out good with white gloves and the ladies in veils and all. Then I says to 'em that the hunt staff of these here South Dorchester Rat Hounds is going to look neat or we don't be goin' to hunt, no by no manner o' means, and that they got to take care of their huntin' clothes and keep 'em hung up and brushed, and trees into their shoes, and all of that. It be the orfulest thing the way some people let children come out huntin' in rat catcher clothes, nothin' clean and smart, but I don't lay to let these here children get any such notions.

I bought four tins of saddle soap and new sponges and when we be through huntin' we all come in the tack room, and the young gentlemen got to clean their huntin' shoes good, and I clean Miss Aleece's and mine, 'cause I see it be easier for children to do somethin' when everybody is doin' the same thing. There don't be anybody tries to clean his shoes good like Master John.

Resp.

EDDIE

An S. P.

Maybe your honor wouldn't want me to say this but the ladies in those English magazines what ride astride look turrable, 'long side of those ladies what ride side-saddle so could I have a side-saddle for Miss Aleece?

To

HIS HONOR COLONEL WEATHERFORD, M.F.H.

SIR:

Yesterday I couldn't' report on our run 'cause I writ too much about the ridin' and leppin', but I do it now.

Around four o'clock the terriers poked a rat out of the south side of Miss Molly Crawford's covert. The rat didn't take a line like usual but pointed clean away for the stone wall along the state road. Master John saw him go away and tally-hoed extra good but by the time Master Cabot gets the terriers on the line the rat be most to the road, we boilin' along after him. All to once a automobile stops quick like, brakes hollerin', and a perticeler big gentleman jumps out, runs to the wall, climbs over, and I see it's Mr. Henry Vaughan, what I knows 'count of him bein' over to Millbeck with your honor. I touches my hat and he says "Well, well, well! What's a goin' on here?" Please, if Mr. Vaughan weren't standin' right where the rat was headin', right on the line, so Master Cabot calls out, "Hold hard, sir, or you'll turn him."

The rat comes up to Mr. Vaughn, sees him, and turns west towards the Stick Heap covert. Master Cabot sounds three quick, short notes like I taught him, the terriers come flyin' to the horn knowin' that Master Cabot be goin' to show 'em the rat, and off it is we are for the Stick Heap! "Come on, sir, come on, come on," Master Cabot sings out to Mr. Vaughan. "Come up front with me so you can see better."

We sail on down to the Stick Heap wide open, the terriers huntin' fine and drivin' along, and we could have killed in the open only there be a patch of sedge grass right in front of that covert, so the terriers don't see so good. Mr. Vaughan, 'count of bein' extra perticeler tall, views the rat breakin' out of the far side of the sedge, settin' his head for the Stick Heap and hollers out fine, "Tally-ho! Tally-ho! Tally-ho for'ard!" and Scalper is 'most on the rat's back when he slips in.

I never saw our terrier so keen and givin' such tongue. Please sir, you could have heard 'em a mile away. All this noise drove two rats out of the far side of the covert. One of 'em was a King George rat, and he don't head for Miss Molly Crawford's covert like your honor would think he would, but straight for Dedham stream. It were Miss Aleece viewed him sneakin' away, and tally-hoed, and Mr. Vaughan turned, looked at her and says, "God bless me," two times 'count of the way Miss Aleece can tally-ho.

We raced down to the stream as fast as we could. There don't hardly be any water in her this time o' year and the rat went slippin' along between the dry stones. We're in the mud, then in the water, then on the bank, the terriers flyin' every which way. When we saw the rat we tally-hoed, Master Cabot would lift the terriers to the view, and it was flyin' on we were again, jumpin' from stone to stone, fallin' down, leppin' from one bank to the tuther, cheerin' the terriers on, till we hunted clean down the falls, killin' on a nice spit of sand, and Master Cabot gives Mr. Vaughan a trophy what he said he was glad to have and would keep.

When things was quieted down I tell the children who Mr. Vaughan is; how he was a M. F. H. himself, and president of all the other Masters. The children act very good and Master John, 'count of him pretending' he were Mr. Vaughan, like I writ you, was kind o' excited, and took off his cap and says he's sorry Mr. Vaughan got all his good clothes messed up and hopes he wasn't goin' to some party, and he lends Mr. Vaughan his huntin' crop what don't be no good to Mr. Vaughan, 'count of it bein' so small.

It's late and we have to take terriers home so the children can do the school work. Please, I wish your honor could have seen our pack goin' back to kennels. Everything looked just perticiler smart, sir, the six little white terriers with their tails curled over their backs extra high, the children turned out in grey clothes and velvet caps, all neat and proper, and walkin' where they belong, same as a beagle hunt staff. Mr. Vaughan and me, bein' the field, walked behind.

When we get to the kennels Master Cabot, M. R. T., stands in front of the door, with Miss Aleece, first whipper-in, on one side, Master John, second whipper-in, on tuther side, and everybody works hard to hold the terriers steady and give 'em manners. I go around back, open the door, and Master Cabot waves 'em in. Your honor wouldn't know what a scramble and throwin' of tongues there be.

When we were back in the tack room hangin' up our crops, leashes, and the horn, Mr. Vaughan says it is maybe twenty-five years since he's had so good sport and wants to come again. He thinks as how he will go in to have some tea with Miss Weatherford, who he hasn't seen in a long time. I hope he said somethin' good for rat huntin'.

Resp.

Eddie

An S. P.

Miss Weatherford said we could use a rug and some of the furniture from the porch to fix up our tack room. The children brought down their horse pictures and it looks orful nice. They now got to callin' it The South Dorchester Hunt Club. Master John don't have any horse pictures and worries about it, so he brings a lot of shells he picked up at the seashore, and a tame English black-bird what Mr. Framington gave him. The shells be kind of a nuisance in a tack room but it's all right. Master John sets powerful store by that black-bird.

Please sir, another S. P.

When we was holdin' hard by the sedge, Mr. Vaughan, wantin' to help all he could, kept a walkin' about and standin' up on his toes tryin' to see the rat, and Master Cabot says, "Please sir, stand steady. If you keep movin', the terriers will get to lookin' at you, thinkin' you are goin' to show 'em the rat, and won't work good." Mr. Vaughan only says, "Sorry, sir," and looks over at me.

When Mr. Vaughan saw Master Cabot in a velvet cap, with the ribbons turned, a master's way, he took his hat off to him nice and proper, but Master Cabot didn't take his cap off to Mr. Vaughan, so I had to tell him, but I don't do it till we get back to the tack room.

Another S. P. please.

Would your honor be havin' a book what Albert could send Master Cabot tellin' about hare huntin'? It would help the children in their learnin' if we hunted fox-rats one week, then hare-rats one week, and please, maybe there would be a otter book so we could hunt otter-rats. When the young gentlemen and Miss Aleece would be goin' to Ireland to hunt I want 'em to do good. I don't lay to have 'em tally-hoin' no otter nor hare, nor toodley-dooin' a fox, not by no matter o' means. Seems like the way that King George rat run the river maybe we could have some good otter huntin', so I am havin' the children make some of those long poles what otter hunters carry in Ireland to help 'em lep across the ditches.

The children be excited 'cause Mr. Framington is comin' here tomorrow. I don't know who this Mr. Framington is but it don't seem like the children could be more upside down were Santa Claus comin'.

Resp. one more time

EDDIE

PART III
STORIES

THIRTEEN

TING-A-LING

David Gray

They were sitting on the balcony which distinguished the bridal suite, in the sun of the June morning. Below was the main street, animated mildly with the shopping of a dormant New England community. A few ancient carriages, reliquaries of the first families, mingled with the buggies and the delivery-wagons, and at dignified intervals a horse-car jingled past and disappeared in the vista of the elms.

"It's ten minutes past eleven," he observed, looking at his watch. "We have five hours to wait for the fourteen train, but I believe we *dine* at twelve."

"Are you hungry?" she asked. "I dare say we could get something even before dinner—perhaps a pie."

They both laughed. "This is an awful place," he said, "isn't it? No more historic New England for me."

They leaned lazily upon the balcony rail, and sat with their heads together, looking down into the street. A grocer's clerk was putting things into a wagon, and they wondered who was going to have asparagus, and how big a family it might be which needed six quarts of strawberries. Presently, with the noises of the street, came the jingling of the periodic horse-car, and they turned and watched it approach.

"That is not a bad-looking horse," he said.

"Look!" she exclaimed. There was a note of pity and indignation in her voice. The car, as it drew near, appeared to bulge with passengers.

"It's rather a joke," he said. "Those are women delegates to the Society for the Prevention of Cruelty to Animals convention."

"It's shameful," she said.

The car stopped on the corner in front of the hotel for another passenger to worm himself into the jam on the rear platform. The horse, a big, showy chestnut, stood panting, his nostrils red and dilated. His neck was white with lather. Wet streaks extended up his ears. His body dripped, and the sweat was running down his legs.

As the two strokes of the conductor's bell gave the signal to start, he plunged forward almost before the driver had loosened the brakes. There was a clatter of hoofs on the cobblestones, and a mighty straining. The heavy car began to move, and the chestnut horse went trotting down the street, tail up and neck arched like a cavalry horse on parade.

"He's game," he said.

She put her hand on his arm. "I can't bear to see it," she whispered.

He looked down at her. Her eyes were brimming.

"Don't be a little goose," he said gently; but there was a queer feeling in his throat. He rose to his feet. "I'll be back in a few minutes," he added. "I want to go down to the office." He bent down and kissed her, and left the balcony.

She waited half an hour, and then went down to the corridor. He was not at the office. She decided to go out. As she was on the hotel steps, she met him coming in, and at the same moment a coach-horn sounded, and they saw a coach and four come around the corner.

He looked back. "O Lord!" he exclaimed, "we're caught. There's your brother, and the Appleton girls, and Frank Crewe, and Winthrop, and most of your bridesmaids. I suppose they are on their way to Lenox."

"What shall we do?" she asked.

A great uproar arose from the people on the coach.

"Hello!" said Curtis.

"Hello!" yelled the people on the coach. Mr. Crewe got possession of the horn and produced fragments of the "Lohengrin Wedding March." The people in the street and the hangers-on about the hotel began to gather around.

Her brother waved his hand from the coach. "Well," he said, "how are you getting on? Quarreled yet? I am sorry, but we are completely out of rice."

"I don't understand," said Curtis, looking at the crowd in dismay. "This is a beautiful county, Willie. Historic battle-fields and all that sort of thing; besides, they breed some good horses all about here. We have been picking up one or two."

"For the bride!" called Winthrop, and he generously threw her an enormous bunch of wild roses which Crewe that morning had patiently pulled from the roadside bushes at the cost of no small suffering, and had presented to the elder Appleton girl.

Curtis ignored the episode. His eye at the moment caught a stable-boy leading a big chestnut horse toward the hotel. "Here's one we've just bought," he said. "I think he's likely to make a jumper." He felt his hand, which was behind him, squeezed surreptitiously, and he was aware of beaming some-what foolishly. He was glad that the people on the coach had turned their attention to the horse.

"Where did you find that?" asked Winthrop.

Curtis hesitated a moment. "Over that way," he said vaguely, waving his hand over an arc which extended from east to west. "It's a great country for horses."

Her brother had been inspecting the horse in silence. "My son," he said to the stable-boy, "how did you gall that race-horse's shoulder?"

"That's a collar-mark," said the boy. "Pulling a street-car is hard work."

Peals of laughter came from the coach.

"You needn't laugh," said the boy. "He's a horse all right."

She had moved to the horse's head. "I believe you," she said to the boy. "He's game."

"He is ma'am," said the boy.

"Well, Ting-a-ling," said her brother, addressing the chestnut horse, "we can't stop to admire you all day. You're not a bad-looking horse, but if you are a street-car horse, as unfortunately you are, you have the nature that will jump until you get tired, and then you'll roll over things, and make my sister an attractive widow. I wouldn't have you at any price."

"Then everybody is satisfied," said Curtis.

"I am, " she said. She gave him a little look that meant that she was sat-isfied with him, and Curtis felt that he was beaming again. He turned away.

The horse began to rub his nose against her arm and sniffed.

"He's looking for sugar," said the boy. "I give it to him sometimes."

"You are a very nice boy," she said. "What's your name?"

"Tim," said the boy.

"Let's have him take the horse down for us," she said to her husband. "We might keep him, too."

"All right," he said. "But let's get out of this crowd." They slipped away and hurried around the block.

"You were good to get him," she said in a low tone. "The way he acted made me feel that he wasn't meant for street-car work. What shall we call him?"

"I am afraid that brother Willie has already named him," he answered.

"What?" she demanded.

"Ting-a-ling," he replied.

"But he ought to be called Sultan or Emperor, or something like that," she insisted.

"You and I," he said, "we know what a heart he has; but, after all, he *is* a street-car horse. We'd better accept the facts."

"Well, then it's Ting-a-ling," she said.

IT was November; three years had slipped away. The race for the Hunt Club cup was coming off in the afternoon, and everybody was lunching at the club. She was patiently chaperoning the elder Appleton girl and Frank Crewe at a table on the glass-closed veranda overlooking the polo-field.

"We'll give you some lunch," she said to Winthrop, who was passing.

"I'm with Willie," he answered.

"Willie can come too," she said.

He thanked her and sat down.

"Is Ting-a-ling pretty fit?" he asked.

"I think so," she replied; "but of course he's never been steeplechased, so we don't know what he can do."

"He is certainly a good horse to hounds," said Winthrop.

"He's never been down," she said.

"Please don't say that on the day of the race," he interrupted; "it's unlucky."

Just then Willie joined them.

"Still talking steeplechase," he observed. "I suppose your husband is going to win."

"I don't know about that," she answered; "but he'll beat you."

"I'll bet he won't," he retorted. "It's a sure thing. I am not going to ride. They tell me that I am too fat, but that isn't the reason. I am afraid. Hello! here's the steeplechase jockey," he said to Curtis, who came in.

"Have you provided liberally for me in your will? Haven't I always been a good brother-in-law?"

"Always," said Curtis, "and no doubt you need the money; but I am not making wills today."

"You'd better," said Willie, cheerfully. "I'd hate to have that street-car horse roll you out and have no other consolation than the thought that you had loved me." His tone became less playful. "Bequeath me my nephew, and your widow can take the property."

"If that blessed boy of yours," Crewe said to Mrs. Curtis, "isn't ruined by the indulgence of his foolish old uncle, I shall be much surprised."

"*Taisez-vous!*" retorted Willie, "and get a nephew of your own."

Winthrop turned to Curtis. "How has the horse shown in his training?" he asked.

"He rates pretty well, and I have a good deal of confidence in his jumping," Curtis answered. "He's rather a pet, you know, so that perhaps my judgment is prejudiced."

"He'll go until he gets tired," put in Willie, "and then he'll shut up and go through his fences. Those big half-breds are all alike."

"How do you know he's a half-bred?" said Curtis.

"I don't know that he is anything," Willie retorted. "You got him out of a street-car."

"I think we would better change the subject," said his sister; "you're becoming disagreeable. Remember," she added to the party, "you are all coming in this evening to play bridge. You can't come to dinner, because the cook is sick."

From the hill back of the club-house they watched the race. A horse of Winthrop's with Crewe up, made the running for the first mile. Then Curtis took Ting-a-ling out of the bunch, and went away apparently without effort. At the two-mile flag Curtis was a hundred yards in the lead. The other horses seemed to be racing for the place.

"He seems to have things all his own way," said Winthrop to Mrs. Curtis. "My horse is done."

"He *is* going well," she whispered. She was very much excited.

Toward the middle of the third mile the four horses that were running in the second flight drew up, and it became a race again. Her heart almost stopped beating. "Is he tiring?" she murmured. The five went at the board fence near the third mile flag in a bunch. As they took off, there was crowding on the outside. Then four horses jumped cleanly; one fell, and the four went on again.

A rustle of apprehension ran through the crowd.

"Who's down?" exclaimed the elder Appleton girl in a low tone.

"Is he hurt?" said her sister.

"It's Ting-a-ling!" murmured Mrs. Curtis.

The horse got up, and galloped riderless after the leaders. A moment later the rider got up and started across the field on foot.

"He's not hurt," said Winthrop. "I'm awful sorry. He would have won."

"That's good of you," she replied. But she suspected that he was only softening the bitterness of the disappointment. Willie was right. The horse ran himself tired and stopped. She felt that she was very white and made an effort to talk. "That's your horse ahead with Frank Crewe," she said; "he's got the race."

It was so, and the crowd was already surging down to the finish-flags to congratulate the winner. Mrs. Curtis drove her cart across the meadow to meet the dismounted rider.

Their eyes met as she pulled up.

"It's too bad," she said. "Are you hurt?"

"I think my collar-bone is gone," he answered. "I'll see Tim and send the horse home, and then I'll go to the club and get bandaged."

He gave his orders to the boy.

"You was fouled, sir," said Tim. He was much excited. "I seen Mr. Crewe pull across you about two lengths from the fence."

"Not at all," said Mr. Curtis, shortly. "Walk him home at once and do him up."

"Is it so?" she asked. "Were you fouled?"

"I don't think I'd say it," he answered. "I rode very badly. It was my fault. I shouldn't have pulled back into the crowd."

She said nothing. She saw that he was very much disappointed. But the hardest for her to bear was that confidence in Ting-a-ling was gone.

At the club-house Willie was on the veranda.

"I am awfully sorry," he said. "But, seriously, you had better shoot the horse. You'll not be so lucky another time."

Curtis looked up angrily to reply, and then turned away with his lips tightly closed.

"I'll be ready in half an hour," he said to his wife.

In rather less than that time he came from his dressing-room, his arm in bandages and the hand in a sling. He sent for his trap, and found Mrs. Curtis in the tea-room.

"I think we had better go," he said. "They have just telephoned from the house, saying the baby isn't very well. I told the doctor to come along as soon as he could. Don't say anything to Willie about the little chap," he added. "He'll tag along and make a fuss and irritate me."

She rose and followed him. The trap was at the door, and they drove away.

Earlier, the November afternoon had been flooded with a damp sunshine, and there had been a still and unnatural mildness in the air. Toward four, as they left the club, the sky became overcast, and out of the West a mass of blue-black cloud began to rise and stretch across the horizon. Soon it threw the western part of the plain and the hills beyond into darkness. Overhead it was still light, but the shadow drew on and began to chill the day.

Curtis looked apprehensively toward the west and touched the horse with the whip. His wife had the reins.

"It's growing colder," she said.

He bent forward and tucked the robe about her feet.

Uncertain drafts of wind rattled the brown leaves on the oaks and made the dead goldenrods along the roadside bow excitedly.

"I am afraid that we are going to get wet," he said.

The gusts became stronger. The blackness from the west had spread until it was overhead, and light clouds were moving eastwardly across the face of the sky.

"I felt a drop of rain," she observed.

He urged the horse to a gallop.

"So did I," said he a moment later.

"It will be a good night to stay at home and read," he went on. "Don't you think I am getting to be quite a reader? Two books already this month; one of them had three hundred and twelve pages. But there were a good many pictures," he added conscientiously.

She smiled, but said nothing.

He watched her as they drove along. Presently he broke the silence.

"I wouldn't worry about the baby," he said. "Probably he has a little cold or a stomach-ache. The nurse is terrified if he sneezes."

"That's probably all," she said; "you know what a goose I am."

As they turned into the driveway the rain began to pour down. Under the porte-cochere she got out of the trap and went in while he held the horse.

Presently a man came from the stable, and he too went in. He was taking off his coat when his wife came down from the nursery.

"Well?" he asked.

"He's about the same," she answered. "He seems to have a little fever. What time did the doctor say he would be here?"

"About six," said Curtis. He looked at his watch. "It will be an hour yet. It's begun to snow," he added.

They went to the library, which looked toward the west, and watched the breaking storm.

"It was too bad about Ting-a-ling," she said after a pause.

"Well," he answered, "we have to take things as they come. I should like to have shown what a horse he is. We shall next year."

"I wish you would promise never to ride him in a race again," she said.

"I don't think you ought to ask that," he answered sharply. "For the horse's sake, I want him to have a chance to redeem himself. Don't you?"

"Isn't it wrong to take unnecessary risks?" she replied.

He made no answer.

The rain had changed to sleet, and the ground was already white. The bare elms on the lawn were creaking dismally. They could see the stiff shrubs in the garden bend to the gusts. The storm beat on the windowpanes, and in the fierce blasts the house trembled. As they stood by the window, the man brought lighted lamps, and they realized that the night had set in.

"Suppose we have a look at him," he said. By "him" he meant Ting-a-ling. "Won't you come? If the doctor arrives, they can send for us."

"I'd like to," she said.

On the way out, she went to the pantry and took some lumps of sugar.

The stable servants were at supper, and the stable was still except for the sound of the horses munching at their oats. As he drew the door open the grinding hushed except in the two stalls where the phaëton ponies ate stolidly on. The line of dusky heads was lifed and thrust curiously forward. From the box-stall in the corner came a low whinny, and in the dim light of the wall lamp they saw a long neck stretched out and two pointed ears cocked forward. It was Ting-a-ling.

"You beggar!" said Curtis. "You know what we've got." He went into the stall and stripped off the blankets. She followed him. "Hello!" he exclaimed. His arm was nipped gently. "You have very bad manners." The horse drew back, tossed his head, and pawed.

"Look here," Mrs. Curtis said. She held out a piece of sugar. A soft muzzle touched her hand, the lips opened and scraped across her palm, and there was a crunching sound.

"You baby!" she said, and gave him a second piece. "I'm very fond of you," she added under her breath, "in spite—" She stopped.

"He seems to be feeding well," said Curtis.

He put his hand into the manger. It touched the clean, moistened boards of the bottom.

"You're a pig!" he exclaimed. "He's put away five quarts already," he said to his wife. "Doesn't he look fit?"

They drew back and looked the horse over. The legs were clean, the great muscles stood out on forearm and quarter, the flesh was hard and spare.

"He's a great type," said Curtis, "isn't he? But if he were three-cornered I'd like him just as well. I'm ashamed to care so much for him."

"Do you remember the day we got him?" she asked.

He stepped back and put his arm around her.

"It seems yesterday, dear," he said. "How the years go by!" He put back the blankets, and stood a moment fastening the surcingle.

"Barring accidents, old horse," he muttered, "we'll have your name on the cup yet."

A swelling feeling came into his throat, and he put his face against the sleek neck. He straightened up quickly as he heard the doors slide apart and somebody come in.

"Mr. Curtis," called a voice. It was Tim.

"Hello!" said Curtis.

"The doctor's come," said Tim.

"All right," answered Curtis.

He drew his wife's wraps about her, and they made their way back to the house.

The doctor met them at the door of the nursery.

"This child is sick," he said. "The temperature has gone up in a way I don't like. We've got to operate."

"Operate!" Curtis exclaimed. He put his hand upon the banister. "What do you mean?"

"Yes," said the doctor.

"When?" said Mrs. Curtis.

"Lamplight is bad," said the doctor, "but we must do the best we can. It ought to be done before ten o'clock. I should be afraid to wait longer."

Neither husband nor wife spoke. The doctor looked at his watch.

"Whom would you rather have?" he asked.

"Have?" repeated Curtis. A gust rattled the windows at the end of the hall, and as it died away he heard the *tick-tick* of the sleet on the pane. He looked at the doctor with a white face.

"Can't *you* do it?" he asked. "Suppose we couldn't get any one from town by ten o'clock?"

"We must," said the doctor, cheerfully. "I'm not a surgeon, and there is none in the village. Would you rather have Anderson, or Tate?"

"Dr. Anderson," said Mrs. Curtis.

"He must get the train that leaves town at eight o'clock," said the doctor. "There is no other until midnight."

"It's quarter past six now," said Curtis. "That gives us just an hour and three quarters. I'll telephone at once." He left the room and went to the telephone.

After some delay the village operator answered.

"You can't get the city," said the girl; "the wires are down. I have been trying to get them for an hour for the telegraph people. Their line is closed, too."

"When do you expect your wires to be repaired?" he asked.

"Can't say," the operator replied. "Not to-night, though. The lineman can't work to-night."

"Thank you," said Curtis. He hung up the receiver and stood blankly before the instrument. He was about to move away when he heard a footstep. He turned, and his wife was standing beside him.

He put a cigarette in his mouth and struck a match.

"Is anything the matter?" she asked. "Won't he come?"

"He'll come," he answered. "I'm going to the station for him myself. I'll dine when I come back. You and the doctor get the things ready." He went into the smoking-room and walked the length of the room and back. "Six miles, ten, fifteen, and six more downtown," he said aloud. He looked at his watch again. It was twenty minutes past six. "Start at half-past," he went on; "that's twenty-one miles in an hour and a quarter—and these roads!" He went to the wall and rang a bell. "Twenty-one miles in an hour and a quarter," he repeated. "Searchlight can't do it, nor Xerxes, nor Huron, nor the roan mare."

A servant appeared.

"Tell Hobson," he said, "to saddle Ting-a-ling at once. Tell him to hurry, and send Tim here."

Tim came, and Curtis explained.

"Can he do it?" asked Curtis.

"I don't know, sir," said the boy.

"He's got to do it," said Curtis. "Do you understand?"

"Yes, sir."

They hurried to the stable, and found Hobson buckling the throat-latch.

"All ready, sir," he said.

Tim climbed into the saddle and gathered up his reins. Then Hobson threw open the door, and the horse and boy clattered out and disappeared in the storm.

Curtis looked at his watch. It was twenty-eight minutes past six. "Have the bus and a pair at the house at eight," he said, and went back to the house.

He met his wife in the hall.

"Is there any change?" he asked.

She shook her head.

"Suppose he should miss the train?" she suggested.

"He won't," said Curtis.

She sighed, and was silent for a pause. "What a wonderful thing the telephone is!" she said. "What would we have done without it?"

"That's so," said Curtis. "I'm going to the station at eight," he added.

At ten minutes of nine she was standing with her face against the window-pane, where the lights of the station bus in the driveway glimmered through the storm. She went to the head of the stairway and waited breathless.

"Suppose," she thought, "he has missed the train!"

Presently there sounded the crunching of wheels on the gravel under the porte-cochere. This meant that the bus was stopping at the house. Then the door opened.

"Come along," said her husband's voice.

"Thank God!" she murmured. She sat down for a moment, and then went to the nursery, which had been made into a hospital.

There was the tramp of ascending feet on the stairs, and then the surgeon and the village doctor came in and asked her to leave the room.

It seemed a long time, but it was only half an hour, when Dr. Anderson came out.

"It's all right," he said.

"What are the chances?" she asked.

"There aren't any," he replied; "that is, perhaps only one in a million—"

She looked alarmed.

"Of anything unpleasant happening," he went on. "We got it just in time. Your son is better off than other boys who wear their appendices. His is in a bottle."

The door-bell sounded faintly from the rear of the house, and they both listened. A moment later the front door opened, and she heard voices in the lower hall.

"They're a lot of people who've come in to play bridge. I'd forgotten about them," she said. "Will you tell them I'll be down presently?"

She went into the nursery, and Dr. Anderson went down-stairs.

When she came down she found them in the dining-room, watching the surgeon and Curtis eating supper, and asking them questions about the operation.

Her eyes caught Willie's. He was quiet and white.

He drew a chair for her, and she sat down next him. She put her hand in his.

"It's all right," she said.

"It was an awfully close shave," he whispered.

"Yes, it was," she answered.

She turned to Dr. Anderson. "You were good to come," she said. "I wonder what we would have done if you hadn't been at home when Mr. Curtis telephoned?"

"Telephone?" he repeated.

Curtis got up and went to the sideboard for a whisky-decanter.

"Yes, telephone," she said.

The surgeon looked at Curtis.

"Mary," said Curtis, "the telephone wires were down. Tim went to town for the doctor."

She looked around in amazement.

"But we didn't know till nearly half-past six," she exclaimed. She turned to Dr. Anderson. "You caught the eight o'clock train. How did Tim go?"

"On horseback," said Curtis.

"But that's twenty miles!" said Willie.

"Twenty-one," said Curtis; "he went in an hour and a quarter."

There was a silence for a moment. Then she spoke.

"What horse did he ride?" she demanded.

"What horse have we that could have done it?" replied Curtis.

She looked at him for a moment in apprehension. "Is he all right?" she asked.

"I don't know," said Curtis. "Tim came back by train."

"Send for Tim," she said to the butler.

When the bell rang he staggered a step forward. *By Paul Brown*

Tim came, and stood fumbling with his cap, which was soggy with melted snow.

"Weren't you frozen?" she asked.

"No, ma'am," the boy answered.

"Tell me about it," she said.

"Tell about it?" repeated the boy. "Why, ma'am—" He grew confused and stopped.

"But tell me—" she hesitated, and her lip trembled—"tell me how Ting-a-ling is."

The boy made no answer, but looked toward the surgeon.

She turned to Dr. Anderson. "What is it?" she demanded.

"I was starting to dine," said the surgeon, "when a policeman came to the door and said there was a sick horse on the corner, and a boy with him who wanted to see me. I went and found them both there."

"Well?" said Mrs. Curtis.

"Well," said the doctor, "as I reached the corner the cross-town trolley-car was letting off a passenger. When the bell rang to start, the horse in the street lifted his head, scrambled to his feet, staggered a step forward, and came down again. He was dead."

There was a stillness in the room, and the crying of a sick baby sounded faintly from up-stairs. Presently it ceased. For an instant the wife's eyes met those of her husband. Then resting her elbows on the table, she hid her face in her hands.

"God forgive me!" they heard Willie murmur in a queer voice. "That *was* a horse!"

"A street-car horse," said Curtis gently.

No one spoke again, but each rose and left the dining-room.

FOURTEEN

PHILIPPA'S FOX-HUNT

Somerville and Ross

No one can accuse Philippa and me of having married in haste. As a matter of fact, it was but little under five years from that autumn evening on the river when I had said what is called in Ireland "the hard word," to the day in August when I was led to the altar by my best man, and was subsequently led away from it by Mrs. Sinclair Yeates. About two years out of the five had been spent by me at Shreelane in ceaseless warfare with drains, eaveshoots, chimneys, pumps; all those fundamentals, in short, that the ingenuous and improving tenant expects to find established as a basis from which to rise to higher things. As far as rising to higher things went, frequent ascents to the roof to search for leaks summed up my achievements; in fact, I suffered so general a shrinkage of my ideals that the triumph of making the hall-door bell ring blinded me to the fact that the rat-holes in the hall floor were nailed up with pieces of tin biscuit boxes, and that the casual visitor could, instead of leaving a card, have easily written his name in the damp on the walls.

Philippa, however, proved adorably callous to these and similar shortcomings. She regarded Shreelane and its floundering, foundering ménage of incapables in the light of a gigantic picnic in a foreign land; she held long conversations daily with Mrs. Cadogan, in order, as she informed me, to acquire the language; without any ulterior domestic intention she engaged kitchen-maids because of the beauty of their eyes, and housemaids because they had such delightfully picturesque old mothers, and she declined to correct the phraseology of the parlor-maid, whose painful habit it was to whisper "Do ye choose cherry or clarry?" when proffering the wine. Fast-days, perhaps, afforded my wife her first insight into the sterner realities of Irish housekeeping. Philippa had what are known as High Church proclivities, and took the matter seriously.

"I don't know how we are to manage for the servants' dinner to-morrow, Sinclair," she said, coming in to my office one Thursday morning; "Julia says she 'promised God this long time that she wouldn't' eat an egg on a fast-day,' and the kitchen-maid says she won't eat herrings 'without they're fried with onions,' and Mrs. Cadogan says she will 'not go to them extremes for servants.'"

"I should let Mrs. Cadogan settle the menu herself," I suggested.

'I asked her to do that," replied Philippa, "and she only said she 'thanked God *she* had no appetite!'"

The lady of the house here fell away into unseasonable laughter.

I made the demoralizing suggestion that, as we were going away for a couple of nights, we might safely leave them to fight it out, and the problem was abandoned.

Philippa had been much called on by the neighbourhood in all its shades and grades, and daily she and her trousseau frocks presented themselves at hall-doors of varying dimensions in due acknowledgment of civilities. In Ireland, it may be noted, the process known in England as "summering and wintering" a newcomer does not obtain; sociability and curiosity alike forbid delay. The visit to which we owed our escape from the intricacies of the fast-day was to the Knoxes of Castle Knox, relations in some remote and tribal way of my landlord, Mr. Flurry of that ilk. It involved a short journey by train, and my wife's longest basket-trunk; it also, which was more serious, involved my being lent a horse to go out cubbing the following morning.

At Castle Knox we sank into an almost forgotten environment of draught-proof windows and doors, of deep carpets, of silent servants instead of clattering belligerents. Philippa told me afterwards that it had only been by an effort that she had restrained herself from snatching up the train of her wedding-gown as she paced across the wide hall on little Sir Valentine's arm. After three weeks at Shreelane she found it difficult to remember that the floor was neither damp nor dusty.

I had the good fortune to be of the limited number of those who got on with Lady Knox, chiefly, I imagine, because I was as a worm before her, and thankfully permitted her to do all the talking.

"Your wife is extremely pretty," she pronounced autocratically, survey-ing Philippa between the candle-shades; "does she ride?"

Lady Knox was a short square lady, with a weather-beaten face, and an eye decisive from long habit of taking her own line across country and else-where. She would have made a very imposing little coachman, and would have caused her stable helpers to rue the day they had the presumption to be born; it struck me that Sir Valentine sometimes did so.

"I'm glad you like her looks," I replied, "as I fear you will find her thor-oughly despicable otherwise; for one thing, she not only can't ride, but she believes that I can!"

"Oh come, you're not as bad as all that!" my hostess was good enough to say; "I'm going to put you up on Sorcerer to-morrow, and we'll see you at the top of the hunt—if there if one. That young Knox hasn't a notion how to draw these woods."

"Well, the best run we had last year out of this place was with Flurry's hounds," struck in Miss Sally, sole daughter of Sir Valentine's house and home, from her place half-way down the table. It was not difficult to see that she and her mother held different views on the subject of Mr. Flurry Knox.

"I call it a criminal thing in any one's great-great-grandfather to rear up a preposterous troop of sons and plant them all out in his own country," Lady Knox said to me with apparent irrelevance. "I detest collaterals. Blood may be thicker than water, but it is also a great deal nastier. In this country I find that fifteenth cousins consider themselves near relations if they live within twenty miles of one!"

Having before now taken in the position with regard to Flurry Knox, I took care to accept these remarks as generalities, and turned the conversation to other themes.

"I see Mrs. Yeates is doing wonders with Mr. Hamilton," said Lady Knox presently, following the direction of my eyes, which had strayed away to where Philippa was beaming upon her left-hand neighbour, a mildewed-looking old clergyman, who was delivering a long dissertation, the purport of which we were happily unable to catch.

"She has always had a gift for the Church," I said.

"Not curates?' said Lady Knox, in her deep voice.

I made haste to reply that it was the elders of the Church who were venerated by my wife.

Lady Knox

"Well, she has her fancy in old Eustace Hamilton; he's elderly enough!" said Lady Knox. "I wonder if she'd venerate him as much if she knew that he had fought with his sister-in-law, and they haven't spoken for thirty years! though for the matter of that," she added, "I think it shows his good sense!"

"Mrs. Knox is rather a friend of mine," I ventured.

"Is she? H'm! Well, she's not one of mine!' replied my hostess, with her usual definiteness. "I'll say one thing of her, I believe she's always been a sportswoman. She's very rich, you know, and they say she only married old Badger Knox to save his hounds from being sold to pay his debts and then she took the horn from him and hunted them herself. Has she been rude to your wife yet? No? Oh, well, she will. It's a mere question of time. She hates all English people. You know the story they tell of her? She was coming home from London, and when she was getting her ticket the man asked if she had said a ticket for York. 'No, thank God, Cork!' says Mrs. Knox."

"Well, I rather agree with her!" said I; "but why did she fight with Mr. Hamilton?"

"Oh, nobody knows. I don't believe they know themselves! Whatever it was, the old lady drives five miles to Fortwilliam every Sunday, rather than go to his church, just outside her own back gates," Lady Knox said with a laugh like a terrier's bark. "I wish I'd fought with him myself," she said; "he gives us forty minutes every Sunday."

As I struggled into my boots the following morning, I felt that Sir Valentine's acid confidences on cub-hunting, bestowed on me at midnight, did credit to his judgment. "A very moderate amusement, my dear Major," he had said, in his dry little voice; "you should stick to shooting. No one expects you to shoot before daybreak."

It was six o'clock as I crept downstairs, and found Lady Knox and Miss Sally at breakfast, with two lamps on the table, and foggy daylight oozing in from under the half-raised blinds. Philippa was already in the hall, pumping up her bicycle, in a state of excitement at the prospect of her first experience of hunting that would have been more comprehensible to me had she been going to ride a strange horse, as I was. As I bolted my food I saw the horses being led past the windows, and a faint twang of a horn told that Flurry Knox and his hounds were not far off.

Miss Sally jumped up.

"If I'm not on the Cockatoo before the hounds come up, I shall never get there!" she said, hobbling out of the room in the toils of her safety habit. Her small, alert face looked very childish under her riding-hat; the lamp-light struck sparks out of her thick coil of golden-red hair: I wondered how I had ever thought her like her prim little father.

She was already on her white cob when I got to the hall-door, and Flurry Knox was riding over the glistening wet grass with his hounds, while his whip, Dr. Jerome Hickey, was having a stirring time with the young entry and the rabbit-holes. They moved on without stopping, up a back avenue, under tall and dripping trees, to a thick laurel covert, at some little distance from the house. Into this the hounds were thrown and the usual period of fidgety inaction set in for the riders, of whom, all told, there were about a half-a-dozen. Lady Knox, square and solid, on her big, confidential iron-grey, was near me, and her eyes were on me and my mount; with her rubicund face and white collar she was more than ever like a coachman.

"Sorcerer looks as if he suited you well," she said, after a few minutes of silence, during which the hounds rustled and crackled steadily through the laurels; "he's a little high on the leg, and so are you, you know, so you show each other off."

Sorcerer was standing like a rock, with his good-looking head in the air and his eyes fastened on the covert. His manners, so far, had been those of a perfect gentleman, and were in marked contrast to those of Miss Sally's cob, who was sidling, hopping, and snatching unappeasably at his bit. Philippa had disappeared from view down the avenue ahead. The fog was melting, and the sun threw long blades of light through the trees; everything was quiet, and in the distance the curtained windows of the house marked the warm repose of Sir Valentine, and those of the party who shared his opinion of cubbing.

"Hark! hark to cry there!"

It was Flurry's voice, away at the other side of the covert. The rustling and brushing through the laurels became more vehement, then passed out of hearing.

"He never will leave his hounds alone," said Lady Knox disapprovingly.

Miss Sally and the Cockatoo moved away in a series of heraldic capers towards the end of the laurel plantation, and at the same moment I saw Philippa on her bicycle shoot into view on the drive ahead of us.

"I've seen a fox!" she screamed, white with what I believe to have been personal terror, though she says it was excitement; "it passed quite close to me!"

"What way did he go?" bellowed a voice which I recognized as Dr. Hickey's, somewhere in the deep of the laurels.

"Down the drive!" returned Philippa, with a pea-hen quality in her tones with which I was quite unacquainted.

An electrifying screech of "Gone away!" was projected from the laurels by Dr. Hickey.

"Gone away!" chanted Flurry's horn at the top of the covert.

"This is what he calls cubbing!" said Lady Knox "a mere farce!" but none the less she loosed her sedate monster into a canter.

Sorcerer got his hind-legs under him, and hardened his crest against the bit, as we all hustled along the drive after the flying figure of my wife. I knew very little about horses, but I realised that even with the hounds tumbling hysterically out of the covert, and the Cockatoo kicking the gravel into his face, Sorcerer comported himself with the manners of the best society. Up a side road I saw Flurry Knox opening half of a gate and cramming through it; in a moment we also had crammed through, and the turf or a pasture field was under our feet. Dr. Hickey leaned forward and took hold of his horse; I did likewise, with the trifling difference that my horse took hold of me, and I steered for Flurry Knox with single-hearted purpose, the hounds, already a field ahead, being merely an exciting and noisy accompaniment of this endeavor. A heavy stone wall was the first occurrence of note. Flurry chose a place where the top was loose, and his clumsy-looking brown mare changed feet on the rattling stones like a fairy. Sorcerer came at it, tense and collected as a bow at full stretch, and sailed steeply into the air; I saw the wall far beneath me, with an unsuspected ditch on the far side, and I felt my hat following me at the full stretch of its guard as we swept over it, then, with a long slant, we descended to earth some sixteen feet from where we had left it, and I was possessor of the gratifying fact that I had achieved a good-sized "fly," and had not perceptibly moved in my saddle. Subsequent disillusioning experience has taught me that but few horses jump like Sorcerer, so gallantly, so sympathetically, and with such supreme mastery of the subject; but none the less the enthusiasm that he imparted to me has never been extinguished, and that October morning ride revealed to me the unsuspected intoxication of fox-hunting.

Behind me I heard the scrabbling of the Cockatoo's little hoofs among the loose stones, and Lady Knox, galloping on my left, jerked a maternal chin over her shoulder to mark her daughter's progress. For my part, had there been an entire circus behind me, I was far too much occupied with ramming on my hat and trying to hold Sorcerer, to have looked round, and all my spare faculties were devoted to steering for Flurry, who had taken a right-handed turn, and was at that moment surmounting a bank of uncertain and briary aspect. I surmounted it also, with the swiftness and simplicity for which the Quaker's methods of bank jumping had not prepared me, and two or three fields, traversed at the same steeplechase pace, brought us to a road and to an abrupt check. There, suddenly, were the hounds, scrambling in baffled silence down into the road from the opposite bank, to look for the line they had overrun, and there, amazingly, was Philippa, engaged in excited converse with several men with spades over their shoulders.

"Did ye see the fox, boys?" shouted Flurry, addressing the group.

"We did! We did!" cried my wife and her friends in chorus; "he ran up the road!"

"We'd be badly off without Mrs. Yeates!" said Flurry, as he whirled his mare round and clattered up the road with a hustle of hounds after him.

It occurred to me as forcibly as any mere earthly thing can occur to those who are wrapped in the sublimities of a run, that, for a young woman who had never before seen a fox out of a cage at the Zoo, Philippa was taking to hunting very kindly. Her cheeks were a most brilliant pink, her blue eyes shone.

"Oh, Sinclair!" she exclaimed, "they say he's going for Aussolas, and there's a road I can ride all the way!"

"Ye can, Miss! Sure we'll show you!" chorussed her *cortège.*

Her foot was on a pedal ready to mount. Decidedly my wife was in no need of assistance from me.

Up the road a hound gave a yelp of discovery, and flung himself over a stile into the fields; the rest of the pack went squealing and jostling after him, and I followed Flurry over one of those infinitely varied erections, pleasantly termed "gaps" in Ireland. On this occasion the gap was made of three razor-edged slabs of slate leaning against an iron bar, and Sorcerer conveyed to me his thorough knowledge of the matter by a lift of his hind-quarters that made me feel as if I were being skillfully kicked downstairs. To what extent I looked it, I cannot say, nor providently can Philippa, as she had already started. I only know that undeserved good luck restored to me my stirrup before Sorcerer got away with me in the next field.

What followed was, I am told, a very fast fifteen minutes; for me time was not; the empty fields rushed past uncounted, fences came and went in a flash, while the wind sang in my ears, and the dazzle of the early sun was in my eyes. I saw the hounds occasionally, sometimes pouring over a green bank, as the charging breaker lifts and flings itself, sometimes driving across a field, as the white tongues of foam slide racing over the sand; and always ahead of me was Flurry Knox, going as a man goes who knows his country, who knows his horse, and whose heart is wholly and absolutely in the right place.

Do what I would, Sorcerer's implacable stride carried me closer and closer to the brown mare, till, as I thundered down the slope of a long field, I was not twenty yards behind Flurry. Sorcerer had stiffened his neck to iron, and to slow him down was beyond me; but I fought his head away to the right, and found myself coming hard and steady at a stonefaced bank with broken ground in front of it. Flurry bore away to the left, shouting something that I did not understand. That Sorcerer shortened his stride at the right moment was entirely due to his own judgment; standing well away from the jump, he rose like a stag out of the tussocky ground, and as he swung my twelve stone six into the air the obstacle revealed itself to him and me as consisting not of one bank but of two, and between the two lay a deep grassy lane, half choked with furze. I have often been asked to state the width of the

I felt as if I were being skilfully kicked downstairs

bohereen, and can only reply that in my opinion it was at least eighteen feet; Flurry Knox and Dr. Hickey, who did not jump it, say that it is not more than five. What Sorcerer did with it I cannot say; the sensation was of a towering flight with a kick back in it, a biggish drop, and a landing on cee-springs, still on the downhill grade. That was how one of the best horses in Ireland took one of Ireland's most ignorant riders over a very nasty place.

A sombre line of fir-wood lay ahead, rimmed with a grey wall, and in another couple of minutes we had pulled up on the Aussolas road, and were watching the hounds struggling over the wall into Aussolas demesne.

"No hurry now," said Flurry, turning in his saddle to watch the Cockatoo jump into the road, "he's to ground in the big earth inside. Well, Major, it's well for you that's a big-jumped horse. I thought you were a dead man a while ago when you faced him at the bohereen!"

I was disclaiming intention in the matter when Lady Knox and the others joined us.

"I thought you told me your wife was no sportswoman," she said to me, critically scanning Sorcerer's legs for cuts the while, "but when I saw her a minute ago she had abandoned her bicycle and was running across country like—"

"Look at her now!" interrupted Miss Sally. "Oh!—oh!" In the interval between these exclamations my incredulous eyes beheld my wife in mid-air, hand in hand with a couple of stalwart country boys, with whom she was leaping in unison from the top of a bank on to the road.

Every one, even the saturnine Dr. Hickey, began to laugh; I rode back to Philippa, who was exchanging compliments and congratulations with her escort.

"Oh, Sinclair!" she cried, "wasn't it splendid? I saw you jumping, and everything! Where are they going now?"

"My dear girl," I said, with marital disapproval, "you're killing yourself. Where's your bicycle?"

"Oh, its punctured in a sort of lane, back there. It's all right; and then they"—she breathlessly waved her hand at her attendants—"they showed me the way."

"Begor! you proved very good, Miss!" said a grinning cavalier.

"Faith she did!" said another, polishing his shining brow with his white flannel coat-sleeve, "she lepped like a haarse!"

"And may I ask how you propose to go home?" said I.

"I don't know and I don't care! I'm not going home!" She cast an entirely disobedient eye at me. "And your eye-glass is hanging down your back and your tie is bulging out over your waistcoat!"

The little group of riders had begun to move away.

"We're going on into Aussolas," called out Flurry; "come on, and make my grandmother give you some breakfast, Mrs. Yeates; she always has it at eight o'clock."

The front gates were close at hand, and we turned in under the tall beech-trees, with the unswept leaves rustling round the horses' feet, and the lovely blue of the October morning sky filling the spaces between smooth grey branches and golden leaves. The woods rang with the voices of the hounds, enjoying an untrammeled rabbit hunt, while the Master and the Whip, both on foot, strolled along unconcernedly with their bridles over their arms, making themselves agreeable to my wife, an occasional touch of Flurry's horn, or a crack of Dr. Hickey's whip, just indicating to the pack that the authorities still took a friendly interest in their doings.

Down a grassy glade in the wood a party of old Mrs. Knox's young horses suddenly swept into view, headed by an old mare, who, with her tail over her back, stampeded ponderously past our cavalcade, shaking and swinging her handsome old head, while her youthful friends bucked and kicked and snapped at each other round her with the ferocious humour of their kind.

"Here, Jerome, take the horn," said Flurry to Dr. Hickey; "I'm going to see Mrs. Yeates up to the house, the way these tomfools won't gallop on top of her."

From this point it seems to me that Philippa's adventures are more worthy of record than mine, and as she has favored me with a full account of them, I venture to think my version may be relied on.

Mrs. Knox was already at breakfast when Philippa was led, quaking, into her formidable presence. My wife's acquaintance with Mrs. Knox was, so far, limited to a state visit on either side, and she found but little comfort in Flurry's assurances that his grandmother wouldn't mind if he brought all the hounds in to breakfast, coupled with the statement that she would put her eyes on sticks for the Major.

Whatever the truth of this may have been, Mrs. Knox received her guest with an equanimity quite unshaken by the fact that her boots were in the fender instead of on her feet, and that a couple of shawls of varying dimensions and degrees of age did not conceal the inner presence of a magenta flannel dressing-jacket. She installed Philippa at the table and plied her with food, oblivious as to whether the needful implements with which to eat it were forthcoming or no. She told Flurry where a vixen had reared her family, and she watched him ride away, with some biting comments on his mare's hocks screamed after him from the window.

The dining-room at Aussolas Castle is one of the many rooms in Ireland in which Cromwell is said to have stabled his horse (and probably no one would have objected less than Mrs. Knox had she been consulted in the matter). Philippa questions if the room had ever been tidied up since, and she endorses Flurry's observation that "there wasn't a day in the year you wouldn't get feeding for a hen and chickens on the floor." Opposite to Philippa, on a Louis Quinze chair, sat Mrs. Knox's woolly dog, its suspicious little eyes peering at her out of their setting of pink lids and dirty white wool. A couple of young horses outside the windows tore at the matted creepers on the walls, or thrust faces that were half-shy, half-impudent, into the room. Portly pigeons waddled to and fro on the broad window-sill, sometimes flying in to perch on the picture-frames, while they kept up incessantly a hoarse and pompous cooing.

Animals and children are, as a rule, alike destructive to conversation; but Mrs. Knox, when she chose, *bien entendu,* could have made herself agreeable in a Noah's ark, and Philippa has a gift of sympathetic attention that personal experience has taught me to regard with distrust as well as respect, while it has often made me realize the worldly wisdom of Kingsley's injunction:

"Be good, sweet maid, and let who will be clever."

Family prayers, declaimed by Mrs. Knox with alarming austerity, followed close on breakfast, Philippa and a vinegar-faced henchwoman forming the family. The prayers were long, and through the open window as they progressed came distantly a whoop or two; the declamatory tones staggered a little, and then continued at a distinctly higher rate of speed.

"Ma'am! Ma'am!" whispered a small voice at the window.

Mrs. Knox made a repressive gesture and held on her way. A sudden out-cry of hounds followed, and the owner of the whisper, a small boy with a face freckled like a turkey's egg, darted from the window and dragged a donkey and bath-chair into view. Philippa admits to having lost the thread of the dis-course, but she thinks that the "Amen" that immediately ensued can hardly have come in its usual place. Mrs. Knox shut the book abruptly, scrambled up from her knees, and said, "They've found!"

In a surprisingly short space of time she had added to her attire her boots, a fur cape, and a garden hat, and was in the bath-chair, the small boy stimulating the donkey with the success peculiar to his class, while Philippa hung on behind.

The woods of Aussolas are hilly and extensive, and on that particular morning it seemed that they held as many foxes as hounds. In vain was the horn blown and the whips cracked, small rejoicing parties of hounds, each with a fox of its own, scoured to and fro: every labourer in the vicinity had left his work, and was sedulously heading every fox with yells that would have befitted a tiger hunt, and sticks and stones when occasion served.

"Will I pull out as far as the big rosydandhrum, ma'am?" inquired the small boy; "I seen three of the dogs go in it, and they yowling."

"You will," said Mrs. Knox, thumping the donkey on the back with her umbrella; "here! Jeremiah Regan! Come down out of that with that pitch-fork! Do you want to kill the fox, you fool?"

"I do not, your honor, ma'am," responded Jeremiah Regan, a tall young countryman, emerging from a bramble brake.

"Did you see him?" said Mrs. Knox eagerly.

"I see himself and his ten pups drinking below at the lake here yester-day, your honour, ma'am, and he as big as a chestnut horse!" said Jeremiah.

"Faugh! Yesterday!" snorted Mrs. Knox; "go on to the rhododendrons, Johnny!"

The party, reinforced by Jeremiah and the pitchfork, progressed at a high rate of speed along the shrubbery path, encountering *en route* Lady Knox, stooping on to her horse's neck under the sweeping branches of the laurels.

"Your horse is too high for my coverts, Lady Knox," said the Lady of the Manor, with a malicious eye at Lady Knox's flushed face and dinged hat; "I'm afraid you will be left behind like Absalom when the hounds go away!"

"As they never do anything here but hunt rabbits," retorted her lady-ship, "I don't think that's likely."

Mrs. Knox gave her donkey another whack, and passed on.

"Rabbits, my dear!" she said scornfully to Philippa. "That's all she knows about it. I declare it disgusts me to see a woman of that age making such a Judy of herself! Rabbits indeed!"

Down in the thicket of rhododendron everything was very quiet for a time. Philippa strained her eyes in vain to see any of the riders; the horn blowing and the whip cracking passed on almost out of hearing. Once or twice a hound worked through the rhododendrons, glanced at the party, and hurried on, immersed in business. All at once Johnny, the donkey-boy, whispered excitedly:

"Look at he! Look at he!" and pointed to a boulder of grey rock that stood out among the dark evergreens. A big yellow cub was crouching on it; he instantly slid into the shelter of the bushes, and the irrepressible Jeremiah, uttering a rending shriek, plunged into the thicket after him. Two or three hounds came rushing at the sound, and after this Philippa says she finds some difficulty in recalling the proper order of events; chiefly, she confesses, because of the wholly ridiculous tears of excitement that blurred her eyes.

"We ran," she said, "we simply tore, and the donkey galloped, and as for that old Mrs. Knox, she was giving cracked screams to the hounds all the time, and they were screaming too; and then somehow we were all out on the road!"

What seems to have occurred was that three couple of hounds, Jeremiah Regan, and Mrs. Knox's equipage, amongst them somehow hustled the cub out of Aussolas demesne and up on to a hill on the farther side of the road. Jeremiah was sent back by his mistress to fetch Flurry, and the rest of the party pursued a thrilling course along the road, parallel with that of the hounds, who were hunting slowly through the gorse on the hillside.

"Upon my honour and word, Mrs. Yeates, my dear, we have the hunt to ourselves!" said Mrs. Knox to the panting Philippa, as they pounded along the road. "Johnny, d'ye see the fox?"

"I do, ma'am!" shrieked Johnny, who possessed the usual field-glass vision bestowed upon his kind. "Look at him over-right us on the hill above! Hi! The spotty dog have him! No, he's gone from him! *Gwan out o' that!*" This to the donkey, with blows that sounded like the beating of carpets, and produced rather more dust.

They had left Aussolas some half a mile behind, when, from a strip of wood on their right, the fox suddenly slipped over the bank on to the road just ahead of them, ran up it for a few yards and whisked in at a small entrance gate, with the three couple of hounds yelling on a red-hot scent, not thirty yards behind. The bath-chair party whirled in at their heels, Philippa and the donkey considerably blown, Johnny scarlet through his freckles, but as fresh as paint, the old lady blind and deaf to all things save the chase. The hounds went raging through the shrubs beside the drive, and away down a grassy slope towards a shallow glen, in the bottom of which ran a little stream, and after them over the grass bumped the bath-chair. At the stream they turned sharply and ran up the glen towards the avenue, which crossed it by means of a rough stone viaduct.

" 'Pon me conscience, he's into the old culvert!" exclaimed Mrs. Knox; "there was one of my hounds choked there once, long ago! Beat on the donkey, Johnny!"

At this juncture Philippa's narrative again becomes incoherent, not to say breathless. She is, however, positive that it was somewhere about here that the upset of the bath-chair occurred, but she cannot be clear as to whether she picked up the donkey or Mrs. Knox, or whether she herself was picked up by Johnny while Mrs. Knox picked up the donkey. From my knowledge of Mrs. Knox I should say she picked up herself and no one else. At all events, the next salient point is the palpitating moment when Mrs. Knox, Johnny, and Philippa successively applying an eye to the opening of the culvert by which the stream trickled under the viaduct, while five dripping hounds bayed and leaped around them, discovered by more sense that that of sight that the fox was in it, and furthermore that one of the hounds was in it too.

"There's a sthrong grating before him at the far end," said Johnny, his head in at the mouth of the hole, his voice sounding as if he were talking into a jug, "the two of thems' fighting in it; they'll be choked surely!"

"Then don't' stand gabbling there, you little fool, but get in and pull the hound out!" exclaimed Mrs. Knox, who was balancing herself on a stone in the stream.

"I'd be in dread ma'am," whined Johnny.

"Balderdash!" said the implacable Mrs. Knox. "In with you!"

I understand that Philippa assisted Johnny into the culvert, and presume that it was in so doing that she acquired the two Robinson Crusoe bare footprints which decorated her jacket when I next met her.

"Have you got hold of him yet, Johnny?" cried Mrs. Knox up the culvert.

"I have, ma'am, by the tail," responded Johnny's voice, sepulchral in the depths.

"Can you stir him, Johnny?"

"I cannot, ma'am, and the wather is rising in it."

"Well, please God, they'll not open the mill dam!" remarked Mrs. Knox philosophically to Philippa, as she caught hold of Johnny's dirty ankles. "Hold on to the tail, Johnny!"

She hauled, with, as might be expected, no appreciable result. "Run, my dear, and look for somebody, and we'll have that fox yet!"

Philippa ran, whither she knew not, pursued by fearful visions of bursting mill-dams, and maddened foxes at bay. As she sped up the avenue she heard voices, robust male voices, in a shrubbery, and made for them.

Advancing along an embowered walk towards her was what she took for one wild instant to be a funeral; a second glance showed her that it was a party of clergymen of all ages, walking by twos and threes in the dappled shade of the over-arching trees. Obviously she had intruded her sacrilegious presence into a Clerical Meeting. She acknowledges at this awe-inspiring spectacle she faltered, but the thought of Johnny, the hound, and the fox, suffocating, possibly drowning together in the culvert, nerved her. She does not remember what she said or how she said it, but I fancy she must have conveyed to them the impression that old Mrs. Knox was being drowned, as she immediately found herself heading a charge of the Irish Church towards the scene of disaster.

Fate has not always used me well, but on this occasion it was mercifully decreed that I and the other members of the hunt should be privileged to arrive in time to see my wife and her rescue party precipitating themselves down the glen.

"Holy Biddy!" ejaculated Flurry, is she running a paper-chase with all the parsons? But look! For pity's sake will you look at my grandmother and my Uncle Eustace?"

Mrs. Knox and her sworn enemy the old clergyman, whom I had met at dinner the night before, were standing, apparently in the stream, tugging at two bare legs that projected from a hole in the viaduct, and arguing at the top of their voices. The bath-chair lay on its side with the donkey grazing beside it, on the bank a stout Archdeacon was tendering advice, and the hounds danced and howled round the entire group.

"I tell you, Eliza, you had better let the Archdeacon try," thundered Mr. Hamilton.

"Then I tell you I will not!" vociferated Mrs. Knox, with a tug at the end of the sentence that elicited a subterranean lament from Johnny. "Now who was right about the second grating? I told you so twenty years ago!"

Exactly as Philippa and her rescue party arrived, the efforts of Mrs. Knox and her brother-in-law triumphed. The struggling, sopping form of Johnny was slowly drawn from the hole, drenched, speechless, but clinging to the stern of a hound who, in its turn, had its jaws fast in the hindquarters of a limp, yellow cub.

"Oh, it's dead!" wailed Philippa, "I *did* think I should have been in time to save it!"

"Well, if that doesn't' beat all!" said Dr. Hickey.

FIFTEEN

A NINETEENTH-CENTURY MIRACLE

Somerville and Ross

Captain "Pat" Naylor, of the —th Dragoons, had the influenza. For three days he had lain prostrate, a sodden and aching victim to the universal leveler, and an intolerable nuisance to his wife. This last is perhaps an over-statement; Mrs. Naylor was in the habit of bearing other people's burdens with excellent fortitude, but she felt justly annoyed that Captain Pat should knock up before they had fairly settled down in their new quarters, and while yet three of the horses were out of sorts after the crossing from England.

Pilot, however, was quite fit, a very tranquillising fact, and one that Mrs. Pat felt was due to her own good sense in summering him on her father's broad pastures in Meath, instead of "lugging him to Aldershot with the rest of the string, as Pat wanted to do," as she explained to Major Booth. Major Booth shed a friendly grin upon his fallen comrade, who lay, a deplorable object, on the horrid velvet-covered sofa peculiar to indifferent lodgings, and said vaguely that one of his brutes was right anyhow, and he was going to ride him at Carnfother the next day.

"You'd better come too, Mrs. Pat," he added; "and if you'll drive me I'll send my chap on with the horse. It's too far to ride. It's fourteen Irish miles off, and fourteen Irish miles is just about the longest distance I know."

Carnfother is a village in a remote part of the Co. Cork; it possesses a small hotel—in Ireland no hostelry, however abject, would demean itself by accepting the title of inn—a police barrack, a few minor public-houses, a good many dirty cottages, and an unrivalled collection of loafers. The stretch of salmon river that gleamed away to the distant heathery hills afforded the *raison d'être* of both hotel and loafers, but the fishing season had not begun and the attention of both was therefore undividedly bestowed on Mrs. Naylor and Major Booth. The former's cigarette and the somewhat Paradisaic dimensions of her apron skirt would indeed at any time have rivalled in interest the landing of a 20-lb. fish, and as she strode into the hotel the bystanders' ejaculatory piety would have done credit to a revival meeting.

"Well, well, I'll say nothing for her but that she's quare!" said the old landlady, hurrying in from her hens to attend to these rarer birds whom fortune had sent to her net.

Mrs. Pat's roan cob had attacked and defeated the fourteen Irish miles with superfluous zeal, and there were still several minutes before the hounds could be reasonably expected on the scene. The soda was bad, the whisky was worse. The sound of a fiddle came in with the sunshine through the open door, and our friends strolled out into the street to see what was going on. In the centre of a ring of onlookers an old man was playing, and was, moreover, dancing to his own music, and dancing with serious, incongruous elegance. Round and round the circle he footed it, his long thin legs twinkling in absolute accord with the complicated jig that his long thin fingers were ripping out of the cracked and raucous fiddle. A very plain, stout young woman, with heavy red face and discordantly golden hair, shuffled round after him in a clumsy pretence of dancing, and as the couple faced Mrs. Pat she saw that the old man was blind. Steam was rising from his domed bald head, and his long black hair danced on his shoulders. His face was pale and strange and entirely self-absorbed. Had Mrs. Pat been in the habit of instituting romantic parallels between the past and the present she might have thought of the priests of Baal who danced in probably just such measures round the cromlechs in the hills above Carnfother; as she wasn't, she remarked merely that this was all very well, but that the old maniac would have to clear out of that before they brought Pilot round, or there'd be trouble.

There was trouble, but it did not arise from Pilot, but from the yellow-haired woman's pertinacious demands for money from Mrs. Naylor. She had the offensive fluency that comes of long practice in alternate wheedling and bullying, and although Major Booth had given her a shilling she continued to pester Mrs. Pat for a further largesse. But, as it happened, Mrs. Pat's purse was in her covert coat in the dog-cart, and Mrs. Pat's temper was ever within easy reach, and on being too closely pressed for the one she exhibited the other with a decision that contracted the ring of bystanders to hear the fun, and loosened the yellow-haired woman's language, till unfortunate Major Booth felt that if he could get her off the field of battle for a sovereign it would be cheap at the price. The old man continued to walk round and round, fingering a dumb tune on his fiddle that he did not bow, while the sunlight glistened hot and bright in his unwinking eyes; there was a faint smile on his lips, he heard as little as he saw; it was evident that he was away where "beyond these voices there is peace," in the fairy country that his forefathers called the Tir na'n Oge.

At this juncture the note of the horn sounded very sweetly from across the shining ford of the river. Hounds and riders came splashing up into the village street, the old man and his daughter were hustled to one side, and Mrs. Pat's affability returned as she settled her extremely smart little person on Pilot's curveting back, and was instantly aware that there was nothing present that could touch either of them in looks or quality. Carnfother was at the extreme verge of the D— Hounds' country; there were not more than about thirty riders out, and Mrs. Pat was not far wrong when she observed to Major Booth that there was not much class about them. Of the four or five women who were of the field, but one wore a habit with any pretensions to conformity with the sacred laws of fashion, and its colour was a blue that, taken in connection with a red, brass-buttoned waistcoat, reminded the severe critic from Royal Meath of the head porter at the Shelburne Hotel. So she informed Major Booth in one of the rare intervals permitted to her by Pilot for conversation.

"All right," responded the gentleman, "you wait until you and that ramping brute of yours get up among the stone walls, and you'll be jolly glad if she'll call a cab for you and see you taken safe home. I tell you what—you won't be able to see the way she goes."

"Rubbish!" said Mrs. Pat, and, whether from sympathy or from a petulant touch of her heel, Pilot at this moment involved himself in so intricate a series of plunges and bucks as to preclude further discussion.

This first covert—a small wood on the flank of a hill—was blank, and the hounds moved on across country to the next draw. It was a land of pasture, and in every fence was a deep muddy passage, through which the field splashed in single file with the grave stolidity of the cows by whom the gaps had been made. Mrs. Pat was feeling horribly bored. Her escort had joined himself to two of the ladies of the hunt, and though it was gratifying to observe that one wore a paste brooch in her tie and the other had an imitation cavalry bit and bridle, with a leather tassel hanging form her pony's throat, these things lost their savour when she had no one with whom to make merry over them. She had left her sandwiches in the dog-cart, her servant had mistaken whisky for sherry when he was filling her flask; the day had clouded over, and already one brief but furious shower had scourged the curl out of her dark fringe and made the reins slippery.

At last, however, a nice-looking gorse covert was reached, and the hounds threw themselves into it with promising alacrity. Pilot steadied himself, and stood with pricked ears, giving an occasional snatch at his bit, and looking, as no one knew better than his rider, the very picture of a hunter, while he listened for the first note that should tell of a find. He had not long to wait. There came a thin little squeal from the middle of the covert, and a hound flung up out of the thicker gorse and began to run along a ridge of rock, with head down, and feathering stern.

"They've got him, my lady," said a young farmer on a rough three-year-old to Mrs. Pat, as he stuffed his pipe in his pocket. "That's Patience; we'll have a hunt out o' this."

Then came another and longer squeal as Patience plunged out of sight again, and then, as the glowing chorus rose from the half-seen pack, a whip, posted on a hillside beyond the covert, raised his cap high in the air, and a wild screech that set Pilot dancing from leg to leg broke from a country boy who was driving a harrow in the next field: "Ga—aane awa—ay!"

Mrs. Pat forgot her annoyances. Her time had come. She would show that idiot Booth that Pilot was not to be insulted with impunity, and— But here retrospect and intention became alike merged in the present, and in the single resolve to get ahead and stay there. Half a dozen of Pilot's great reaching strides, and she was in the next field and over the low bank without putting an iron on it. The horse with the harrow, deserted by his driver, was following the hunt with the best of them, and, combining business with pleasure, was, as he went, harrowing the field with absurd energy. The Paste Brooch and the Shelburne Porter—so Mrs. Pat mentally distinguished them—were sailing along with a good start, and Major Booth was close at their heels. The light soil of the tilled field flew in every direction as thirty or more horses raced across it, and the usual retinue of foot runners raised an ecstatic yell as Mrs. Pat forged ahead and sent her big horse over the fence at the end of the field in a style that happily combined swagger with knowledge.

The hounds were streaking along over a succession of pasture fields, and the cattle gaps which were to be found in every fence vexed the proud soul of Mrs. Pat. She was too good a sportswoman to school her horse over needless jumps when hounds were running, but it infuriated her to have to hustle with these outsiders for her place at a gap. So she complained to Major Booth, with a vehemence of adjective that, though it may be forgiven to her, need not be set down here.

"Is *all* the wretched country like this?" she inquired indignantly, as the Shelburne Porter's pony splashed ahead of her through a muddy ford, just beyond which the hounds had momentarily checked; "you told me to bring out a big-jumped horse, and I might have gone the whole hunt on a bicycle!"

Major Booth's reply was to point to the hounds. They had cast back to the line that they had flashed over, and had begun to run again at right angles from the grassy valley down which they had come up towards the heather-clad hills that lay back of Carnfother.

"Say your prayers, Mrs. Pat!" he said, in what Mrs. Pat felt to be a gratuitously offensive manner, "and I'll ask the lady in the pretty blue habit to have an eye to you. This is a hill fox and he's going to make you and Pilot sit up!"

Mrs. Pat was not in a mood to be trifled with, and I again think it better to omit her response to this inconvenient jesting. What she did was to give Pilot his head, and she presently found herself as near the hounds as was necessary, galloping in a line with the huntsman straight for a three-foot wall, lightly built of round stones. That her horse could refuse to jump it was a possibility that did not so much as enter her head; but that he did so was a fact whose stern logic could not be gainsaid. She had too firm a seat to be discomposed by the swinging plunge with which he turned from it, but her mental balance sustained a serious shake. That Pilot, at the head of the hunt should refuse, was a thing that struck at the root of her dearest beliefs. She stopped him and turned him at the wall again; again he refused, and at the same instant Major Booth and the blue habit jumped it side by side.

"What did I tell you!" the former called back, with a laugh that grated on Mrs. Pat's ear with a truly fiendish rasp; "do you want a lead?"

The incensed Mrs. Pat once more replied in forcible phraseology, as she drove her horse again at the wall. The average Meath horse likes stones just about as much as the average Co. Cork horse enjoys water, and the train of running men and boys were given the exquisite gratification of a contest between Pilot and his rider.

"Howld on, miss, till I knock a few shtones for ye!" volunteered one, trying to interpose between Pilot and the wall.

"Get out of the way!" was Mrs. Pat's response to this civility, as she crammed her steed at the jump again. The volunteer, amid roars of laughter from his friends, saved his life only by dint of undignified agility, as the big horse whirled round, rearing and plunging.

"Isn't he the divil painted?" exclaimed another in highest admiration; "wait till I give him a couple of slaps of my bawneen, miss!" He dragged off his white flannel coat and attacked Pilot in the rear with it, while another of the party flung clods of mud vaguely into the battle, and another persistently implored the maddened Mrs. Pat to get off and let him lead the horse over "before she'd lose her life:" a suggestion that has perhaps a more thoroughly exasperating effect than any other on occasions such as this.

By the time that Pilot had pawed down half the wall and been induced to buck over, or into what remained of it, Mrs. Pat's temper was irretrievably gone, and she was at the heel instead of the head of the hunt. Thanks to this position there was bestowed on her the abhorred, but not to be declined, advantage of availing herself of the gaps made in the next couple of jumps by the other riders; but the stones they had kicked down were almost as agitating to Pilot's ruffled nerves as those that still remained in position. She found it the last straw that she should have to wait for the obsequious runners to tear these out of her way, while the galloping backs in front of her grew smaller and smaller, and the adulatory condolences of her assistants became more and more hard to endure. She literally hurled the shilling at them as she set off once more to try to recover her lost ground and by sheer force of passion hustled Pilot over the next broken-down wall without a refusal. For she had now got into the stony country whereof Major Booth had spoken. Rough heathery fields, ribbed with rocks and sown with grey boulders, were all round. The broad salmon river swept sleekly through the valley below, among the bland green fields which were as far away for all practical purposes as the plains of Paradise. No one who has not ridden a stern chase over rough ground on a well-bred horse with his temper a bit out of hand will be able at all fitly to sympathize with the trials of Mrs. Naylor. The hunt and all that appertained to it had sunk out of sight over a rugged hillside, and she had nothing by which to steer her course save the hoof-marks in the occasional black and boggy intervals between the heathery knolls. No none had ever accused her of being short of pluck, and she pressed on her difficult way with the utmost gallantry; but short of temper she certainly was, and at each succeeding obstacle there ensued a more bitter battle between her and her horse. Every here and there a band of crisp upland meadow would give the latter a chance, but each such advantage would be squandered in the war dance that he indulged in at every wall.

At last the summit of the interminable series of hills was gained, and Mrs. Pat scanned the solitudes that surrounded her with wrathful eyes. The hounds were lost, as completely swallowed up as ever were Korah, Dathan and Abiram. Not the most despised of the habits or the feeblest of the three-year-olds had been left behind to give a hint of their course; but the hoof-marks showed black on a marshy down-grade of grass, and with an angry clout of her crop on Pilot's unaccustomed ribs, she set off again. A narrow road cut across the hills at the end of the field. The latter was divided from it by a low, thin wall of sharp slaty stones, and on the further side there was a wide and boggy drain. It was not a nice place, and Pilot thundered down towards it at a pace that suited his rider's temper better than her judgment. It was evident, at all events, that he did not mean to refuse. Not did he; he rose out of the heavy ground at the wall like a rocketing pheasant, and cleared it by more than twice its height; but though he jumped high he did not jump wide, and he landed half in and out of the drain, with his forefeet clawing at its greasy edge, and his hind legs deep in the black mud.

Mrs. Pat scrambled out of the saddle with the speed of light, and after a few momentous seconds, during which it seemed horribly likely that the horse would relapse bodily into the drain, his and Mrs. Pat's efforts prevailed, and he was standing, trembling, and dripping, on the narrow road. She led him on a for a few steps; he went sound, and for one delusive instant she thought he had escaped damage; then, through the black slime on one of his hind legs the red blood began to flow. It came from high up inside the off hind leg, above the hock, and it welled ever faster and faster, a plaited crimson stream that made his owner's heart sink. She dipped her handkerchief in the ditch and cleaned the cut. It was deep in the fleshy part of the leg, a gaping wound, inflicted by one of those razor slates that hide like sentient enemies in such boggy places. It was large enough for her to put her hand in; she held the edges together, and the bleeding ceased for an instant; then, as she released them, it began again worse than ever. Her handkerchief was as inadequate for any practical purpose as ladies' handkerchiefs generally are, but an inspiration came to her. She tore off her gloves and in a few seconds the long linen hunting-scarf that had been pinned and tied with such skilled labour in the morning was being used as a bandage for the wound. But though Mrs. Pat could tie a tie with any man in the regiment, she failed badly as a bandager of a less ornamental character. The hateful stream continued to pump forth from the cut, incarnadining the muddy road, and in despair she took Pilot by the head and began to lead him down the hill towards the valley.

Another gusty shower flung itself at her. It struck her bare white neck with whips of ice, and though she turned up the collar of her coat, the rain ran down under the neckband of her shirt and chilled her through and through. It was evident that an artery had been cut in Pilot's leg; the flow, from the wound never ceased; the hunting-scarf drenched with blood, had slipped down to the hock. It seemed to Mrs. Pat that her horse must bleed to death, and, tough and unemotional though she was, Pilot was very near her heart; tears gathered in her eyes as she led him slowly on through the rain and the loneliness, in the forlorn hope of finding help. She progressed in this lamentable manner for perhaps half a mile; the rain ceased, and she stopped to try once more to readjust the scarf, when, in the stillness that had followed the cessation of the rain, she heard a faint and distant sound of music. It drew nearer, a thin, shrill twittering, and as Mrs. Pat turned quickly from her task to see what this could portend, she heard a woman's voice say harshly:—

"Ah, have done with the thrash of music; sure, it'll be dark night itself before we're in to Lismore."

There was something familiar in the coarse tones. The weirdness fell from the wail of the music as Mrs. Pat remembered the woman who had bothered her for money that morning in Carnfother. She and the blind old man were tramping slowly up the road, seemingly as useless a couple to any one in Mrs. Pat's plight as could well be imagined.

"How far am I from Carnfother?" she asked, as they drew near to her. "Is there any house near here?"

"There is not," said the yellow-haired woman; "and ye're four miles from Carnfother yet."

"I'll pay you well if you will take a message there for me—" began Mrs. Pat.

"Are ye sure have ye yer purse in yer pocket?" interrupted the yellow-haired woman with a laugh that succeeded in being as nasty as she wished; "or will I go dancin' down to Carnfother—"

"Have done, Joanna!" said the old man suddenly; "what trouble is on the lady? What lamed the horse?"

He turned his bright blind eyes full on Mrs. Pat. They were of the curious green blue that is sometimes seen in the eyes of a grey collie, and with all Mrs. Pat's dislike and suspicion of the couple, she knew that he was blind.

"He was cut in a ditch," she said shortly.

The old man had placed his fiddle in his daughter's hands; his own hands were twitching and trembling.

"I feel the blood flowing," he said in a very low voice, and he walked up to Pilot.

His hands went unguided to the wound, from which the steady flow of blood had never ceased. With one he closed the lips of the cut, while with the other he crossed himself three times. His daughter watched him stolidly;

The Blood-Healer. *By E.O.E. Somerville*

Mrs. Pat, with a certain alarm, having, after the manner of her kind, explained to herself the incomprehensible with the all-embracing formula of madness. Yes, she thought, he was undoubtedly mad, and as soon as the paroxysm was past she would have another try at bribing the woman.

The old man was muttering to himself, still holding the wound in one hand. Mrs. Pat could distinguish no words, but it seemed to her that he repeated three times what he was saying. Then he straightened himself and stroked Pilot's quarter with a light, pitying hand. Mrs. Pat stared. The bleeding had ceased. The hunting-scarf lay on the road at the horses' empurpled hoof. There was nothing to explain the mystery, but the fact remained.

"He'll do now," said the blind man. "Take him on to Carnfother; but ye'll want to get five stitches in that to make a good job of it."

"But—I don't understand—" stammered Mrs. Pat, shaken for once out of her self-possession by this sudden extension of her spiritual horizon. "What have you done? Won't it begin again?" She turned to the woman in her bewilderment: "Is—is he mad?"

"For as mad as he is, it's him you may thank for yer horse," answered the yellow-haired woman. "Why, Holy Mother! did ye never hear of Kane the Blood-Healer?"

The road round them was suddenly thronged with hounds, snuffing at Pilot, and pushing between Mrs. Pat and the fence. The cheerful familiar sound of the huntsman's voice rating them made her feel her feet on solid ground again. In a moment Major Booth was there, the Master had dismounted, the habits, loud with sympathy and excitement, had gathered round; a Whip was examining the cut, while he spoke to the yellow-haired woman.

Mrs. Pat, tie-less, her face splashed with mud, her bare hands stained with blood, told her story. It is, I think, a point in her favour that for a moment she forgot what her appearance must be.

"The horse would have bled to death before the lady got to Carnfother, sir," said the Whip to the Master; "It isn't the first time I seen life saved by that one. Sure, didn't I see him heal a man that got his leg in a mowing machine, and he half-dead, with the blood spouting out of him like two rainbows!"

This is not a fairy story. Neither need it be set lightly down as a curious coincidence. I know the charm that the old man said. I cannot give it here. It will only work successfully if taught by man to woman or by woman to man; nor do I pretend to say that it will work for every one. I believe it to be a personal and wholly incomprehensible gift, but that such a gift has been bestowed, and in more parts of Ireland than one, is a bewildering and indisputable fact.

SIXTEEN

THE BROOKE HOUND

Gordon Grand

Drawing by Eleanor Iselin Mason

To

HIS HONOR COLONEL WEATHERFORD, M.F.H. AND ESQ.

MILLBECK, NEW YORK.

SIR:

I tried Judge Culpeppers' grand looking, big brown colt for your honor and will report on him and report on the hunt like you told me to do.

The horse wouldn't suit you honor, not by no manner o' means at all, at all. He is no Master's horse, doesn't like to go out front, jumps sticky, unless he has other horses a-front of him and jumps sticky even then. I don't think he will ever have heart enough to suit your honor and Judge Culpepper says he doesn't think so either. It's too bad. Now please sir, about the hunt.

There is an old gentleman, Mr. Cavendish Brooke, who lives away back in the country, twenty miles from La Marquisville. He is a friend of Judge

Culpepper and the Judge says that maybe Mr. Brooke is the finest gentleman in the whole State of Virginia.

Well, this old gentleman has been owing the Judge a little mite of money for a long time and couldn't pay it and it's been worrying him.

Last week he wrote Judge Culpepper asking could he pay the money by letting the Judge have some hounds. The Judge sees right away that this business is worrying the old gentleman, who he says hasn't any money, so he writes him that he will come over and take three hounds and fix everything up good.

Judge Culpepper and the Sheriff went over to Mr. Brooke's and took me along so that I could help with getting the three hounds home in the back of the car.

While we were driving over, Judge Culpepper told the Sheriff that he thought Mr. Brooke was the best hound man in Virginia and that it was too bad, seeing as how he was so poor, that he didn't go into the business of breeding and selling hounds but that he wouldn't do it. The Judge said that Mr. Brooke didn't like to sell hounds, or sell anything but only to give 'em away and that when he did sell a hound, he wouldn't sell any except the best one he owned and would never ask only a few dollars, what was rediciloos.

If your honor would excuse me, I will report on these hounds. They are called Brooke hounds and come from Maryland, where most of Mr. Brooke's family live. They are mostly white with little patches of lemon on 'em and never in my life altogether did I see hounds with such grand heads and eyes. They have been bred by the Brooke family for all kinds of years.

Judge Culpepper says there be no hounds that can outrun Mr. Brooke's pack, 'cause one day Mr. Brooke runs 'em in a rocky, extra perticiler steep mountain on grey foxes; next day in swamps on greys, then in a hilly farm country on red foxes. They are powerful fit.

Judge Culpepper looked all the hounds over, picked two grand ones and then a small runty hound. I said to myself that it was sure nice of the Judge to take that no account hound when he could have any one in the kennels.

We started home and hadn't got to the front gate afore the Sheriff started giving the Judge a most orful talking to for picking out the little hound. The Judge didn't say anything for a long time then told the Sheriff that if anybody ever said that he could have the pick of a good kennel he should pick out the most no account looking hound he could find because a good hound man never keeps a no account looking hound in a pack unless it is extra perticiler good. He told the Sheriff that if he hadn't been afraid of making Mr. Brooke feel bad, he would have picked the three worst looking hounds in the pack. All the Sheriff said was that it was too bad to see a gentleman like the Judge get so old that he was muddled in his head.

We hunted this morning away over in Saint Alban's Parish, a rough wild country, and the Judge took the three new Brooke hounds. It isn't real fox-hunting in that parish, not lots of galloping and jumping which is what I like, but mostly listening to hounds hunting a long way off.

We were standing in a meadow, the hounds off by themselves away up on a mountain. All to once we heard them. I was 'long side of Slim and Double Slim, and Double told me that that mountain was the worst place for a hound to get through that ever he had been in. He said that two or three times the Judge had sent him up on the mountain afoot to blow for hounds and that he would rather go to gaol than fight those briars and grape vines and pull himself up those rock ledges.

Slim and Double Slim and me were talking, when all to a sudden the Sheriff starts hallooing so you could hear him clear to Richmond. The fox was crossing the meadow, right in front of us. For the Sheriff to halloo so loud right then was a bad business. The fox stopped. Judge Culpepper called out, "Go on Walsh! Go on! Go on!" I went as fast as my horse could lay foot to the ground and got between the fox and the mountain. The fox looked at me, looked over towards the gentlemen, turned, layed his ears flat back on his head and started in the direction he was running when the Sheriff scared him. He was throwing gravel, sir.

I went back to the field and we all waited quiet. Hounds were still up on the mountain but we could hear them coming a mite closer. That fox was a powerful way ahead of 'em.

Your honor wouldn't know how the gentlemen bet, one with the other, on which hounds would come driving out in the meadow first. Judge Westmoreland writ all the bets down in a book so the gentlemen wouldn't forget 'em.

Nobody wanted to bet that any special one of their hounds would be first out of covert 'cause they had done that lots o' times and lost and couldn't get big enough odds to make it a good bet.

The Sheriff bet Major Padget a gallon that he would have more hounds in the first ten than Major Padget would. They both had three couple running.

Mr. Cavendish bet Mr. Stringfellow two gallons that his *Trumpeter* would be closer to the fox than Mr. Stringfellow's *John*. When the gentlemen were all finished, Judge Westmoreland told 'em that fifty-three gallons had been wagered.

Judge Culpepper hadn't said anything. He was standing away off by himself listening to the hounds. Pretty soon he rode over to the gentlemen and asked 'em what odds on one of his hounds being first out of covert. The gentlemen stopped talking, each one took his horse away from the other horses, so they could hear and went to listening to see could they tell which hound was out front. They are scared to bet against the Judge. Nobody could tell one hound from another so they rode back, talked it over, then Mr. Templeton Randolph said that if one of the Judge's hounds was the first out of covert every gentleman would give him one old gallon and that if some other gentleman's hound was first then the Judge was to give every gentleman a quart, a year old.

Then they all went to listening again. It seemed like the hounds must have come over the top of some ridge 'cause we could hear 'em a lot better. Judge Culpepper said there were more than thirty-five couple running. The cry was getting louder every second. Please sir, they were just tumbling down off that steep mountain—just tumbling. Major Padget who gets orful excited stood up in his stirrups and hollered out, "It's a waterfall of hounds! It's a waterfall!"

Every hound was giving cry, such a cry that our horses went to twisting, turning, grabbing for their heads; a couple of 'em kicked and my young horse made a powerful lunge out into the meadow.

To a sudden Judge Westmoreland jumps up in his saddle and goes to cheering and cheering, and please sir, he had a right to cheer. There were as good hounds as any in the world on that mountain and we could hear Judge Westmoreland's *Gabriel* away out front, all by himself, *Westmoreland's Gabriel* he is registered in the book. He won the Virginia open stake two years ago. No hound around La Marquisville has the same kind of voice so everybody could tell it was him in the lead.

The Sheriff is the only moosician among the gentlemen, and he hollered out that he would bet fifty gallons against any gentleman in Kentucky that there wasn't a July, Trigg or Walker hound in Kentucky that could sound so low a note and so high a note and so many notes in between.

Please sir, everybody was standing up in their stirrups. Double Slim's mouth was twitching and he kept saying over and over, "Lawd God, *Gabriel*—push him hound—drive him. You is up front. Show 'em the light. Show 'em the light. Lead 'em out of Egypt, hound dog." I never heard any suck rediciloos talk, so I rid away.

Gabriel wasn't more than two hundred yards from the meadow and dead on the line where the fox had come out of the woods. Judge Westmoreland rode up in front of all the gentlemen 'cause the gentleman whose hound is first has the right to cheer first. Judge Westmoreland took off his hat, cleared his throat so he could cheer good. The gentlemen want their hounds to hear 'em when they are in the lead.

It sounded like *Gabriel* must be right at the edge of the woods now. Judge Westmoreland held his hat ready, took a long breath, then, then sir, to a sudden there was a cheer right 'long side o' me that I won't ever forget as long as I live. Old Judge Culpepper was standing in his stirrups, his big black hat up in the air, "Whee ow—ow—ow—hi ow—forrard. Whee ow—whee ow—whee ow."

And there sir, please, racing across that meadow, making such a cry as never was—a hundred yards affront of the nearest hound, was the little hound we brought home from Mr. Brooke's.

I hope your honor will excuse me for making this report so long. I won't report any more about the run. It lasted over four hours, nearly five hours. The gentlemen said it was one of the longest and hardest on hounds ever they remembered. I didn't see the end. Judge Culpepper sent me home 'count of my colt getting tired. All I know is that when the fox went to earth at a quarter past six, the little hound, *Jack Bentley,* they call him, after the great baseball player, 'cause the Bentleys have been breeding this Brooke strain of hounds over in Maryland, was the first hounds at the earth.

I got just one more thing to report. About nine o'clock at night, Uncle Up came to my room. I was in bed, orful tired. He said the Judge wanted to see me, so I got dressed.

When I went in the library the Judge was in his big armchair and little *Jack Bentley* was sitting up in front of him, looking at him. The Judge has a trick of sort of tickling a hound, very soft like, back of the ears, that they like. Every time the Judge would stop doing this, *Jack Bentley* would look up at him and lift his paw and put in on Judge Culpepper's knee.

The Judge asked me if I could find my way back to Mr. Brooke's. I told him I could. "All right," he says. "Take this hound back to Mr. Brooke in the morning, tell him that Judge Culpepper presents his compliments and would like to have some other hound, and will Mr. Brooke please pick out another one for Judge Culpepper. Good night, Walsh," he said.

Resp.

EDDIE

SEVENTEEN

THE HUNTING IF

Angela Shortt

If you can hunt and stay among the leaders,
And yet not thrust nor override the hounds;
If you can take a dozen nasty "headers,"
Yet never let your temper out of bounds:

If, at the Meet, some inexperienced fellow
Backs into you and trouble is astir,
If you can merely smile and do not bellow:
"Damnation! Where is your red ribbon, Sir?"

If you can see that chap you've always hated
Sent flying in the mud by playful buck,
And do not laugh aloud nor feel elated,
But stop and help him up and say: "Hard luck:"

Or if the girl you loathe is the aggressor,
"Cuts in," and leaves you lying in the ditch,
If you can say: "That girl rides well, God bless her!"
Instead of calling her "a naughty Witch!"

If you should feel at times your nerve is breaking,
Yet take yourself in hand ere 'tis too late,
And jump the monstrous fence that sets you quaking,
Nor look with longing eyes at gap or gate:

If when you feel your horse is blown and jaded
Just near the finish of a glorious run,
You can leave off, with thought of self all faded,
And pat his heaving flanks and say: "Well done!"

And if, when the shades of night are falling,
You're jogging homeward with a well-earned thirst,
And, though a steaming bath and drink are calling,
You see your mount is fed and watered first:

If when at last before the fire contented,
While telling others all about the ride,
You leave that bank the height that nature meant it,
Nor let that four-foot ditch grow twelve feet wide:

If you are always loyal to your Master,
And never brag about the things you'd do,
Then, in the face of any dire disaster,
You'll be a Sportsman and a Marvel too!

EIGHTEEN

TRYING

Gordon Grand

Had you been prying about, which you wouldn't have been doing, among our Millbeck hills on a certain Friday evening preceding our Cup Race and chanced upon the snug cottage of that fine old huntsman, Will Madden, and peeped through the crack at the bottom of the kitchen window, this is what you would have seen. The brightest, cleanest, homiest kitchen in our county. Will Madden sitting on a low rush bottom rocking chair with his slippered feet spread toward the stove, a copy of "Horse and Hound" on his lap, his aged briar pipe in his mouth and back of him his estimable wife Meg doing up the dishes and putting things to rights.

I don't know whether you are interested in the character, personality, and physical appearances of huntsmen, but I am a hero worshiper and had you, as I suggested, been peeking under the blind you would have seen a small, wizened, tanned man of uncertain age with closely cropped, gray streaked hair and a furrowed face dominated by small, deep-set, active eyes. There was that about the mouth line which told of independence and determination—a man to keep trying on.

The low unpainted rush bottom chair kept rocking backwards and forwards as the man smoked in communion with himself. Finally the silence was broken. "It's nothing you have said about the run, Will, what with all the visitors being out and it being a race week. Tim O'Connor was saying it were no sort of a day you had. I'm right sorry, Will, that you and the master should be disappointed what with all the ladies and gentlemen out. Tim was after remarking that hounds had no try to 'em."

Silence hung heavy in the kitchen, broken only by the sound of the rocking chair, for time was of little moment in that peaceful room. The blue-tinted smoke from Will's pipe drifted languidly upwards. Then, if you had been following the disintegrating clouds as they soared ceiling-ward you would have noticed a break in the series, for Will was holding his pipe in his hand.

"Meg, how long be it since rain?"

"I don't know rightly, Will, but Mr. Malloney at the store says it's been no rain since St. Bartholomew's Day—that be three months, likely."

"And was it that hounds had no manner o' try to 'em? Be that what Tim said, Meg?"

"Aye, Will, it's what he said, right sure."

A very slim little cloud of smoke started falteringly upward—then became engulfed in two impetuous clouds that raced angrily ceiling-ward in a whirligig of disorder.

Will Madden rested his now hot and gurgling pipe on the table, went to a corner cupboard, extracted a pair of boots such as farmers wear in bad weather, kicked off his slippers, drew on the boots, encased himself in an old brown melton great-coat and picked up his pipe. "I be going to have a look at the hounds, Meg," he said, and left the kitchen.

Arrived at the kennels he entered a small office set apart for Colonel Weatherford, the M.F.H., and himself. The huntsman put a match to the fire, stepped into an adjoining room, and returned with a green plaid horse blanket which he placed in front of the fire. Three times he laid the blanket on the floor and as many times picked it up mumbling to himself: "It don't look handy. Not handy like would make a body comfortable." Then by a turn of fortune the blanket fell in smooth, soft folds. "Aye, that would lie comfortable, that would."

The blazing white birch logs were now filling the small room with a myriad of shadows which played up and down the walls, touching here and there a sporting print or fox's mask. The huntsman moved a leather armchair close to the fire, looked once again at the blanket, noticed that a section of hard, yellow braid lay stretched kitty-cornered across it, and reached down to smooth out the braid. He then opened the door, passed through the cook room, down a narrow passage on the walls of which hung a row of white kennel coats looking stark and cold in the dim light, across a small court where hounds were shown on the flags, and entered the kennels.

Farmers tucked away in our snug valleys, deep in "The Rural New Yorker," or listening, and mind you, listening thoughtfully and very knowingly to expositions of our national problems, raised their heads and listened; for as the huntsman's hand touched the latch music spread afar. Will Madden stood surrounded by his hounds. Soft, sensitive paws rested on him to his very shoulder for he was small of stature. "Gently lads, gently," and he touched a hound here and another there.

They had all come to him—all but one. A solitary hound still stood on the bench, an animal with a face and expression which would have sunk deep into the memories of all true hound men. There was no time of offishness or indifference about the hound as he stood there alone, for his every

Woodsman. *By J. Alden Twachtman*

fibre was tingling. His very intensity seemed to freeze him to the bench. The muscles of his forearm shook as with the ague. "Gently hounds—gently. Woodsman," he called. The words were hardly uttered before the white hound on the bench was at the huntsman's side, his face upturned; that long face—some say the longest ever seen on an American foxhound, with deep, pensive, sensitive eyes. "Kennel up, kennel up, hounds. Woodsman lad, come with me." And the white hound followed him through the gate and to the tiny, fire-lit office.

The grizzly-haired man, an old man he seemed in that flickering light, sat down in the leather chair, took the long, upturned head in his hands, and those two old fox hunters looked understandingly into each other's faces.

"Woodsman, lad—that Tim O'Connor—him I got the job of whipper-in to me, has a mind I be too old—too old, Woodsman, to hunt hounds. It's a year now he's bin a-sayin', quiet-like, I be too old. A-sayin' of it quiet-like. A sort o' hintin' of it to the young uns what likes to gallop. He told the missus that today were no sort of a day—that hounds had no manner o' heart nor try to 'em. That's what he said. No try to 'em. He wants to be huntsman. Wants it powerful strong. It's eatin' of him, lad. Eatin' of him hard.

"The Missus says there been no rain since St. Bartholomew's Day. Three months without rain and he said hounds had no try.

"Woodsman, lad, do you mind where we met this mornin'? Right here at the kennels it were. It's race day amorro—race day—country full o' visitors so must keep hounds near to home. All sorts of crocks out—-borrowed horses, jobbed horses, riff-raff—ridden by trippers—week-end people. That's what they be, trippers aridin'o' riff-raff.

"Cars and lights through the woods all night—owners—trainers—gentlemen jocks with their ladies—a dance agoin' on over to the club house. 'Where will we go? 'What'll we do?' they be askin' of themselves. 'Over to the kennels,' they say. 'Come on, we'll take a ride. Let's be goin' to see the race horses stabled over to the kennels.' Four o'clock in the mornin' it be. Then stable boys, visitin' stable boys a-comin' home. Cars and lights right through the kennel covert all night. Seven o'clock, Mr. Pettibone Lithgow—three cars of people—his week-end trippers—party clothes on to 'em at seven o'clock in the mornin'—come right through the covert to see his race horse. Right through the covert. I'm out on the grass at four o'clock—five o'clock—six o'clock—a-feelin' of it—hands all over it. No dew. God, it's dry, burned, hot.

"I draw the covert. Nothing there. Not even a night line to work up on. The ground like the cobbles affront o' Buckingham Palace. Drew on north a-tward the Stickheap. Took hounds along the stream bottom. Nothing but sand and gravel in the stream bottom now. Then the patch o' grass where the apple tree stands what has a limb broke and layin' on the ground. You mind the spot well, Woodsman. The others were across the stream bed and you found—found right there where the grass was green and you could smell him. You found him, Woodsman man, and opened. They all honored, and we run him up the left side of the stream and I blew 'gone way—gone away' to Colonel Weatherford.

"Then the line turned left-handed and ran up the cliffs a-tward the Stickheap. The ground all baked—gray—hard, and hounds faltered at the bottom. I stood still and let 'em try and they tried all over the place. They kinda knowed they couldn't touch it again. They knew. And I couldn't find you and kept a-lookin' for you and kind o' needin' of you an' was thinkin' I would start sort o' slow up towards the top hopin' we might touch it; then I heard you—heard you way up on the top a-callin' of me—high up where them three old pine trees stand. It's dark under them trees—the sun don't get in there. May be there be a might o' damp there in the mornin' or may be the fox lay down in the pine needles. That's where you touched it again— right under them three pine trees, and I brought hounds up the cliff. What a climb that would be when it's burned! Three trippers came off, and on the top the grass ain't cut. Two years now it's not cut—and you were goin' on alone—catchin' o' body scent from the tall grass and a-callin' every step for me to come on and bring hounds and tellin' me it were all right and to come on—and me with eighty-three people a-pressin' of me—and you sayin' 'Come on—I have it. It's all right.' And we come clear 'cross the top o' the Stick— hounds a-feelin' their way and you a little mite on in front but sure you were right—that's the whole thing—sure you were right—then you had to stop.

"You lost it and were tryin' hard—tryin' every blade and the grounds all covered with weed smells on account of no frost and the grass not bein' cut— golden rod smells, milk weed smells—all kind o' smells but fox smells. May be we'd lose it entirely and couldn't go on. It were a-hangin by a cobweb, it were. Then HE galloped up on you—the young tripper—galloped right at you. I was a-leanin' way forrard on old Timemaster's off side a-watchin' of you, hopin' and hopin', and seen him gallop at you and you had to make way and I said 'God, how will he ever find that patch again?' Then I see Colonel Weatherford a-standin' in his stirrups. He's a big man, Woodsman—a powerful man. I hear him holler 'Hold hard, sir, hold hard, I say.' Man how he hollered at him. But you found it again and worried it along to the lane.

Sloanly Lane. It's moister in the ruts o' that lane. An old spring sort o' makes up in there—that's it—an old spring, and you carried it across the lane and the trippers had to jump the in-and-out. They thought it were an ordinary in-and-out but it's not, Woodsman boy. No, it's narrow—powerful narrow—no use a-goin' at it hard—it's too narrow; must pop in—pop out. The Colonel had it right—trot up slow, in—out; he knows. Trippers gallopin' wide open—in, horses hookin' knees a-getting' out and loose horses sky-larkin' about.

"Do you mind all them cattle tuther side the lane—Andrew Haightman's cattle—runnin'—soilin' the line? I was a watchin' you. No scent—nothin'! Hounds tryin' all over the place—all tryin'—but you sort o' creepin' along a step at a time—tryin' to find it. Then that little Fantasy bitch, your daughter —man, what a lady she be! Makes me think of a princess a-drivin' in a coach, so dainty she be. It looks like you were tippin' her to try the green patch for-rard. I seen that green patch across the wall—old ruins and fresh grass where the garden used to be—earth damp and deep under them old gardens. Farmers' women worked hard. Likely place for a fox to cross, that green patch. Woodsman, you're not jealous, lad. That's the thing, not jealous. You let the bitch try forrard in the green grass while you stayed on in the burned stuff with the cattle. Then she hit it. Her first season, and she hit it and opened—opened wide. A high anxious kind o' little voice she have and every hound honored her—every hound, Woodsman—they believed her, and it be her first season. Man, what a bitch she be and how they flew to her and we went on—hittin' it—losin' it, but tryin'—tryin' for it every foot o' the way and O'Connor said hounds had no try today!

"Where did we carry it to, Woodsman? That's it, where did we carry it to? Seven miles right to the foot o' Pugsley Hill. That's where it were. Man, what a hill that be and what did they all say? That a fox would never go over the top on a day like this. That's what they said and wanted me to try around the bottom and Tim said as how there was no manner of use a-going' to the top 'cause if the fox be there the hounds couldn't hunt him. But I was a-lookin' at you— watchin' of you close. I saw the very spot you lost him. I saw you a-stand-in' there with your legs all spread out not darin' to move. You couldn't touch it on ahead. Then that clump o' golden-rod. I seen 'em—them with the briar patch back on 'em. I seen that white stern o' yours start movin' slow, back and forth, and I said, 'Wait, he be touchin' it sure.' Then you see the line o' stones buried in the briars where they had took down the old stone wall, only leavin' the big foundation stones. No oxen to drag the big stones away these days. That was a smart place for the fox to turn and run that old wall hidden in weeds; and you clumb up on the first big stone but you couldn't be sure. I was a-lookin' at you. Man, I hoped you would strike it. I looked back and there be Colonel Weatherford a-holdin' all those people quiet. Eighty odd of 'em. Everything a-waitin' on you, Woodsman. Then you went on to the next stone just sort o' half movin'; and stopped and looked back at me and old Timemaster, kinda like sayin' to me 'I don't know but it seems sort o' likely.' Then you went along the wall to where the milkweed grew up close. That's where you spoke to it good and opened and hounds went to you and Fantasy flew on up the wall and hit it where the wall dropped down to the swamp.

"Man but we run him good across the bottom right straight for the big hill, right to the very bottom of it. And Steadfast and Rowdy carried it on up to the top o' Pugsley. Right away to the top. That hit the trippers, that did. Then on the top the wind blowed. How it blowed! Hot, dry and the ground all sheep cropped. Scent all blowed away. Hounds couldn't do nothin'. Heads up one after another, seemed like we was beat. Two hundred acres she be on the top and not a stick or stone to be seen. The fox might ha' gone off the hill in any direction. I cast 'em over the whole top, it looked to me. Then I could-n't see you no place. I stood up in my stirrups but couldn't find you and I said to Tim, 'Step over the north lane and see if you can find Woodsman' and I come slowly after him castin' hounds and pretty soon I heard Tim a crackin' of his thong and bellowin' and ratin', 'Leave it, leave it. Get away back to him,' he hollers. Colonel Weatherford says to me, 'What is that jackass of a whip doin'?' That's what he said; 'Jackass of a whip,' and I said, 'I sent him on over to see if he could find Woodsman.' 'Woodsman,' 'e says, 'Well, God bless my soul, Madden. What's he mean by ratin' o' that hound?' I didn't stop to make no answer to him but took hounds over across the lane at a gallop 'cause I knew you had touched it forrard.

"Man what a powerful stone wall that be where Timemaster and me lep it, and there you were a-standin' steady like with Tim a-crackin' and bel-lowin' and we come up and that old Traveler hound spoke to it a spell to one side of you. It were more like a whimper and we run him right smart down the north slope through Oak Spring bottom across the Hotchkiss Place, and then swung a big half circle to Squire Thornley's hills. Two miles we run him across them hills. Black cattle every place, but not a hound's head goes up. There be no sweeter place topside o' this earth to see hounds race forrard than be the Squire's hills. Man, but we rattled him good across them big fields; with every hound a-feelin' the line, and then we come to the plow at Stanwich Hall—fifty acres o' plow maybe, and all gray dust. When he sees it Colonel Weatherford come up 'longside o' me on that old Athelstane horse of his. 'We be beat, Madden. The damn thing will beat us sure,' he says, and we galloped down to the plow with hounds but a spell in front o' us and you run him clean across the plow without hangin' a minute. Man, there be no other pack o' hounds in the world would carry that line across fifty acres o' dust without hangin'. Then he turns into that bit o' covert to the west, and you and Traveler and Rowdy—I seen you when you went in—you druv him clean through the covert without a check. It don't happen that way once in a season, leastwise not in no rough covert like that one be.

"Then out he comes in the open, out where it be all rocks and briars, 'No Man's Land' they call it, with 'Poor Man's Acres,' the black swamp at the bottom. A rough, hard country it be and we were slow trailin' down through the rocks when of a sudden I hear your voice change, change quick and loud-like, and you be runnin', runnin' hard, rocks everywhere and I see Blatchford, our den hound, fly forrard to you. Then I knew. 'God,' I said, 'we've a-marked him'—marked him to earth at last, marked him sure, and I kicked old Timemaster up to the earth and see Blatchford with most of hisself down the earth, diggin' like he do and gettin' madder and madder. Then Colonel Weatherford galloped up and cheered. He always cheers good at an earth to encourage hounds. 'Whoop, whoop, whoop, have at him lads, have at him.' What a grand voice he have!

"Fourteen miles we be trailin' him, pokin' him along, runnin' him—no scent—wind all hot, no rain since St. Bartholomew's Day. Hounds always tryin'. God, how you tried, and that Tim O'Connor says it were no sort o' day. 'Hounds had no try to 'em,' was what he said."

The old huntsman held the hound's head in his two gnarled hands and looked fixedly into its eyes. "Woodsman man, some o' the young uns are a-thinkin' and sayin' I be too old to hunt hounds. They want to see hounds drawn on the run. They don't want to let hounds try—want 'em lifted all the while, want 'em hunted like they be in England. Woodsman man, they'll never kill no foxes in this dry country except by hounds tryin'. Man's tryin' won't do, and there don't be a farmer standin' in every field and on top o' the hills like in England to show where the fox be gone.

"This Tim O'Connor wants to hunt hounds. He reckons some o' the young uns want him—wants to see him spoil the best pack o' hounds in this 'ere country. They want to see him get hounds so their heads be always up a-lookin' for him to show 'em the fox.

"Woodsman lad, it don't seem like I could stand a-seen' that O'Connor's wife a-livin' in my Meg's kitchen. Don't seem like I could stand it. Twenty-three years come next month my Meg be a-livin' in that kitchen. But what Tim don't reckon on is the old master. The Colonel knows when hounds be tryin'. He knows. 'Will,' he says to me comin' home with the hounds, 'Will, there be no pack of hounds in this country with the nose, drive, and the manners o' this pack, and you made 'em, Will. You made 'em. They never quit tryin', he says. And Woodsman, do you mind the Colonel a-sayin' to me: 'What that jackass of a whip O'Connor a-doing'?' Do you mind him a sayin' that to me a-top o' Pugsley?

"Woodsman man, I be tired—powerful tired I be. Mind it ain't that I be old. It ain't that, mind. It's the drought maybe what makes me tired so my vittles don't taste good. We best turn in, lad, but I feel a power better now, I do. That Tim O'Connor a-huntin' o' these hounds and his missus a-living' in my Meg's kitchen while Colonel Weatherford be master? God! He said my hounds had no try. That be what he said."

NINETEEN

THE SILVER HORN

Gordon Grand

On a sparkling summer morning in early September I was breakfasting under the fine old gnarled apple tree that stands off the corner of my house. I was in a tingling, buoyant state and well I might be for we had had a rare cubbing morning and many pleasant things had contributed to my well-being since my return, and other pleasant things were in the immediate offing. Those that had happened included a swim in the pool, the feel of a fresh pongee suit, the taste of an iced cantaloupe, and a first cup of coffee. Those in the offing were two boiled eggs whose natal day I vouch for, three slices of crisp bacon, a second cup of coffee, a smoke, and the morning paper.

I was in the act of pouring the second cup of coffee when the morning mail was placed on the table. The mail had no interest for me until I noticed a generous envelope postmarked London and addressed in Colonel John Weatherford's handwriting.

When I had finished breakfast I lit a cigarette, took my coffee and the letter over to a comfortable lounge chair, opened the letter and read:

Dear Pendleton:

   I had a delightful chance meeting with Florence in London the other morning. The enclosed tells the story. "Good hunting" to you. I will be home soon.

   Faithfully,

   J.W.

THE SILVER HORN

A nocturne of old London town

I said to the head waiter of that venerable hotel on Albemarle street, "Make my compliments to the lady who has just come in to breakfast and is sitting over in the corner and say I very particularly commend broiled finnan haddie."

The pompous and ponderous dignitary returned a moment later. "The lady is much obliged, Sir, but told me to say, Sir, that she has quite a different idea about her breakfast. Quite different, if I might say so, Sir—thank you, Sir—and the lady says, Sir, as how she would be obliged if you would stop and speak with her on your way out, Sir."

When I had finished my own finnan haddie, I stopped to wish Florence "the top of the morning."

"A man who will eat finnan haddie," she said mysteriously, "doesn't deserve to hear hunting horns under a summer moon."

"What do you mean?" I asked.

"Didn't you hear him?"

"Hear whom?"

"The lone huntsman of Albermarle street?"

"No, my rooms are on the Dover street side."

"Oh," said Florence, "what bad luck! You missed the most delightful thing." And then she told me this story:

Returning from the theater and supper she had drifted off into a sound sleep, from which she was gently and fancifully awakened without sensing the cause. Her watch showed three o'clock. The roar and rumble of London had faded to its lowest murmur. A midsummer moon filtered through and illuminated the street below. What was it that had so illusively awakened the sleeper? Again she listened. The faint mellow note of a hunting horn drifted up from Piccadilly.

Now a hunting horn is one thing to some people, and a very different thing to some other people. In Mrs. Grundy's family it represents only a noise; in Florence's family and to Florence herself it is a mystic spring which unlocks myriad memories and pictures; so at 3 a.m. Florence was hanging far out of a front window of her hotel, her eyes searching the moonlit London street.

A solitary figure was strolling at his leisure up the center of the street. To the tutored eye of the lady of the balcony, there was the slightest tinge of a roll to his gait. There is much of romance in Florence, and her coffee grew colder and colder as the description ran on. The gleam of his white waistcoat, the cut of his dress coat, the sheen of his silk hat worn just a bit toward the back of the head, the cane hooked over his left arm, and—touch of touches —the gleam of a silver horn tucked between the white tie and top shirt stud. "Mind you," said Florence, "just exactly where a huntsman would carry it. Oh, it was too delicious." Well, this reveler of the night halted in front of Florence's window. Why just there, I did not inquire, but Florence had said she was hanging out of the window.

With feet far apart and leaning back on his cane, the gentle reveler plucked forth his horn, and made old Albermarle street resound. Twang. Twang. Twang. Then he warmed to his task. "Hoick, Hoick! Furrier has it. Hoick! For'ard to Furrier! Hold hard, gentlemen! Hold hard, please! Ah, Rattler Boy. Hoick! For'ard to Furrier! Steady, gentlemen, please. Let hounds get out of covert. Let them get straightened away. Please don't press hounds." And then, in a glorious, resounding voice that rolled on from street to street, "Gone away—gone away—Hoick! For'ard!" After three more sharp notes of the horn indicating that hounds had found and gone away, and as a signal and final exhortation to any hounds that might be left in covert, the horn was once more inserted between the white tie and top shirt stud.

The lone Huntsman, cheering and encouraging his hounds, passed on toward Grafton street. Hounds ran a burning line with fine head up Albermarle street, but at The Royal Institute they dwelled on the line and faulted.

"Hold hard, Sir. Dash it, Sir! Don't you see hounds are casting? You will have their heads up in a minute. Hold hard!"

Then Furrier opened, the pack honored, and away they flew toward Grafton street. Of course, Albermarle street ends at Grafton, and there was a great to-do as to whether the fox had turned right-handed to Old Bond street or left-handed to Dover street. Again hounds faulted and up went their heads. Again the twang of the horn calling hounds to him, and then patiently he cast a little way toward Old Bond—then a little toward Dover—and finally a bit back on Albermarle. On this latter cast he encountered the old guardian of the venerable Institute standing in the middle of the road, his eyes agog.

"That's right, my man, that's right. Never fuss about when hounds are at fault."

"Of course, I think he should have cast first toward Dover street," said Florence, "because the breeze was blowing toward Hyde Park corner."

Then he cast them up on to the porch of Quaritch's, that great book shop on Grafton street, into Bunting's, the bootmaker's on Dover, and even as far back as Boss's, the master gunmaker's shop on Albermarle, probably thinking that the fox might have been turned at the Institute and headed back toward Piccadilly.

At last the riddle was solved. The true line ran toward Dover street and so down Little Hay Hill where Huntsman and horn drifted out of hearing; but Florence said she heard the horn once more across Berkeley Square and about opposite Dartmouth House on Charles street. She said she then went to bed and to sleep, but I rather think she fell to romancing.

When Florence told me this tale, and I thought of those hounds of the imagination casting for the line around Quaritch's, I could but wonder what all the old English worthies depicted in word and illustration in Quaritch's first editions would have thought of that young English blade of this year of grace alone at three o'clock in the morning hunting his hounds in the heart of moonlit old London town. I do believe that there must have been many a good British sportsman tucked away in his bed close to the line of the hunted fox that night, whose heart beat a bit faster as he listened to the twang of that horn and the cheery "Hoick! For'ard!" and those who had long since resigned from the pigskin must have had mellow memories of their own youth awakened.

When I stopped at the mail desk, a ruby-faced old gentleman was saying to the mail clerk, "I say, what a go that young chap was having last night— splendid voice for a huntsman—splendid! Reminded me of my days with the Earl of Fitzwilliams' hounds. When I heard him turn down Little Hay Hill I said to myself, "Ah, now there's a sweet stretch to watch hounds race down.' Blest if I could get back to sleep for an hour. Of course, I thought it a bit nervy to call his hound Furrier, after George Osbaldeston's great hound, but it might jolly well be that he thought he was the Squire or old Meynell. Oh, youth—that's the thing—youth! When you get to be my age it's a grand thing to know that you made good use of it."

The old gentleman pulled on his gloves, squared his shoulders, slipped his stick on his arm, and marched off, looking, I thought, very fit.

TWENTY

COLONEL WEATHERFORD'S BRUSH

Gordon Grand

The morning's mail brought me an invitation to dine at Colonel Weatherford's. It was one of those lugubrious things which start off—"Mr. John Weatherford requests" and so forth. Two or three times a year the Colonel girded up his loins and did this sort of thing. I don't think he enjoyed the functions but those who attended them did. If you were gastronomically minded you had a splendid time, and if you were of the younger generation you saw how your forebears were supposed to have dined and wined and were privileged to say to Smith the next day that you had toyed with some of old Weatherford's tawny port of '63 the night before.

As I started to accept the invitation I noticed that the dinner was being given on the Colonel's birthday. As he was never known to mention or refer to this day I thought it odd that he should commemorate it by a formal dinner. I had only learned of the date myself through a chance remark of one of his relatives.

When the evening of the dinner arrived we had hopped into our Indian summer and the weather was extremely close. It was with reluctance if not actual irritation that I encased myself in evening clothes. I would not have associated a dinner jacket with the state of the weather, but I am of that illogical majority who are persuaded that a dress coat is a smothering thing to wear.

When I arrived at the house the only car in sight was Enid Ashley's much used station wagon. I was then a few minutes late and I commented adversely upon the growing habit of people being late for dinner. After offering an ardent prayer that I might draw Enid at dinner I essayed the door. "They are in the library, Sir," the man said, and led the way. An odd place to receive, thought I. When I reached the library, a room which seemed as much mine as the Colonel's so much time did I spend in it, there was Enid

Ashley, little Mary Sedgwick and Colonel Weatherford. The sight of Mary at such a supposedly old folks gathering surprised me. I had hardly more than shaken hands when the Colonel said, "Pendleton, if you will take Enid, and Mary will do me the honor, we will go in to dinner. This is our party. There is an old saying, 'the more the merrier, the fewer the better fare.' We are going to prove that it should run, 'the fewer the merrier the more the better fare.' The fare may be frugal but I feel exceedingly merry."

The Colonel had said that he felt merry and he did. There is no cut and dried rule by which one can organize, promote or guarantee merriment. It slips quietly into the midst of all sorts of gatherings, at all sorts of places, and under all sorts of circumstances, causing people to expand and to think kindly of friends and neighbors and to go home convinced that this old world of ours is a grand place in which to have one's being.

We four had much in common. Each had a good horse and at least three of us knew one when we saw it, and I was learning. We thoroughly enjoyed foxhunting and were keenly interested in our hounds and what they did. We could have sat together hour after hour following a good run and argued and expounded the doings of the fox and the pack. Foxhunting is a great leveler of ages. No one was young and no one was old. We were just four enthusiastic foxhunters.

When we were back in the library after dinner, Mary, who was sitting on the couch between Enid and me, got up, walked over to the back of the Colonel's chair, put her hands on his shoulders and said, "Colonel Weatherford, Mr. Pendleton whispered to me that this is your birthday. I'm awfully sorry I didn't know about it. I guess it's too late for me to do anything now, but I have a wonderful idea. You know, they say it's better to give than to receive. Would you promise to give me something if I wanted it very much?" The conservatism of a lifetime slipped from the Colonel or was it that he knew the child so well. He hit his knee a fine round whack and vowed that Mary should have anything she wanted.

Mary looked up over the fireplace and said, "Colonel Weatherford I want the story of your brush more than anything I can think of. I have never seen the brush before but I often hear people talk about it. Will you tell it to us? Please do. I know Mrs. Ashley wants to hear it. She told me so. We've had such a wonderful time and if we could only hear how you got the brush, your birthday party would be perfect; and please Colonel Weatherford, couldn't we come here just like this every year on your birthday—just we four?"

When we in our hunting country wished to convey the thought that a thing would probably not come to pass, we were wont to say, "Oh, it will happen when Colonel Weatherford tells how he won his brush."

This saying had even filtered down into the vocabulary of small children, for I heard my nephew, aged eleven, say to his sister, "I do wish Dad would let me hunt *Old Piedmont,* but I don't suppose he ever will until Colonel Weatherford tells how he won his brush."

The brush in question hung in a specially constructed niche over the library fireplace, where in Italy or Spain one would have expected to see a small polychromed figure of a Saint.

Weatherford never gave the impression of being the least secretive regarding the trophy, but rather waved the subject aside as being of no moment, or too long a story to tell. Yet one could not help feeling that a man who had hunted all his life, and went as well as he did, would never display a solitary brush in such a conspicuous manner unless it had a worthy history.

If this matter had assumed undue importance, I think it was because a number of women had from time to time made trifling wagers that they would pry the story loose.

There was an uncomfortably long silence, then the Colonel said, "Mary, the only objection I have felt about telling the story is that I'm just a bit sentimental about the little affair, and one is sometimes reluctant to air such things. I will, however, gladly tell you about it if you wish, and if you will all bear with me in the telling."

The Story of the Brush

She was a bewitching little English girl of twelve whose lot had been temporarily cast in these alien United States through the business of her father, a dominant figure in the world of shipping.

At the hoary age of two and fifty I had fallen head-over-heels in love with her and found myself playing the roles of sporting companion, admirer, and father confessor. It is hard to recall, and harder to explain, how such affairs have their beginnings. I presume the child supplied a want the very existence of which was unknown to me until she so winsomely crept into my heart.

Horses had become her all absorbing passion, and that which should have been but a minor interest had become a too engrossing theme. We all recognized this, but only when it was too late, and I who had so fervently aided and abetted it had somewhat to regret. That she was more intense than other children we knew, but where was the yardstick with which one might measure such intensity?

For two years she and I had reveled in a rollicking welter of horse lore. We read all manner of books on horses and hunting. We recited verses, sang songs and pored over pictures featuring the horse.

On my visits to her parents she would resort to all the feminine sub-terfuges of the ages to get me alone, and then in that serious, quizzical way of hers would press her search. What did the book you brought me last week mean when it said so and so? Why did it say that a huntsman should never do this or that? She toiled through Beckford, devoured Lord Willoughby deBroke, and caused my copy of Henry Higginson's *The Hunts of the United State and Canada,* to look like a nursery copy of the *Water Babies.* Whyte-Melville's *Riding Recollections* she could quote ad lib. Even the ancient spelling and letters of my first edition of Somerville's great poem could not discourage her.

It would have been her greatest joy to have squeezed in between Dick Christian and The Druid when they took their famous trip in the gig through Leicestershire, preparing Dick's lecture. It might or might not have pleased Harry Worcester Smith and Harry Page to have known that she considered them to be of the same era as John Mytton and Captain John White. A pic-ture of Mr. Smith on *The Cad* was one of her treasures but she seemed intol-erant of the idea that both horse and rider were not of the later eighteenth century. I once pointed out Henry Vaughan to her, whom she knew to be a real, live, present-day M.F.H. She fairly glued her eyes on his spectacular height, accentuated by his gray top hat, and said she wished she lived next door to Mr. Vaughan so she could see him start off every single morning in his pink coat and on Sundays with his gray hat.

With a child's love of the superlative she used to ask, "Who do you sup-pose was the greatest rider in all the world? I mean ever and ever? Who do you guess was the greatest huntsman that ever was known in the very whole world? Don't you think that there must have been some horse some time that was just ever so much the greatest hunter in the world? Don't you know which one it was, Colonel John? You have read all of the books. Don't you know? Do you think it might have been some horse of Squire Osbaldeston's or Mr. Assheton Smith's, or maybe Mr. Whyte-Melville's? Somebody just must have had the greatest hunter."

I once asked her why she wanted so much to know, and she told me it was because when she went to bed she would close her eyes and play a game pretending, and would pretend that she was hunting with the great Will Long, who must always be on his white mare, *Bertha,* just as they looked in the pic-ture in her room. And there would be Squire Osbaldeston, Assheton Smith, Dick Christian, Mr. Meynell, Whyte-Melville. She said the only thing she had to ride was Squire Osbaldeston's *Slasher,* and that surely in all the world I must know of a greater horse than *Slasher,* and that it would spoil her pretending if she did not know that she was on the greatest horse of all time. I felt like telling her that each and every one of my friends—men and women—particularly the latter, would confess to being the owner of the dream-horse needed for her pretending.

I had carried her off to witness all sorts of sporting events. I had held a feverish little hand at international polo matches, and the running of the Brook Steeplechase. We had run ourselves breathless to keep horses in view at amateur race meets, and burst into convulsive sobs when a horse was killed. We had junketed to the Genesee Valley and Virginia in search of an ideal horse for her and were pleased to think we had found it,—and carefully planned to see the Maryland Cup en route.

All these things were wondrous good fun, yet deep down in our hearts we knew that they were but the forerunners of our high and all absorbing ambition, our first foxhunt. What hours and hours we had spent discussing this project! I longed to take her hunting as I have longed for few things before or since, yet I rather dreaded the event. The responsibility gave me concern, as she seemed too young for the pitfalls of the hunting field; yet I think I feared more the risk of disappointment to her. She was fairly steeped in the traditions of the shires of England. Her mind was aglow with the rich panoply of the hunt with all its color, action and thrills, and I flunked at the risk of disillusionment. However, I well knew that the day could not be indefinitely postponed.

At the time of which I tell I was maintaining a small weekend establishment in one of the older hunting countries, to which I would motor over the week-ends and on such other hunting days as I could get away. A flare-up in my menage had temporarily discommoded me, and pending the procuring of new servants I had closed the cottage.

On a Friday, toward the end of October, I dropped in for luncheon with Maida Elizabeth's parents, en route to the country where I had planned to spend the night with the M.F.H., hunt in the morning and perhaps stay on for a few days. We dawdled through luncheon, and just as I was preparing to leave I felt a soft little arm steal around my neck, and what to me were the most adorable brown curls in the world tickling my ear, the whole resulting and terminating in my being kissed. Maida Elizabeth had returned from school. Was I going to hunt on the morrow? When, Colonel John, could she come hunting? Why hadn't I been in to see her for ever so long? Had I kept my hunting diary after every single run this autumn as I had promised, and please wouldn't I bring it to her the very next time?

"Maida Elizabeth," I said, 'if I had any one in that cottage of mine to take care of us and cook for us, I would take you up with me this very day if your mother and father would let you go. Indeed I would."

She lapsed into silence while I talked with her parents. I can see her so plainly, even now, sitting on a low stool, leaning forward, and apparently reviewing some weighty matter. A half century of bachelorhood may suggest some discrimination in the matter of the feminine eye, and I say in all seriousness that neither before nor since have I seen such expressive, questioning, searching eyes. She was wont to look down when thinking, then raise a pair of very telling eyelashes and look straight at and into you. A Russian painter who made an impress through his work in this country, told me that he thought the child had one of the most beautiful faces he had ever seen and with great tenacity badgered her mother without avail to permit Madia Elizabeth to sit for him as a model.

When the general conversation lapsed she came over, sat down beside me and snuggling her hand into mine as she did on rare occasions, said, "Colonel John, I can cook a little; I could wash and put away the dishes, and I learned all about making beds when I went to camp. Don't you think if I worked and tried as hard as anything I could take care of just you and me, just for one day—just for one day. Colonel John? Don't you think maybe I could?"

That was too much. In thirty minutes I had her in the car, bag and baggage, and as Scott said of Marjorie Fleming when he carried her off on winter nights, "We'll hep'it up."

Perched on the back seat, and also off for their first hunt, were a pair of diminutive black boots with brass plates on the trees proclaiming them to be the property of Maida Elizabeth Barminster. An indulgent father had failed to realize that $110 boots and hollow trees that fit at twelve years may not fit at fourteen.

We motored a long time in silence. She was never wont to chatter. Knowing her so well I understood that her feelings were very tense, and that no one could possibly appreciate how momentous an event this seemed to her.

Of our adventures at light housekeeping I will say little. I retain a happy picture and remembrance of it. I recall entering my bedroom hours after she had gone to the land of nod and finding the bed neatly turned down, a pair of companionable old red slippers poking their worn toes out from under the bed, and on the night table a vase of fall asters.

She ate practically no dinner, saying she felt all tight and funny inside. I knew the symptoms. I too had felt "sort of sicky and funny inside," just before riding my first race years ago.

We awoke to as perfect a hunting day as this well-favored land of ours can produce.

While dressing and contemplating the problems incident to preparing palatably a breakfast which would tide us over until our return at perhaps four or five o'clock, I heard a decidedly authoritative bustling going on in the kitchen.

Mrs. Tim Templer, bless her heart, had come over from the kennels to get breakfast for us.

She had heard in that mysterious way in which country people hear so much that we were "in residence" and, as she said, "like enough to be helpless."

Tim told me that he had won Mrs. Tim away from a belted Earl. After that breakfast I was surprised that the Magna Charta, the Bill of Rights, or even the Writ of Habeas Corpus, had saved Tim after stealing such a cook from an Earl.

I was perplexed at first as to which of my horses would best carry Maida Elizabeth, but fixed upon a fourteen-year-old clean bred horse called *Lord Autumn,* doing his ninth season. He was a safe, capable, courageous horse but inclined to be a trifle domineering.

At the Meet I was punctilious in introducing Maida Elizabeth to the Master and the more gallant of our first flighters. I knew she would place much stress on this formality.

A good many years have rolled by since that morning, but I remember feeling inordinately proud of her. It was odd that so retiring and silent a child should invariably make such an impression upon people. She had an exquisite immaculateness in putting herself together, difficult to describe and impossible to emulate.

We moved off and drew a nearby covert but with no success. Then for two hours we drifted mile upon mile across a red and golden landscape, drawing as we went. Many of the field dropped out in favor of bridge and tea. Others as usual grumbled at the lack of foxes and talked of other days, but hounds drew on.

From time to time I would ride up to Maida Elizabeth just for the pleasure of watching her. She seemed absorbed and disinclined to talk. Only once she spoke, "Colonel John, isn't it more glorious than anything else in the whole world?" and smiled in a way which suggested that we alone of all the field, yes of all the fields of the world, knew the joys of fox hunting.

The hoped for "two o'clock fox" failed us.

At three o'clock we were drawing an important covert from which if a fox were found and bustled out we were reasonably sure of some sort of a run. The field had dwindled to not above a dozen.

Of a sudden a hound opened at the far end of the covert. I recognized it to be *Big Echo,* a hound I had walked for the Hunt, and so named by reason of a loud and resounding voice, and I knew from many talks with old Tim Templer, the huntsman, that this hound never opened unless sure he was right. I also knew that Tim, from somewhere in the labyrinth of the covert, was cocking his ear and making it his business to move up nearer to the hound.

Drawing a little to one side I signaled to Maida Elizabeth to come with me. I then very casually and in as off hand manner as possible, edged down towards the woods. The rest of the field continued "coffee-housing" but then they were all old stagers and did not have a Maida Elizabeth to save from the disappointment of a blank day or losing a run.

Again the deep voice of *Big Echo* resounded and a second later a hound with a thin, choppy, impatient voice honored.

The covert was on my right. The M.F.H. was some way on in front, talking to an apparently agitated farmer. I noticed him turn, look towards the covert as the hound spoke, and knew he was casting about for a method of terminating his conversation. I felt apprehensive about behind so far from the center of action at this particular covert, so, at the risk of teaching my little charge bad hunting manners, and having a bad five minutes myself with the Master, I decided to slip into the covert and be prepared to go out on the far side in good company with hounds should they break that way. I was determined on this day of all days to get well away if I could possibly manage it.

We had not ridden above a few hundred years in covert when hounds opened with a great resounding burst of music and seemed fairly to crash out of the far side. As I looked up I saw old Tim directly ahead of us on his redoubtable grey horse, *Suds*. A hard pair of old timers, those two.

Maida Elizabeth snuggled into Tim's "pocket," and we scurried through a long wood ride towards the open country. Looking ahead I saw a break in the tree tops indicating cleared land, and just in front a formidable barway of new, black, whippy saplings dividing the covert from the open pastures.

Tim was setting a terrific pace, and in no very good humor, having been delayed in covert through bustling up a dead end wood ride which took him nowhere. He was now bent on getting on good terms with his hounds.

Tim was a better huntsman than he was a rider, particularly in moments of high stress. He approached the barway with his horse extended and not a leg under him with which to jump. *Suds* hit the barway to an extent which caused the saplings, as is ever the way of saplings, to bend and rattle but not break. The grey horse, to whom this experience was no novelty, pecked on to his nose, scraped and bumped along the rocky wood ride for some distance, now on his knees, then on his chin, encouraged to do his best or worst by Tim's dictatorial voice and virile language. Tim's legs were dangling about in a seemingly futile effort to synthesize them with his fluttering stirrup irons.

Maida Elizabeth pulled *Lord Autumn* down to a walk to give Tim and *Suds* room in which to complete their evolutions. When they were out of the way she took the old horse by the head, him who they all said had no mouth, and brought him into the barway beautifully collected. They made a perfect jump and were gone. I scrambled over after them.

We were now crossing a grand bit of turf, with hounds well on and carrying a good head. For myself I was none too well fixed for a big run. I was riding a spectacular looking five-year-old that had sold for a King's ransom at Saratoga as a yearling. A knowledgeable trainer had discarded him as a racing prospect and I was trying to make a hunter of him. He was a delightful ride for as long as he lasted, but seemed to have little interest in the sport.

We raced along over Twyford Bottom with Mellick's Woods two miles ahead and to the west. I rather thought the fox might den in those woods and that we should call it a day. Instead of that the line scouted the woods for its entire length and then veered northeast towards Steeptoe Hill. This was two miles as the fox ran, but we, to avoid Mulgrave Swamp, had to tack on an extra mile and at a pace which boded no good for me.

I heard horses behind me and saw the M.F.H. and five of the hard riding brigade pounding after us pretty much wide open, as though they expected the thing to be over any minute. Little did they guess what they were in for.

By the time we had reached the stone-strewn sheep pasture that lies at the foot of Steptoe, the Master and Maida Elizabeth were both in Tim's "pocket," while I was laboring in the rear with a rapidly tiring young horse under me.

There is a famous earth in a rocky ledge in that sheep pasture. I knew the spot well. Surely I thought, he will go to earth there. Standing up in my stirrups I located the rocks, but even as I looked hounds passed them by and were a hundred yards beyond. They were running beautifully packed with great drive and heading north. I could see the white steeple of Smithborough Church far ahead.

We had entered a cattle country where farmers insisted on stout enclosures, and the fences took a bit of real doing. I was perceptibly dropping to the rear. The hard riding brigade had been reduced to three, but those were well up and in front of me. If ever I detested a horse it was that magnificent looking, 16.2 hand chestnut thoroughbred. He had hit the last three fences fore and aft. He was now proceeding on the theory that it was entirely my duty and responsibility to hold his head up for him and was leaning on the bit accordingly.

I could still see old Tim pounding along on his white horse with Maida Elizabeth and the Master in his wake. Of a sudden an urge came over me to be up front and share the child's feelings. I wanted so much to see her in a role we had often pictured in our talks. If I were ever to make it I must act promptly, for I was fast getting to the bottom of my horse.

I judge it to have been a long time since any one had been rough with

COLONEL WEATHERFORD'S BRUSH

that colt. His good looks and amiable disposition had insured him an easy life; but now he had an interesting experience for about five minutes. I rode him with determination and a disregard of consequences. He hit a stiff, upstanding post-and-rail fence so hard that he twisted and cork-screwed until I had nothing between me and the ground, but he managed to disentangle one foot in time to use it as a prop and so stood up.

I at last drew up with *Lord Autumn* and my reward was worth many times the effort. I wish a master might have produced a picture for me of Maida Elizabeth as I saw her at that moment. I think I had counted on seeing a hot, wide-eyed, disheveled little child. Instead I looked upon a face that was just as I had seen it when I first beckoned her to follow me. Her great eyes were looking far ahead towards the hounds. Her exquisite chin was tilted up as though trying to make herself taller and so see farther. She was sitting as nonchalantly as in an armchair. Such composure and ease I think I never saw on a galloping horse. The usually domineering and self-willed *Lord Autumn* was striding along with hardly a touch on the reins. The horse had never performed so since he was foaled. I was conscious of experiencing a tinge of uneasiness as I looked at her. People didn't cross difficult countries in terrific runs on strange horses or on any other horse that way. The Master, a two-fisted and essentially practical person of no imagination, didn't like it either, and when I asked him long afterwards what he didn't like, he was unable to tell me, but said he felt as though he had Joan of Arc beside him for all those miles, and would never again speak of it, which perplexed me.

Hearing me come alongside, she turned, and again her look was suggestive of a great and glorious secret between us; but neither of us spoke. We galloped side by side for a few fields, then I again dropped back. The colt had shot his bolt.

We had left the hamlet of Smithborough on our right, and hounds were still running hard, with the line bending to the northeast. About three miles on was as far as our hounds had ever hunted to the north. Then *terra incognita*.

There was one thing I could do which might at least keep me in distant touch with the fun. It was a meagre chance but better than giving up.

On my left was a high, wooded ridge extending well to the north but no more than half a mile in width. Should the fox continue north and round the point of the ridge he might then head south or east, permitting me to nick in again.

I took a clumsy fall in reaching a grassy lane to which I could find no barway or gate. Picking myself up, I jogged down the lane towards the ridge. Before entering the woods I climbed a knoll to have one final look at the disappearing field. At the far end of an extensive meadow I saw the Master on the ground and the last of the hard-riding brigade standing with him. Whatever had happened, they were both now out of the run. This put another aspect on the matter. As long as the Master had kept going I felt reasonably comfortable above Maida Elizabeth, but now she was following the most devil-may-care rider in seven states over a difficult country, and approaching a region unknown to any of us. She was undoubtedly riding a tired horse. I was in a blue funk.

There appearing nothing that could do better than what I was doing, I pressed on through and over the ridge hoping against hope.

The wood ride was longer and rougher than I had expected. When I finally emerged into the open and pulled up, I was standing at the top of a long rise from where I could view the country to the north, south and east.

A fine October day was rapidly drawing to a close, and as I stood there nothing broke the stillness but the faint chirping of a bird in the bushes back of me, and the far away lowing of a cow complaining of a tardy farmer.

I scanned the horizon for any moving object and strained my ears in listening, but it was evident that no hounds were running on that side of the ridge.

Surely there is no lonesomeness met with in any our games or sports like unto that which creeps over him who in the hour of twilight seeks alone for hounds on the line of the hunted fox.

I took out my pipe and as I lifted my head from lighting it, I was looking towards the north. Far in the distance something was moving across a field. I finally made it out to be cattle. Perchance hounds had disturbed them. I kept looking until my eye caught also a rapidly moving white horse and something following close behind. Hounds were plainly still running hard and heading somewhat north.

Below in the valley a dusty country road meandered into the North Country and I determined to take it and plug on. I cajoled the disheartened son of a St. Leger winner into a toe-stubbing jog and essayed the endless looking road.

I had progressed in this fashion for some way when a boy passed me in a car and directly ahead turned into a farmyard. I called to him, asked if I might put my tired horse in his stable and would he, for a consideration, take me a few miles north to search for a little girl for whom I was looking. He agreed and we chugged north. We presently passed the field in which I had seen the cattle moving. They were now complacently huddled together in one corner. From that point we stopped the car every quarter of a mile to listen. As daylight slipped into twilight we came to a gate marking the end of the road through which we passed. From this point the land rose to great stretches of bare hills used only as sheep pastures. It seemed an endless country and very sombre.

The boy said we could run the car most any place on the "barrens" as he called them, so, where did I want to go? I told him to take me to a broad plateau to the north. Upon reaching this I left the car that I might the better listen. The Ford was gurgling, bubbling and panting so plaintively that one could not have heard hounds running fifty yards away. When well clear of the car I listened, and there, far on before me was Tim's horn calling hounds to him. I suppose I have had, I must have had, more stirring thrills than that mellow horn gave me as it floated across the lonely drear hillside in the fading October light, but the memory of no other thrill is quite so clear and persistent.

I sprinted to the car as I had never thought to sprint in top boots and we essayed the alarmingly steep ascent from the plateau to the uppermost reaches of the barrens.

Then we came upon them, a weather-beaten old man in a scarlet coat, and standing beside him with its head between its knees was a very distressed white horse. A few yards away a wee mite of a child was holding a fox's brush with the end tied up in a large, soiled cotton handkerchief. She wore a velvet cap far back on her head, and across her beautiful forehead was a splash of crimson. Tim had blooded her. The hounds were stretched out in the attitudes tired hounds assume.

Off by herself and uttering low yet spiteless growls was a lemon-and-white bitch, *Magic*, with the mask in her mouth. It was her mask for it had been her fox. When *Big Echo* opened she had been the first to honor him. Blessed with a magnificent nose and great foot, she been first out of cover and had stuck relentlessly to the line all through the lengthening hours of that golden afternoon. When her unfathomable instinct told her that the fox—her fox—was sinking, she mustered all her remaining energy, scaled the last ascent and killed him on the crest. It was to Tim Templer's honor that he would ever see justice done, and so *Magic* was alone with her mask.

When I came up Tim looked at me, jerked his finger to his forehead as was his wont, but neither smiled nor spoke. *Lord Autumn* was standing off by himself with the reins tied to a sapling and his girths loosened. He was looking far down the hillside to where some sheep were moving. I put my arm through his reins and led him over and sat down beside Maida Elizabeth. I filled my pipe and when I had it well going she put her arm in mine. I don't know how long we may have sat, nor do I remember that we said anything. From time to time I heard Tim blow his horn, but it seemed far off. I know my pipe burned itself out.

Then Tim moved on leading *Lord Autumn* beside him and the weary hounds in his wake.

It was dark when Tim reached the farm, where I had requisitioned the car and there he stayed the night for the horses could travel no further.

A tired little girl whose fingers twitched every now and then, snuggled down beside me in the car, and slipped her hand into mine. Every so often a sigh would find its way up from the depths of a red blanket loaned us by a friendly but perplexed farmer's wife.

I suppose the turning-in to my driveway was as the slow falling of a curtain at the end of a play. It distinctly marked the end of our first hunt. As we approached the house, I heard: "Oh, Colonel John, it was wonderful. So wonderful I can't talk about it. I never want to talk of it to anybody—not even you. Please, Colonel John, don't let anybody talk to me about it. I want it all for my very own. Perhaps I won't ever want to see Tim or *Suds* again. I want them to be for ever and ever just as they were for all those miles and up that last great hill with the fox in front, and the hounds hardly able to catch him. That was where Tim couldn't go any further and he took off his cap and made me put it on and gave me his horn and said, 'Take 'em, Missie—I never had to do it afore, but take 'em, Missie, and God help you catch him.' That's what he said, and *Lord Autumn* and I went to the top of the hill, and they killed the fox, but I didn't know what to do, and my mouth was all dry and stuck together, and I couldn't make any sound. Then Tim came up and everything."

She said she couldn't even think of *Lord Autumn* without feeling cryey.

When I reached the cottage I tucked her in bed, brought her a light supper, and put a bell on the table so that she could ring for me. When I said good night and stooped to take a last look at those searching eyes which always intrigued me, she seemed fain to let me go.

Fearful that the strain might have been too much for her, I lamented that I had not insisted on her pulling out. Then I thought, "who was I to talk of telling her to pull out who could not even keep her coat tails in view?"

The next morning Mrs. Tim came over, prepared breakfast, and put things in order. As we sat on the lounge together after breakfast, Maida Elizabeth said she wished she could live for ever and ever just with me, and never grow up, and hunt with Tim and me, and that of all things in the whole world she hated birthdays the most, and wished time would stand still so that Tim and *Suds* and *Lord Autumn* and I would not change, and that now she had Tim for her pretend huntsman instead of Will Goodall, and *Lord Autumn* in place of *Slasher,* and was never going to pretend about any one except them and me. Then she was whisked away home in the car.

I moved over to stay with the M.F.H., and the weather remaining fine and the sport good, stayed on about ten days.

Upon reaching home I found a letter from Maida Elizabeth's father written on shipboard telling me that he had been quite suddenly recalled to England, where he hoped I would soon visit them, and thanking me for taking Maida Elizabeth hunting. He was sure she must have had a good time, but she had not been very exhaustive in her description of the visit; that once when her mother had pressed her for an account of the hunt, Maida had burst into tears and left the room, from which they were afraid she had perhaps not conducted herself properly, or had ridden badly.

Each Christmas brought me a card from the family and an invitation to visit them. In October of each year, mailed so as to reach me as near as possible to a certain day, I would receive a letter from Maida Elizabeth. They were long letters telling me the events of her year, but there was never even a veiled reference to our great run or to Tim, or in fact anything connected with our hunt. She was true to her word. She had locked it all in her heart.

Six years rolled away. One fair May morning I received in the mail an envelope addressed in her father's handwriting. It flashed through my mind that it might be an announcement of his intended return to America. A feeling of expectancy stole over me, unlocking countless memories dear to my heart. I found myself projecting all sorts of new adventures with Maida Elizabeth. As a result I felt reluctant to open the letter fearful of disappointment. On the film of the past which was unreeling itself across my memory, was that moment after the greatest run in the history of our hounds, when I had leaned down to kiss her good night, and she in her weariness and tenseness had seemed loath to have me leave her. I knew it to have been the only time in my life that any one had felt this way about me. I finally determined to run over to England during the summer, and as soon as I had decided upon this, I felt reconciled to opening the envelope. It contained a clipping from an English paper.

"On May the first at Higher St. Albans, Dorset, Maida Elizabeth, aged eighteen, the only child of Sir Francis Barminster, Bart., and Lady Barminster."

The obituary told nothing more.

I sat I know not how long, now and again looking up at a photo on my mantel. Then I ordered my horse tacked, and went for a ride.

As I passed the kennels I saw old Tim astride of *Suds*. He was riding back and forth in the far corner of the meadow with his puppies, while two boys followed on foot.

I wanted to talk with some one, so I rode into the meadow and said, "Tim, do you remember the little girl who was with you when you killed the fox that day on the North Barrens?" And Tim said, "Colonel, I've forgot the half of all the ladies and gentlemen who ever hunted with these hounds, but the wee missie is more with me, so help me God, than even my old woman.

It's never into the North Country I get that I don't think on her. I'm an old man getting to be, Sir. It's forty-eight years I've ridden to hounds, and over thirty I've hunted 'em, and there was never the like of the thing that happened to any huntsmans in the old country of this, as when I couldn't go on and gave me cap and horn to that bairn on the sheep hills in the dark and bade her go on to a kill. I knowed I shoulda stopped hounds, Sir—I knowed it, Sir, or leastaways tried to stop 'em—and Colonel, I did blow once, but then she put her hand on my arm and looked at me like I was never looked at afore. Colonel, people like me don't ever have people with them kind of eyes look at 'em that way, and she said, 'Please, Tim, I want just ever so much to go on to the very end. Please, please don't blow.' Those were her very words. It was then I give her me old cap and horn."

"Tim," I said, "the little girl died a week ago in England." And then wished I had never told him.

People like Tim don't do or say anything when they are hurt. "Thank you, Sir," was all he said, and turned back to his puppies.

I rode on in a listless manner for about an hour, then returned to the house and wrote a letter to England.

During each spring season, and upon a day just to my liking, I would go off on an all day riding picnic. This annual event had become a rite which I looked forward to. I had fixed upon the following Sunday for the outing, providing the day proved auspicious.

The weather favoring me on that morning I was up, mounted, and on the road in good season. On these occasions I rode in a well-worn British army saddle, the pouches of which were filled, even including a nip of Amontillado sherry, which the label informed me had been shipped by Mackenzie's Co., Ferez de las Frontera, Spain.

On these rides I would always reach the outer fringe of the hunting country, and very often some miles beyond. I started towards the north and being mounted on a particularly free moving horse, tucked a good many miles behind me by early noon.

I was picking my way over a rocky section of what seemed more like a farm lane than a road, when upon looking up I saw a group of farm buildings, which had a familiar look and I recognized the farm at which Maida Elizabeth, Tim and I had put up our horses. I determined to press on to the hill country, and if possible find the spot where the fox had been killed on that memorable day.

I finally reached the gate marking the end of the lane, let myself through and essayed the long ascent that must have brought old *Suds* to a standstill. I was tugging on up and marveling at the power and endurance of horses and hounds that makes it possible for them to gallop over half a county and at the end face such a hill. I had crossed the plateau from which I had heard Tim's horn and was close to the summit when to my amazement I saw Tim. He was dismounted, with *Suds* standing near by, and evidently engrossed in some activity. My first impulse was to hail him, but on second thought I decided not to. As both Tim and *Suds* had their backs to me, I turned and rode down until I was completely out of sight. There was a meagre plantation of stunted trees and bushes off to my left. I rode back of these, determined to wait until Tim had completed whatever he was doing and had departed. It did not seem as though I wanted to talk to him just then, yet having come so far I wanted to stand alone on the very spot where I had come upon Maida Elizabeth with her brush and Tim's cap and the daub of blood on her forehead.

I had waited perhaps a quarter of an hour, when, peeking through the bushes, I saw Tim riding slowly down. *Suds* had grown very white. In this off season his mane and tail had been allowed to grow. He looked hollow-backed and old, and I thought rather pathetic.

Tim was dressed in disreputable old clothes. The whole picture was rather of a weary farmer plodding his solitary course astride an ancient work horse.

When I thought the way was clear, I took the course Tim had come down. As I reached the summit, I saw ahead of me and slightly to the left, a mound of rough field stones some three feet high. From the center of the mound extended a length of chestnut fence-rail, silvery gray in color, to which a board had been crudely nailed.

I dismounted and walked over to the mound. On the board scrawled in large, ill-formed letters, I read:

> THIS IS WHERE HER AND ME
> KILLED THAT FOX

I followed Tim down the hill.

Towards the end of the following week a package arrived for me. Upon opening it I found a card reading, "These remembrances are forwarded pursuant to the last wish of Maida Elizabeth Barminster."

I sat alone on my terrace through the slowly waning twilight of a June evening, with a fox's brush in my hand and a child's little hunting crop on the seat beside me marked for Tim.

"... and they killed the fox."

TWENTY-ONE

OLD MAN

Gordon Grand

We dropped heavily into Colonel Weatherford's copious leather arm chairs and awaited tea, the sequel to a long, wearing fox hunting day.

The warmth of the fire-lit library after so many hours afield must have made me drowsy, for sounds and movements were as things dreamed. Then I heard the Colonel's voice coming to me as from a great distance. "Pendleton, I have just learned that Algerton Le Courte has been awarded the Victoria Cross for an act of supreme courage out in India."

The mention of a name which had long since dropped from my memory recalled tales of a little English boy who had once tarried in our village for a few years and then journeyed on. I never knew him, but in the passage of time I read of his riding races and hunting hounds in England, and once of his piloting his horse to the victory of victories over the bleak, foreboding Grand National course, with the dour, wind-swept land enveloped in mist and rain. And again I read of him at Gallipoli in the Great War.

To me he was but a legend or as a knight in an old wives' tale. If his name was mentioned a soft, warm, pensive look stole over women's faces as though they took some pleasant memory to their hearts; and he but just a little boy. "Colonel Weatherford," I said, "tell me. Who was Algerton Le Courte?"

The Colonel sat smoking his pipe and gazing into the fire for some time. "Well, Pendleton," he said, "I never quite knew why General Le Courte and his small son came here to Millbeck. They arrived from England one Spring morning accompanied by a family retainer, old Middleton, an excellent servant, and rented the Rose Cottage on Highminster. As soon as they were settled I called to pay my respects to the old General." Colonel Weatherford lapsed into silence, groping in the archives of memory for those word pictures that would best describe his old and valued friend. "Pendleton," he continued, "have you read The Newcomes?" "Yes," I answered. "Well, General Le Courte was made very much in the mold of Colonel Newcome— a quiet, dignified, somewhat old-fashioned gentleman, but Pendleton, a great gentleman, a naturalist, a fine sportsman, and a soldier who had carried on for England in all her hinterlands.

"In a year or two the son entered the Millbeck Academy as a day pupil, and every morning the General would drive him to school in a Mineola cart behind an old-fashioned, smart-moving cob he had picked up some place for a song. I would often meet them bumping over the rough, back country roads as I started off with hounds. They were sufficient unto themselves, those two, and inseparable.

"As time went on the General and I became fast friends. We shot and fished together, and I enjoyed his comments on passing events and the worthwhile books of the day. After some years of this companionship a slow, stealthy change commenced creeping over the General, creeping so slowly at first that it was hardly discernible. He started missing birds he had no right to miss, then making excuses why he could not go shooting. One day, while fishing, he experienced no end of difficulty tying on his flies, and requested my help. If I asked him whether he thought well of a certain book I had loaned him he became evasive and pleaded lack of opportunity to read. In time he gave up driving the Mineola cart and sat as a passenger while old Middleton did the driving. I did not piece two and two together until one day when visiting him I noticed him walk over to the table for a match. The match box was in plain sight but I saw him feeling vaguely for it along the table. He put the matches in his pocket and left the room. When he returned his pipe was going. On a sweet, gentle day in mid-June the last flickering rays of light receded and left him in eternal darkness.

"With a desire to alleviate some of the loneliness, I now saw more of both father and son. Shut off from other contacts and activities the General's thoughts reverted more and more to the boy, his education and future. He wanted him to play at all games and learn of all sports, and his interest and curiosity in the youngster's progress was insatiable. I would now and again take the boy shooting, and the old General would persist in coming along, with Middleton to lead him. If game fell to the boy's gun the father must needs know the length of the shot, was the bird well hit, was it rocketing high overhead or flying low, an in-comer or going away from him; was the boy's stance as it should have been, etc., etc. I can still hear him saying, 'Tell me, Weatherford, did the Old Man do well?' He practically never referred to the boy except as Old Man.

"Pendleton, if you look at the eyes of any noteworthy sportsman who has excelled both in sports and in the playing of games you will read much of the causes of those successes. This boy had just such eyes, and fair hair, fine, true Anglo-Saxon features, and a smile that made you want to go up and put your arm around his shoulder.

"In time he took to playing football and was considered the fastest-running and hardest line-hitting back who ever played for our little pre-preparatory school. Every Fall afternoon the General would have Middleton drive him to the football field. They would poke the pony close up to the side lines and the General would question Middleton, to whom the game was a complete enigma, as to what Old Man was doing now. Had he carried the ball in the last play—how many yards had he made? I once stood by the cart when Middleton was trying to describe a play, 'One of the young gentlemen handed the ball to Master Algy, sir, and Master Algy attempted to pass right up the meadow with it. I'm sure he had every intention of doing so, sir, but some of the other young gentlemen got quite in his way, and in the disturbance was knocked down, sir, and a number of young gentlemen fell on him. I don't think he is harmed, sir, only a trifle soiled. I could brush him off directly, sir, if you wish.'

"During the principal game of the year I sat on a rug with the General out in front of the player's benches. It was the day of our school's supreme effort. The score stood nothing to nothing. There was but five minutes left to play. We had the ball. The signal rang out clear and sharp. It was the Old Man's signal, and the ball was passed to him. He found or made an opening and went through. Boy after boy dove for him and tried for him. On and on he went. Only two players stood between him and the goal and victory. They both tried for him and missed: eighty yards for a winning touchdown. I depicted every move to the blind old warrior beside me. God, Pendleton, the look on the man's face. Automobile horns were screaming all over the place. Every Millbeck boy was on his feet. The cheer leaders jumped to their positions. 'A Millbeck School cheer for Le Courte—everybody in it. Are you ready? One, two, three—Millbeck, Millbeck, Millbeck, Le Courte, Le Courte, Le Courte.'

"Pendleton, I suppose I'm what's known as a crusty, worldly, sophisticated old bachelor, but I am still affected by the picture of the General noiselessly clapping the palm of one hand against the back of the other, not the two palms together. No, no. There must be no noise, no display, no sign of emotion, just clapping gently and saying softly. 'First rate, Old Man, first rate!'

"But the General laid the most stress of all upon the Old Man's riding. He had sold his Purdey gun and put the proceeds into a smart, weedy little thoroughbred horse for the boy. The thing was not much to look at and had very little in the way of manners, but it could positively fly and jump like a disorganized rocket.

"The General had been considered one of the crack horsemen of England, and he tried—tried so hard and so long—to form a satisfactory mental picture of the boy's riding, of his seat and hands and horsemanship.

"I once drove the father in the old pony cart to the very top of Pugsley Hill on a day when his boy was hunting, the hope that he might hear the cry of hounds and the thud of galloping horses.

"It was a warm, fair morning in Indian Summer. We sat in the cart, I smoking and he pulling on his now ever empty pipe while the pony cropped the grass. I had instructed Will Madden, the Huntsman, to draw Peckett's Woods from the north and work on down towards us. As we listened the faint note of the horn would now and again come to us and drift gently by to be lost in the vastness of Malvern Swamp. Suddenly hounds unkenneled their fox. Peckett's Woods awoke. The eager, clamorous cry rolled up towards us, one bellow of sound pressing the one in front until Great Pugsley was enveloped in music—the bass notes of the old dog hounds, the altos and sopranos of the keen, active, flying bitches.

"I stood up in the car. They were racing towards us. 'Look sharp, Weatherford,' called the General. 'Look sharp, old man. You will view the fox. Keep your eyes down wind.'

"'Tally-ho, General. Tally-ho. There he romps,' I sang out. God, Pendleton, but he was a big, strong rover. On came the dull, persisting thud of horses' hoofs. 'Steady boy, steady on,' I called to the pony, and took him by the head.

"'Can you see them, Weatherford? Can you see them yet?'

"'Yes, yes, General. They are heading for the great wall into Malvern lane. Here they come. Will Madden is safe over.'

"'Where is my Old Man, Weatherford? Is he well up with the first flight? Is he over yet? Tell, me, has he a nice light, airy seat? He is not away back in the ruck, is he, Colonel, not milling around with the tail-enders?' 'No, no, General,' I told him. 'He is well over, well over, going brilliantly, magnificently. He is taking his own line. They are turning south straight into the sun and galloping towards the post-and-rail fence with the big drop into Westmoreland Bottom. They are riding too fast. It's a terrible drop. There he is, there he is. There is the Old Man. God bless me, what a jump his horse made. He flew it in his stride and landed going away.'

"They passed from view and were engulfed in the endless swales and woods and uplands that stretch on and on to where even enduring hounds may not explore. Nothing told of their passing beyond a faint suspended cloud of dust over Wendover pastures, and a lone, riderless horse cantering uncertainly in the valley below us.

"But that which touched us closer than all else was the devotion of the boy to his father. No one who lived in Millbeck in those days will ever forget that picture. It was many years later and long after he had left us that I finally evolved the true significance of the boy's character and ideals. Pride of race and background and of one's forebears and their achievements are sometimes very dominant incentives. I would now and again catch the son looking at the blind father. At such moments the boy's forehead would be creased with lines of perplexity and rebellion at so cruel a visitation, but creased too with a great determination to do his part, to live up to all that was expected of him. That was to be his contribution. At such moments the lines about his mouth depicted the things of the spirit.

"The English historian, Trevelyan, described in telling words the charge of the perfectly trained and brilliantly accoutred British troops marching in perfect alignment with steady tramp up the slope of Bunker Hill to be mowed down by skilled marksmen behind embankments. As the front line fell other British troops stepped over them, took their place, and marched gallantly on in the same perfect alignment. The order had been, forward. There were no questions asked. The order had simply been forward on. It was thus Algerton Le Courte marched on. He was gay and playful in his marching, but he had no thought of turning back. With him to give but part of what one had to give, whether it be on the playing field, in the stubble, across country, or in the class-room, would have been as halting on Bunker Hill. His father would not have thought well of that. That's why, Pendleton, you have read of him winning races and hunting hounds in England and facing the Turks at Gallipoli, and why he now wears the Victoria Cross.

"It came on to the Saturday of our cup race. (It was the year my horse, The Woldsman, ran third). It was a wicked day—wind in the northeast and a cold slashing rain. The General would not move about but sat huddled up in the pony cart. He caught cold. Monday night pneumonia set in. On Friday another English gentlemen reported *adsum.* That evening I brought Old Man over here to stay with me.

"The services were set for Sunday. We discussed at some length whether to take hounds out on Saturday, and finally decided to do so informally, the members to ride in mufti. The General was not a landowner or subscriber, nor did he hunt himself, and would have been the last to have wanted hounds kept in kennels on his account. Certainly not with the countryside full of visitors.

"Henry Newcombe was Master that year but was away and I had promised to take the field. As I left the kennels I was surprised and a trifle annoyed to see the Old Man riding up the road. His training should have suggested the impropriety of such an act, even to a boy of fourteen. The thought struck me that if his horse needed exercise he could very easily have found someone to exercise it for him, or at least he could have ridden in some less conspicuous place than around the kennels. And so I dismissed the matter."

The Colonel paused, re-lit his pipe, then looked over at me. "Pendleton, a pack of hounds never burned up a country as the Millbeck hounds burned this country up that day. We met at Upper Standfordville Bridge away over to the northwest.

"Towards late afternoon Will Madden took hounds in to the Oak Spring woods, entering from the north. We had not been in covert a minute or two when I heard halloing from down at the southeast corner. A hound opened and almost instantly the entire pack boiled out of covert. The scent must have been very unusual that day, for I have seldom seen hounds tumble out of woods with such drive and cry. George Ashley had viewed the fox away and told me he was an exceptionally big, strong-running old customer that had set his head straight for Oaklands.

"The fox sank the hill down to Foster's Creek, crossed, went away towards Round Top, which he skirted to the west, then on for Oaklands, as the crow flies. I was splashing through the creek when I heard a horse crossing somewhat below me—crossing wide open, fairly rocketing along, and bless my soul if it wasn't Old Man on that Flying Spinnaker of his.

"Pendleton, I'm not possessed of the best temper in the world, and the very sight of the boy hunting on such a day angered me beyond all reason— the heartlessness of the thing—the indifference. Will Madden was just in front of me. I called out to him to catch the boy and send him back to me. Will was mounted on a thoroughbred horse called Acclaim, by Plaudit. He had won some good races and could fly. Will set sail. Pendleton, he might just as well have chased a rainbow, for by this time the Old Man was the length of Peckett's meadow ahead of us and right on the tail of hounds. Foot is indispensable in a good hunter, but God bless me, there is a pace beyond which no sane man will cross a country. That boy was not riding as a sane person should, and hounds were not running as hounds generally run.

"When we reached Trimble Uplands, close by Oaklands Village, I had a magnificent view. Hounds were tightly packed and fairly driving and pulling each other along, the scent stinging their noses. The Old Man was still on their tails, but Will Madden was two fields behind him, yet riding as few men have ever ridden that country.

"From Oaklands the fox set his head for the Skittles, crossing Jobe Hecker's, Peckham's and Ed Simpson's farms. There was no wire in those days, and chestnut posts and rails were still available. God bless me, but it took a good horse to cross that country. Luck was with me crossing Hecker's farm for I hazarded a guess that the line would bend south, so skirted the hill, and by so doing nicked in with Madden. His horse looked as though he had been through the mill. When we finally worked our way out of the Peckham's peach orchard we saw hounds streaming across the sheep downs beyond on Simpson's farm, and Old Man snuggled right up with them. Dear old Mrs. Estey was out that day. She knew what was going on in my mind and shoved her horse up to me. I can hear her now, saying, 'Colonel, he is only a little boy. We must not be too hard on him. Promise me you won't. He is magnificent.' I suppose I simply grunted at her, but God bless me, my indignation at the boy knew no bounds. We galloped on and on across those far reaches of our north country crowding and taxing our horses, grimly pursuing a fair-haired boy and a streaming, flying pack of hounds.

"By the time we reached the foot of the Skittles most of the field had dropped by the wayside, for we had been running close to an hour without a breather. I had sent my second horse home earlier in the day, and The Woldsman was discouraged at the two hundred pounds he had been lugging at such a pace.

"Due to the light having become exceedingly bad Will Madden's horse, which Will always let step on to his fences too fast, had brought himself up under a big, upstanding post-and-rail fence and turned Will over with a wicked thud. My horse started to jump, found himself in wrong, tried to stop, and slid into the fence, hitting it with his head and off shoulder. He sprawled about but finally lurched up on his legs. Darkness had defeated us. We could go no further. A fence too treacherous and formidable to be jumped in such light stood before us. The members of the field drifted homeward while Will Madden, the Huntsman, and I waited alone in the growing dusk listening.

"Suddenly the hunted line turned and led towards us and the eager, pressing cry became clearer. Then silence settled over all the land. Hounds had lost. They had over-run their line. 'Blow, Will,' I called. 'Quick, man, blow. Blow hounds to us. Call them before they find again.' Will stood up in his stirrups and blew until the hills echoed. We harked. Only Woodsman's daughter, little Fantasy, came to the horn and she falteringly, reluctant, and of two minds. Then from a swale of land at the fringe of the twilight a boy's voice drifted faintly to us. 'Come, come, come—come-ee lads, come, come, come.' He was imitating old Madden, and calling hounds to him. Again the cry of hounds. He had cast them, found the line and they were driving on in the dusk.

"Pendleton, at that moment I could have thrashed the boy, young as he was. The recklessness of the thing, the abandon, the infernal determination of youth for self-assertiveness, and worse, Pendleton, the untimeliness, the impropriety of his riding and playing on such a day; a day on which many had given up their sport out of respect for his father.

"We finally located the road which runs down to Black Tim's Anvil, at Merrittsville, and rode along, harking as we went, but by then the land was quiet as a tomb. When we came to Ed Holcombe's, Ed was standing on his front porch looking into the darkness. I rode in and asked him if he had heard hounds. 'Listen,' he said, and from the hills, far, far to the north, came the distant cry, as faint as a dying note of music. There was no possible chance of our getting to them so we went on towards Merrittsville, blowing from time to time. We stopped at the church this side of the village, but only the far away barking of a house dog and a horse's hoofs on a distant road disturbed the stillness. It would be hard to depict Will Madden's feeling as we stood in the darkening shadow of that old church. I can hear him now. 'Hounds be tired, sir, and the fox be tired. They don't be runnin' him like afore. Do you know what Master Algy be a doin' sir? He be leadin' over the fences—jumpin' on and off and leadin' over. That little, old, wizened up horse is a followin' of him like dog out there in the dark. Leadin' over out there in the dark. It be rough out there, sir. I mind that patch of country. It be mostly slash and rocks and stone walls. He, out there with my hounds in the dark, and me a standin' at this here church.'

"We passed through the village of Merrittsville and heard hounds when we were close to Black Tim's Anvil, and once again a mile beyond, and that was the last we heard of them.

"We poked about here and there in the dark harking, blowing, and asking, but apparently the fox had run steadily away from us. Concluding at last that whatever might have happened, hounds were probably now headed for home, we jogged along over a rough, stony, rutty road, with here and there deep puddles over the surface of which thin skims of ice were forming. It's twelve miles from Merrittsville to the kennels.

"When we came into Bangdollen they told us that hounds were on the road some distance in front of us with a young boy. A man standing by the roadside said, 'and he ha a fox wee him. I see it.' As we jogged on an old couplet came to me,

> 'A hundred horsemen saw him found;
> How many saw him die?'

"I am not proud of my part that night. When we came up with the hounds I asked Old Man if he was all right, for I was deeply concerned; then we rode on together saying little, for I was out of tune with the boy. But when we reached the house and were about to dismount I felt that I could not properly drop the subject of his hunting without some comment, so I said, 'Old Man, I am a bit surprised, perhaps just a bit disappointed about your having been out today.' 'Sorry sir,' was all he answered, and turned towards the house.

"He sent down word by my man that if I would excuse him he would like to have dinner in his room. I dined alone, tormented beyond words at the thought of the boy being by himself on such a night. After dinner I started up to see him, but not wishing to intrude, finally sent the man up to say that I would very much like to sit with him a while either in the library or in his room. He again asked to be excused on the ground that he was tired and had turned in. I tried to read, tried to write, tried thumbing the piano, tried everything. God bless me, but I was upset, and wished I had never taken hounds out. Being tuckered I at length turned in but could not sleep, so crept upstairs to see if by any chance the boy was still awake. The room was in darkness and the door locked.

"I don't know how long I had been asleep or what time it might have been when suddenly I was conscious of someone tapping on the door. I sat up, turned on the night light, and called 'Come in.'

"He had on a blue bath robe, one sleeve of which was empty. He walked to the foot of the bed, stood up very straight, looked squarely at me, and said, 'I'm very sorry, Sir, to have wakened you. I couldn't help it, Sir. I had to. I couldn't stand it any longer, Sir. I can't have you disappointed in me. Dad wouldn't like it. You were very good to him, Sir. I'm sorry, but I had to hunt today.'

"I did not answer him for a moment, determined to think twice before speaking. The boy's appearance alarmed me. He was but fourteen years old, yet as he stood there he might have been of middle age. The constant, haunting thoughts and remembrances of the father lying at the little home on Highminster were tormenting the boy beyond all endurance. From his position I knew that either his shoulder or collar bone was broken, and had now been broken for many hours. 'Old Man,' I said, 'we won't talk about your having hunted today. I shall never refer to it again or think about it, and don't you think about it.'

"The boy took hold of the foot of the bed with his good hand. I could see the knuckles growing white with the intensity of his grip. 'You still don't understand, Sir. Can't you see, Sir? Can't you understand? I should think *you* could understand, Sir,' and there was a note of impatience in the tense, trembling voice. He left the foot of the bed and came close to me. His hand was working convulsively. 'Don't you see, Sir—it was the first time, the only time, he has ever been able to see me ride to hounds. He had been waiting a long time, Sir. I couldn't keep him waiting. It had been a long time, Sir.' He turned, went out of the room, and closed the door very softly. As I reached for the telephone I heard him passing hesitatingly down the hall.

TWENTY-TWO

AND THE SECOND IS LIKE UNTO IT

Gordon Grand

He rode up to me at the meet. "The Herr Secretary?" he asked, removing his ridiculous looking cap. "Please, I would like to be of the hunt. Only for today yet Herr Secretary."

He was an incongruous figure on a horse in his sheepskin coat and black trousers tucked into the tops of a pair of high lumberman's shoes. His hands were encased in new bright yellow gloves with imitation fur at the wrists,— such as were sold to teamsters at country stores. A long, shiny black whip, reminiscent of toy shop windows, hung suspended from his left forearm.

He was of a squat, thick build, with a shaggy, unkempt beard which seemed to cover the greater part of his face. Above the beard sat a dull brown cap with an exaggerated visor and a length of tape around the crown, the purpose of which I did not grasp.

As I was surveying him, Colonel Weatherford, the Master, rode up with hounds. The man turned to me with a glow in his mild blue eyes. "The Herr Mastor?" he enquired anxiously. I nodded. Weatherford drew nearer. The man straightened himself, assumed a military position, and removed his cap. I saw a questioning look pass over the Colonel's face. He surveyed the visitor from head to foot, acknowledged the salute, and rode on.

It would be a long, exhausting task to do justice to the extent to which this man irritated and annoyed the members of the Millbeck Hunt that day. But in fairness to my old friends I plead that their irritation was well founded. The man exercised absolutely no control over his horse. He gave no indication of being sensible of having a horse under him. He climbed on the heels of other horses. He crossed in front of us as we galloped to our fences, endangering our very lives. He twice fell off, necessitating the catching of his horse. His mount stepped on Enid Ashleys horse's hind shoe, twisting and pulling it off so that Enid lost her day's sport. As his final act of devastation he bowled over an exceedingly good hound which was coming in from a wood-ride. It costs a great deal of money to support horses and hounds and all the paraphernalia that goes with a hunt, and when all is said and done those who furnish the sinews are entitled to pursue their sport in some measure of peace and security.

As ill luck would have it, we found a twisting fox in Three Spires Uplands. He doubled and turned and refused to leave the covert, necessitating our galloping up the wood-rides, harking, then, as hounds turned, galloping down again. It is a tremendous covert, and we must have done this half a dozen times, for you dare not let hounds get out of hearing in those woods and every time Colonel Weatherford passed us seeking his place at the head of the hunt the stranger would quickly assure his rigid military seat and remove his cap.

At the end of one of these fruitless pilgrimages the Colonel beckoned to me. I rode over to him. "Pendleton," he said, "if that Bolshevik looking rascal doesn't stop saluting me I will take hounds home." He sat harking to the hounds and glaring straight ahead of him for some time, then turned, and pointing at me with his crop, said, " 'and the second is like unto it. Love thy neighbor as thy self. On these two commandments hang all the law and the prophets.' God bless my soul, Pendleton, it's just this sort of impossible precept which deters a large part of mankind from paying attention to any precepts. It's all damned tommyrot asking people to do the impossible." Hounds turned just below us and again essayed the ridge. The Colonel spun his horse around and jogged off.

Our fox finally broke covert and laid a brilliant course for the foot of Smithboro Hill, with hounds on his back. For thirty exhilarating minutes of a rare, fresh fall day we galloped over one of the fairest lands in Christendom. Then, thinking of his home covert, the fox made a great loop and headed back for Three Spires Uplands.

I was going fast up front with Colonel Weatherford when far off to our right we saw a riderless, galloping horse. If you have hunted all your life, a riderless horse raises a question in your mind; has anyone been hurt? I saw the Colonel looking towards the horse. It was too far off to be recognized. Then we came upon them. The uncouth stranger had her in his arms carrying her across the great upland sheep pasture that runs from Three Spires Hill to Wendover.

The Colonel turned in his saddle, called to the field to go on with hounds, and he and I galloped towards the man. Colonel Weatherford fairly hurled his huge frame to the ground, handed me the reins and strode over to the man. "Here, hand Miss Sedgwick to me, hand her to me. I will carry the child." The man stopped, stood erect, and looked at Colonel Weatherford with those mild blue eyes of his. Something of grandeur touched him. "The Herr Mastor will permit me to carry the liebes Kind. I have knowledge of such things. I am a vatter many times yet and a docktor chemeest."

That man, a stranger, a foreigner, and uncouth-looking was holding in his arms perhaps the most precious thing in the world to John Weatherford. I have known the Colonel for many years and in all this time I seldom knew him to be crossed. His eyes narrowed just a hair's breadth and the two men looked at each other; then the Colonel turned, reached for his horse, and we walked on.

It was a long, trying walk over a very rough stretch of land, yet that squat, powerful German carried the child as a skilled nurse might cross a room with a fretful infant. Mary's eyes were closed and her face ghastly grey, but withal she looked comfortable in his arms, almost as one in a gentle sleep.

Upon reaching the road we found the Colonel's groom standing there with the second horse. The Colonel called him. "Walsh," he said, "get these horses home, and there is another one tied somewhere out at the far end of that sheep pasture, and Miss Mary's horse is running loose. Get someone to help you and get them all home to my stable."

A car came by and we flagged it. "Herr Mastor," said the man, "you will hold the Fräulein, I will myself in the behind seat get. You will hand the liebes Kind to me mit care. You and the Herr Secretary will in the front be." Rebelling inwardly, and within a hair's breadth of exploding, the Colonel complied. As soon as we had started the Colonel turned to the man. "Do you know whether the child is dangerously hurt?"

"Nein, nein, Herr Mastor, nein. I listened to the heart when I was there yet with the sheeps. It is fine yet. The pulse, ach, it is beautiful. I count. Nein, Herr Mastor, the Fräulein, she will be well yet as soon she come to her mooter. The mooter, she will know what to do." It was very odd, but from the moment I first came upon the man with Mary in his arms a feeling of security and assurance came over me.

Upon reaching the house I went ahead to prepare Mrs. Sedgwick. The man handed Mary to the Colonel to hold, but, out of the car, immediately took her from him and carried her up the stairs to where Mrs. Sedgwick was waiting.

We three sat in embarrassed silence awaiting the doctor's verdict. Presently Mrs. Sedgwick entered in search of something. She is a rare person in her composure and dignity and understanding of all things. The man never took his eyes from her during all the time she was in the room. When she had left he moved his chair closer to Colonel Weatherford. He had taken off his sheepskin jacket and appeared in a tight fitting black coat of a most unusual cut, bedecked here and there with black braid. He sat on the very edge of his chair, suddenly pointed his finger at Colonel Weatherford and shook it at him a number of times, a liberty I had never seen taken before. "Herr Mastor, if the Virgin Mary had not been such a kind of a Mooter maybe Jesus Christ would not have been the same man yet."

The Colonel looked at the man for some time, then stood up, moved his chair over directly in front of him, sat down, leaned forward, and tapped the man's knee, saying, "Tell me, why did you want to come fox hunting today? Did you enjoy it? Did you get anything out of it?" A smile passed over the man's face; a really lovely, gentle smile that had its inception in the heart. "Herr Mastor, I am a moosician. I am a docktor chemeest, but first am I a moosician. Herr Mastor, everythings are mooseek—the great city, the quiet country, the water when she moves, the machine when it goes, all are mooseek. But Herr Mastor, three great mooseeks there are. First one is when kleine Kinder play in happiness—the laugh, the quiet voices, the clapping of the hands, one time excited, one time so soft. That is the mooseek of the world when she is growning up.

"Second yet is the mooseek of the chase. That is an old mooseek, Herr Mastor. It tells the story of when mens must hunt; when all things must hunt for their liebes Kinder.

"The last mooseek is the greatest mooseek of the world, Herr Mastor. It is men marching when it is the war. Four years I am of the war. The tramp of men's feet in the night; the wheels of gun carriages on the hard roads, the Herr officer's voice when he makes the command far away. That is the great mooseek of all the world; men going to death.

"Two mooseeks I know—the world growing up like when kleine Kinder play, and the world going down like when men march to war. The chase mooseek I do not know so good yet.

"Herr Mastor, two times I come to Millbeck and stay at Frau Holfstetter's boarding house. I am a shooter. I come to shoot the birds, and every time, Herr Mastor, when I come I see the hunt; the red coats, the many dogs, the horses, the Herr Huntsman. I hear the horses galloping, and the great calling of the dogs and the horn. A long time yet I listen to these things. Many miles I hurry to hear the mooseek. Voonderful it is, Herr Mastor, when one hound waits for the other to make the cry. Does the Herr Mastor think all the hounds make the cry together? Nein, nein, Herr Mastor. The birds, the crickets, the frogs, the hounds in the chase, all things that make mooseek must keep the time. I am a moosician. I am the first violin. Today I ask the Herr Secretary can I please be of the hunt for only one day yet so I know the chase mooseek. Six times yet Herr Mastor have I instruction taken from the Herr professor to make the horse yump. If he yump, Herr Mastor, I am but if he do not yump then sometimes I am not."

I don't know how much time elapsed. It might have been three years, perhaps four. It was the night before Thanksgiving. The telephone rang. "It is the Herr Secretary? Could I again yet be of the hunt tomorrow, please?"

The next morning I went over to the kennels and rode to the Meet with Colonel Weatherford, Will Madden, the Huntsman, and the hounds. Upon arriving at the fixture it was evident that something untoward had happened. Then Clement Hastings rode up to the Colonel. He is a spoiled, over-bearing, dictatorial individual who sends four beautifully bred and schooled horses to Millbeck each season,—and then rarely comes to hunt them.

"Weatherford," he said, "I protest against that man over there riding with this Hunt. I protest against his hunting at all. That hired horse of his is not fit to be around other horses. It has kicked three horses already, including my own. What's the sense of a man having a red ribbon on his horse's tail as a warning that it kicks and then letting it wander all over the place kicking everybody in sight. I subscribe fifteen hundred dollars a year to this Hunt and I protest against that man riding."

Hastings was sorely disgruntled, but then his intriguing brown thoroughbred mare did have a welt on her side the size of a small saucer.

Standing in the middle of the road entirely deserted by the members of the Hunt who were, with just cause, giving him the widest possible berth, stood our visitor. The man's face was wreathed in unhappiness, bewilderment and anxiety. He had heard all that Hastings said, as had the rest of the field.

Hastings rode off, while the Colonel, a very great stickler for propriety in the hunting field, stood quietly in the center of the road looking at the visitor. Memory has an odd little way of recalling things to one's mind. As I stood there watching this trying scene and wondering what was about to happen, the Colonel's words came back to me, "And the second is like unto it." There were a hundred pairs of eyes fixed on John Weatherford. Suddenly I saw him touch his horse lightly with his heel and ride forward. The man in the road watched his approach with evident concern and embarrassment. When he reached the man the Colonel stopped his horse, removed his velvet cap with his right hand, transferred it to his left, in which he held his reins, reached out his hand, and I heard him say in a crisp, hearty voice that all could hear. "Herr Mueller, I make you welcome, Sir. It is a pleasure to see you out with us again. I hope you will dine with me this Thanksgiving day."

There was the same military squaring of the shoulders and the removing of the old brown cap.

The Colonel looked slowly over the entire field. He was apparently in quest of someone. Then he stood up in his stirrups and I saw him signalling with his crop. A groom rode up on the Colonel's second horse. "Walsh, Mr.

Mueller will hunt my horse today. You will exchange with him. Madden, take hounds into the first covert."

Too many Thanksgiving evenings have come and gone for me to remember all the people who dined with Colonel Weatherford that night. George and Enid Ashley were there, and old Madam Estey, Henry and Edith Newcombe, the Reverend Huntington Sedgwick, Mrs. Sedgwick, and Mary. Then there was that old British war horse, Sir Charles Graham-Pierce, who was visiting the Newcombes, and I recall a Belgian baron. His name has escaped me, but he was one of the great archaeologists of his day, and was visiting Colonel Weatherford. The others have been lost in the clouds of old memories.

It was a pleasant gathering of friends and neighbors with many interests and affections in common; the hills of Dutchess County, the hounds that raced across them, and the foxes that bred and lived on their sunny slopes.

To the casual observer the glint showing back of Sir Charles' monocle as he appraised Herr Mueller's sartorial ensemble might have appeared a trifle flinty. But I knew it was only mild surprise for I had once taken a famous British general to view Niagara Falls and he had had the same look as he remarked that the Falls were rather unusual. Madam Estey was the only one perplexed, but that's because she still believed in certain things.

In this present era which sees the renewed abundance of the mediocre in vintages I look back upon the wine of that evening as did the ancients upon the flesh pots of Egypt. "Not now any more, in Europe, Monsieur, not in any place is one honored with such wine." Thus my Belgian neighbor at dinner confided to me with reverence and some emotion in his voice.

Shortly after dinner I missed Colonel Weatherford and Herr Mueller. Glancing towards the hall I saw them in earnest converse, the German with his hands extended in a suppliant attitude as though trying to dissuade the Colonel from some project.

When we were at last all reassembled in the library the Colonel's servant entered the room and handed Herr Mueller a violin case. Formerly of black leather, it was now a dull grey. In place of conventional metal clasps, which had long since disappeared, the case was held together by a length of black braid.

Colonel Weatherford crossed the room, stood with his back to the fireplace, and said, "We had a very good Thanksgiving run today. Hounds ran brilliantly, and we were in a galloping country. It was my pleasure to mount my friend, Otto Fritz Mueller. Mr. Mueller confesses to limited prowess as a horseman, yet has mastered a cardinal objective. He knows enough to let a seasoned horse alone. Because of this he witnessed and enjoyed all that our day's sport had to offer.

"Riding home he told me of having spent some years in endeavoring to portray in music that which a musician hears when he rides to hounds. This is Thanksgiving evening, a friendly, mellow occasion, and I have importuned Mr. Mueller to give the pleasure of hearing his composition to an audience which should be peculiarly appreciative of such music. Herr Mueller."

As I have confessed before, time has obliterated much of that evening, but nothing will dim my picture of Otto Fritz Mueller—his bulging figure, his odd garments, his topsy-turvy beard, his necktie high behind and failing of its principal function in front. But these were of no moment. The man's gentle, kindly smile, the blue of his eyes, the reverent touch of the old violin, his modesty and hesitancy,—theses were things of the very man himself.

Twice he lifted the violin preparatory to playing and twice lowered it, looking earnestly over at Colonel Weatherford. "Please, Herr Mastor, would you say something yet to the people what it is the music tells, please." The Colonel shook his head. "No, Herr Mueller. It will not be necessary to tell them. The music will tell them."

The player seemed not convinced. He looked about the room in a perplexed, troubled air, then said, "Please, it is early morning yet of the hunt day. By the kennels every things are asleep already still."

A soft, dreamy note stole across the room evolving slowly into a gentle lullaby, and I found myself picturing the hounds stretched out on their benches, the Hunt horses in commodious, well-bedded stalls, Will Madden, the Huntsman, and his staff tucked away in snug cottages. Even the kennel cat came to my mind, asleep in a corner of the cook room. The music played on and the Millbeck Hunt slept.

Then a more alert note reached me and I knew that a hound had awakened, stretched himself, left the long bench and whimpered. The instrument suddenly broke into clamorous, vibrating strains, and I saw forty couple of anxious, expectant hounds crowding out into the yard to greet the morning. The kennels were awake. Another hunting day had dawned in Dutchess County.

When the first clamorous cry of hounds had subsided, a busy note of countless comings and goings filled the score, hurried foot-steps between oat bin and stall, the sissing of grooms doing up their horses, the clink of stirrup irons, water splashing into pails. Life at a hunt stable was being unfolded to us.

Again the clamorous cry of hounds. They were being released. Thongs cracked. Will Madden blew three sharp notes on his horn, then the rap-a-tap-tap of the Hunt horses on the hard road, and when at times the music grew very soft we heard hound pads scuffling along.

I was picturing them jogging on to the Meet by Andrew Haightman's farm—a scene I knew so well, when again the music changed. There was a clatter of many horses and the talk of people. Hounds had arrived at the meet. Presently the field jogged slowly down the road. Then the music faded almost away, for hounds had entered covert, and we heard their soft pads on dry, crinkly leaves, and listened to the breeze blowing through oak branches. It was very still in the room, the music hardly audible. Then a new note, one not heard before,—a hound's voice speaking in covert on a fall morning. The player lowered his violin to his side. He waited. We all waited. The room was hushed. A hound had spoken. I did not see the violin lifted, but suddenly the room to its deepest niches was filled with music. Hounds had found. The covert rang with anxious cry. We heard hounds flying toward us, then away from us. The violin gradually softened. They had reached the far edge of the covert. The music sank almost to a whisper. Then we heard the Huntsman's horse, and the strong rustle of other horses' feet in the leaves. The notes of the violin came so fast they crowded one upon another. Little Mary Sedgwick moved far forward on the couch and took my arm. We knew that hounds had reached the open and that the field was with them. I felt the roar of the wind as one gallops into it, and heard the thud of horses' feet.

The man played on and on. I saw old Sir Charles sitting on the edge of his chair, his hands gripping its arms. We hunted that fox in the open, ran him into deep woods and down into quiet, mystic swales. We coursed him to the high hills of Dutchess County and through the swamps that lie at the foot of those hills. Horses sweated and strained, and those who rode them were grim and alert. But through all this great panorama of sport there was brought to us by the strings of the violin a light, soft note, which kept for ever harping in our ears. It was a refrain—a motive, a haunting thing ever repeating itself; I knew well what it was—the feathery touch of a fox pad on the ground. The player produced it by touching the strings with his finger. And as we listened and saw the scene with our mind's eye the beat of the fox pad grew gradually slower—slower yet louder, and ever more insistent. Slower, always slower. I saw Mary's right hand pressing against her forehead. Colonel Weatherford, who had been watching the player intently, took a step or two towards him. Suddenly a cry burst from the violin, an eerie, fateful cry. Little Mary Sedgwick pressed my arm. "Oh, Mr. Pendleton, they have viewed him, they have viewed him. They are running into him." The violin rose and fell with the swaying of the man's body. A great volume of music filled the room and swept on to the upper reaches of the house. Forrard, forrard, forrard! I heard Will Madden's voice, John Weatherford's voice. I heard the struggling, galloping horses and pressing hounds. Then Will's high, tense scream. "Have at him lads. Have at him. Have at him."

The music sank to a plaintive, somber key, gradually fading into nothingness, and then Herr Mueller bowed.

Colonel Weatherford remained standing, evidently turning some project over his mind and appraising the feelings of those in the room. Finally he said, "You all witnessed an unfortunate and exceedingly regrettable incident at the Meet this morning, for which I would like to see amends made. I would also like to see the members of the Hunt record their appreciation of a brilliant musical achievement. I now move you the election of Herr Fritz Mueller as an honorary member of the Hunt."

With the spell of the music still upon us we voted "aye, aye, aye." Old Madam Estey voted aye and clapped her hands. Sir Charles in his bluff way announced that although he had no vote the idea was top hole, top hole, and said bravo, bravo, in a voice that must have carried to the kennels.

We turned to look at Herr Mueller. He was making a series of stiff, formal little bows, his face wreathed in that contagious smile of his. He turned to Colonel Weatherford, saying, "Thank you, Herr Mastor, but I go back to Germany now. What I came to this country for is done. The chemeests every where now know of the things my uncle makes in Hamburg, so I go home. But Herr Mastor, I will accept the honor of a member being. I want very much I should be a member. My vatter, the Count von Bethwig und von Mueller will also much happiness get when I tell him I am a member of the hoont yet.

"Many times now will my vatter tell his friends, 'my son Fritz—he is a sportsman now. He makes his horse yoomp like in England.'

"Herr Mastor I go away in two days now but here is what it is I wish, I wish the Millbeck hounds may have many years of good sport yet. That you, Herr Mastor, will ride always up in the front part—that the hoondts always will go faster and the foxes also. And when, Herr Mastor, you do not be in the front part, then next I wish Fräulein Sedgwick would be in the front part. All the ladies and gentlemens I thank."

TWENTY-THREE

LOSS OF A FRIEND

Tad Shepperd

I knew it when the old vet said:
"Her chances aren't so strong,
"And I'm afraid that she'll be dead
"Before so very long."
Then, as I walked out of the stall,
She breathed a tiny groan.
It seemed as though she'd tried to call:
"Don't let me die alone."
I dropped down in her deep straw bed,
To kneel there by her side
And slowly stroke that lovely head,
Once borne with gallant pride.
The stable noises seemed to bring
A weighty lethargy,
As waters from some Lethean spring,
Inviting reverie.

So there I knelt in drowsy haze,
The while my fancy led
The steeds of memory to graze
In fields of days now sped.
I saw a gangly little shrew
Up on the pasture hill,
A frowzy little drunkard who
Could never drink her fill.
Then she grew to beat damnation,
And her limbs were strong and straight.
She'd her daddy's conformation
And her mammy's lovely gait.
She had wind and speed and fire,
And she'd fiercely roll her eyes,
Spying boogers in the briar
During morning exercise.
I pictured her against the sky
Along the wind-swept ridge,
Aharking to the hounds in cry
Beyond the covered bridge.
I saw her as we'd canter all
Along some woodland ride,
While she'd take fence and ditch and wall,
And never change her stride.
That morning when the "ladies" found
The fox at Hardie's Brae,
And chased him 'til he went to ground
Full fourteen miles away.
And we jogged home as day grew lean
With silent winter dark,

As easily as if she'd been
But for a morning's lark.
And then the Hunt Club races,
Where she gaily spurned the gaps
And kicked dirt in their faces
As she finished under wraps.
And the running of the Barton,
When she floundered through the rain
Like a game and valiant Spartan,
To come in on top again.
And then I saw her as she'd been
That damned and hapless morn,
A justly proud and haughty queen
Who thought of fear with scorn.
And, casting caution to the wind,
I'd answered to her fire
And put her at a panel blind—
To find it topped with wire.
The going had been muddy
And she slithered at the leap,
Then crashed down torn and bloody,
In a writhing, lashing heap.
I came out of my daydream then,
To hear her draw a breath
Like soughing wind in narrow glen,
And felt the wings of Death.
She tried to arch her gallant crest,
And then I saw her yield,

And knew that she had gone to rest
In some Elysian Field.
I knew a trusted friend I'd lost,
The meet was closed and done,
The earthly finish line was crossed,
Her last great race was won.
But Gabriel will find that she
Will gallop through the skies
And keep him up where he can see
The hounds of Paradise,
As they go rolling down the vale
To scramble o'er the rocks
With ringing tongue, upon the trail
Of some celestial fox.
And if she waits the starter's hand
Up There, then when she goes,
Each knowing angel in the stand
Will bet her "on the nose."

PART IV
AMERICAN HUNTING HISTORY
AND PERSONALITIES

TWENTY-FOUR

THE FIRST M.F.H.: ROBERT BROOKE, 1650

J. Blan van Urk

Robert Brooke, Esq., came to Maryland from England in 1650 with a pack of hounds.

> In his desire to increase the population of Maryland, Lord Baltimore appointed Robert Brooke as a member of the "Privy Council of State within our said Province of Maryland" by commission dated September 20, 1649 . . . conferred because he "doth, this next summer's expedition, intend to transport himself, his family and a great number of other persons and good store of provision and ammunition" into Maryland to "settle a considerable plantation."[1]

The plantation, named De La Brooke, consisted of only 2000 acres, but there were some in those days who thought this an enviable hunting ground. On June 30, 1650, Mr. Brooke arrived, bringing with him on his private ship in addition to his hounds, his wife, ten children (eight of whom were boys), twenty-one manservants and seven maidservants—forty persons in all. Not a bad start in populating his new possession!

Incidentally, Lord Baltimore caused many English hounds or "dogs" to be brought to America, since, in his instruction to those about to journey overseas, he specified at least one "dog" to a family as a foremost requirement for colonization.

Because of Mr. Brooke's prominence in Colonial affairs, records of his activities have lived. For this reason he is the first *known* Master of a pack of hounds in America, and the year *1650* must be the *first date* in a chronological history of America foxhunting—"History without chronology is dark and confusing; chronology without history is dry and insipid." That he was the first Master of Foxhounds in the exclusive sense, as some have said, seems to me a bit farfetched. Being a wealthy man, he undoubtedly kept a pack in England, yet his name has never been mentioned as preceding Lowther, Arundel, Boothby and others over there whose hounds have been cited as specialists. Therefore, it is extremely unlikely that his pack should have been kenneled for fox alone upon arrival in this country.

However, Mr. Brooke's contribution to American sport should not be minimized, both for his interest in the chase and for the basic hound blood-strain he introduced, later so important in developing American hounds. His death only five years after coming to the Colonies[2] ended what might well have been a long and merry acquaintance with the fox—and exclusively; but although his life in Maryland was brief, "he left a lasting impression upon the history of his day."[3]

What is more remarkable than any influence Mr. Brooke's five years may have had on early Maryland is the fact that his hounds have lived and been bred by the Brooke descendants right down to the present—*290 years of American breeding* by one family. To be sure there have been many crosses, and other hound-breed reputations have grown to high prominence; but the Brooke hound has been throughout the years, and remains today, a definite entity. As one great hound breeder, student and authority expressed it, "Allowing for the many outcrosses during all these years, there is still resemblance enough to justify these claims . . . and owners of them (Brooke hounds) point with pride to their long unbroken line of ancestry."[4] Who was it said there was nothing traditional in America?

The original Robert Brooke family moved from Prince Georges County (Maryland) to Montgomery County, where they established themselves at Sandy Spring, Brooke Grove and Willow Grove. The eight boys and their sons, and the sons following, all kept and bred hounds—and hunted fox (among other things), some mounted, some afoot; some by day, some by night. Records show that the Brooke hound formed basic stock for such famous strains of American hounds as the Trigg and Walker.

Notes

1. "Maryland under the Commonwealth (1648–1658)," Bernard C. Steiner, Ph.D.; Johns Hopkins University Studies in Historical and Political Science, The Johns Hopkins Press, Baltimore, 1911, Series 29, No. I, pp. 37–38.
2. Genealogical Chart by Ellen Culver Bowen: born, June 3, 1602; B.A., Oxford 1620; M.A., Oxford 1624; died July 20, 1655; buried at Brooke Place.
3. Side Lights of Maryland History, hester Dorsey Richardson; Williams and Wilkins Co., Baltimore, Vol. II, p. 33, 3d edition, 1913.
4. Horse and Hound, Roger D. Williams; privately printed by author, Lexington, Kentucky, 1905.

TWENTY-FIVE

PROMINENT FOXHUNTERS OF AN EARLY DAY

J. Blan van Urk

Among the early great, there is little doubt that George Washington (1732–1799) set the pace in the hunting field as he did in American affairs. It is well known that he was an ardent and active follower of hounds from early boyhood until after the Revolution. "His early education . . . was such as favored the production of an athletic and vigorous body . . . accustomed to the healthful occupations of rural life, and to the manly toils of the chase."[1]

The man responsible for his learning the *Noble Science* at sixteen was Lord Thomas Fairfax, whose own passion for hunting was second to nothing. In 1749 Fairfax came to Virginia—"a man strayed out of the world of fashion at fifty-five into the forests of a wild frontier."[2] Upon his arrival he started keeping horses and hounds in the English manner, and with his style and finesse was a tremendous influence upon neighborhood customs. It was only natural that young Washington should learn a touch of old-world address from Thomas, Lord Fairfax. "When the sport was poor near home (Belvoir), Fairfax would take his hounds to a distant part of the country, establish himself at an inn, and keep open house and open table to every person of good character and respectable appearance who chose to join him in following the hounds."[3]

From 1759 to 1774 Washington devoted all his spare time to foxhunting, and his familiar diary is replete with hunting entries covering this period— the 1768–1769 seasons being most active. Typical notations, selected to give a view of the sport then enjoyed, are the following:

1768[4]—January 8; Hunting again in the same Comp'y. Started a Fox and run him four hours, took the Hounds off at Night.
    February 12; Catch'd two foxes.
    February 13; Catch'd two more foxes.

George Washington invites Lord Thomas Fairfax to follow his hounds.

March 2; Hunting again, and catch'd a fox with a bob Tail and cut Ears after seven hours chase in which most of the Dogs were worsted.

1769[5]—February 18; Went a hunting with Doctr. Rumney. Started a fox, or rather 2 or 3, and catched none. Dogs mostly got after Deer and never joined.

March 27; Went a foxhunting. Found and was run out of hearing by some of the Dogs.

April 11; Went a foxhunting and took a fox alive after running him to a tree. Bro't him home.

April 12; Chased the above fox for an hour and 45 minutes when he treed again; after which we lost him.

1770[6]—March 7; Went a hunting again. Found a Fox and run it 6 hours, and then lost. I returned home this evening.

1773—February 9; After an early Dinner I set off to Mr. Robt. Alexander's upon Foxhunting Party. (This hunt is reported to have continued for three days.)

1774—April 14; Went a hunting. Killed a bitch fox, with three young ones almost hair'd.

That Washington was most particular about all appurtenances to the chase is shown by an invoice to Robert Cary & Company (July 25, 1769) which called for "1 large huntg. Horn bound tight around with sml. brass Wire Slipping." In 1773 (July 10), there was special mention of how a new one was to be "lap'd and secur'd in the strongest manner."[7]

He was also precise in matters of behavior, his code requiring "that every action done in company ought to be with some sign of respect to those that are present."[8] Here we have the Father of our country giving to foxhunters one of the first principles of conduct in the hunting field—*respect* and *consideration*. He had one friend, the eccentric General Charles Lee (1731–1782), who must have been a strange guest in the Washington mansion. General Lee didn't believe in being separated from his pack even for a moment, and always had his "dogs" follow him—legions of them—wherever he went. While visiting people he insisted upon taking them to his host's table as was his custom at home. When chided, his usual reply was, "I must have some object to embrace. When once I can be convinced that men are as worthy objects as dogs, I shall transfer my benevolence and become as staunch a philanthropist as the canting Addison affected to be."[9]

Washington prided himself on his horsemanship, and was a daring rider, although not foolhardy. One day while in the field, a Colonel Humphreys challenged him to follow his lead over a hedge. Humphreys, misjudging the spot, put his mount to it only to find himself "deposited up to his horse's girths" in a quagmire after clearing the obstacle. Washington "either knew the ground better or had suspected something, for, following at an easy pace, he reined up at the hedge, and, looking over at his engulfed aide, exclaimed, 'No, no, Colonel, you are too *deep* for me'!"[10]

He rode "with ease, elegance and power and required but one good quality in a horse—'to go along'." Four of his favorites were *Ajax, Blueskin, Valiant* and *Magnolia,* an Arab. Always perfectly mounted, wearing a "blue coat, scarlet waistcoat, buckskin breeches, top boots, velvet cap," and carrying a "whip with long thong," he tried to plan on at least three days a week for hunting. In addition to this he had many an unplanned chase, for he usually took along some hounds while on inspection tours to distant parts of his estate on the chance of starting a fox. As was the custom, sportsmen exchanged visits to enjoy the chase, frequently taking their own packs with them—many stayed at Mount Vernon for days or weeks at a time, and Washington in turn would visit friends for a change of hunting country. One of the Fairfax family wrote to him in 1768, "I shall be glad of our Company at Towlston when it is convenient to spend three or four days or more. I can't say my hounds are good enough to justifie an Invitation to Hunt."[11] When farther afield, Washington took part in whatever hunting was to be had, as is evidenced by an entry in a Philadelphian's private diary (December 19, 1781) which spoke of the General's presence at a hunt at Frankford (Pennsylvania).[12]

He personally supervised his stables and kennels, and whenever possible visited them morning and evening. Regarding his hounds, it was his boast that they were so "critically drafted, as to speed and bottom, that in running, if one leading dog should lose the scent, another was at hand immediately to recover it."[13] He frequently spoke of being able to cover the pack, when on a line, with a blanket. This boast must have been before absences from home caused his hounds to be neglected, for at one time they became poor and lacked training.

A canter through the *Badminton Magazine* series has revealed that Martha Washington occasionally joined her husband in the chase "clad in a scarlet habit."[14] Also "Billy" Lee, variously described as Washington's Huntsman, friend, neighbor and body servant, rode a great jumping horse called *Chinkling.* This man, whatever his actual capacity or capacities, had his portrait painted by the celebrated Peale.

After the Revolution, the Marquis de Lafayette (1757–1834) sent some "very fierce" French staghounds as a gift to Washington. An entry in the latter's diary dated August 24, 1785, reads, "Received seven hounds sent me from France by the Marqs. de la Fayette, by way of New York, viz. 3 dogs and four Bitches." These hounds, of great size, were very disappointing upon being put to fox—this, despite the fact that they were

. . . Bred out of the Spartan kind,
  So flewed, so sanded; and their heads are hung
  With ears that sweep away the morning dew;
  Crook-kneed and dew lap'd like Thessalian bulls,
  Slow in pursuit, but matched in mouth like bells.

The French hounds liked stag and that was that.

It has been pretty generally stated that, because private affairs and public business required so much of his time, Washington was forced to break up his kennels in 1785; and the entry which is cited as his last hunting reference is the one dated December 22, 1785:

> Went a Fox hunting with the Gentlemen who came here yesterday, together with Ferdinando Washington (his nephew) and Mr. Shaw (his secretary), after a very early breakfast.
>
> Found a Fox just back of Muddy hole Plantation, and after a Chase of an hour and a quarter with my dogs, and eight couple of Doctor Smith's (brought by Mr. Phil. Alexander) we put him into a hollow tree, in which we fastned him; and in the Pincushion put up another Fox which in an hour and 13 Minutes was killed.
>
> We then after allowing the Fox in the hole half an hour, put the Dogs upon his Tract and in half a Mile he took another hollow tree and was again put out of it, but he did not go 600 yards before he had recourse to the same shift. Finding therefore that he was a conquered Fox we took the Dogs off and all came home to Dinner except Mr. Danl. Dulany, who left us in the Field after the first Fox was treed. Lund Washington came home with us to dinner.[15]

However, another and later entry has come to light indicating that Washington continued to hunt for some years after 1785—not often, but whenever he found time to do so. He noted in his diary on February 15, 1788, "Let out a Fox (which had been taken alive some days before) and after chasing it an hour lost it."[16] On this date, Washington was approaching his fifty-sixth birthday. His opportunity to break away from affairs of state for a last fling at the sport he loved so dearly came in the interval between the Constitutional Convention held at Philadelphia and his taking the Presidential oath in New York on April 30, 1789.

Even as late as February 2, 1789, two months before the mantle of the Presidency was placed on his shoulders, he was thinking of matters in the field:

> On my way home met Mr. George Calvert on his way to Arlington with the hounds I had lent him, viz. *Vulcan* and *Venus* (from France), *Ragman* and 2 other dogs (from England) *Dutchess* and *Doxey* (from Philadelphia), *Tryal, Jupiter* and *Countess* (descended from the French hounds).[17]

It is likely that the nostalgic feeling was already beginning to set in and that Washington would have liked to join Calvert and "his" hounds.

The diaries and writings of Washington have been sifted and sorted by so many writers and compilers that it is little wonder some entries are in one collection and some in another. Consequently it was very simple for a mistaken impression to be formed—especially as G. W. Parke Custis, Washington's adopted son, wrote that the year 1787 saw Washington's last hunting. Since the above quoted diary entry of 1788 seems to be authentic, I believe Mr. Custis' observation was incorrect.

It will be of interest to those who do not know of it to learn that the almost perfect citizen, Thomas Jefferson (1743–1826), was also a foxhunter. This fact is not commonly spoken of—probably because so much attention has always been given to George Washington as a sportsman. In his early teens (1757), while attending the Reverend Mr. Maury's School in Virginia (about fourteen miles from the Jefferson farm) where the favorite diversion among the boys was hunting, young Tom was an active participant. He didn't learn *real* hunting then, for this was afoot "on a mountain nearby, which then and long after abounded in deer, turkey, foxes and other game." A little later, however, he rode to hounds and was both enthusiastic and capable.

Being an inveterate student, serious and of scholarly mind, Jefferson didn't feel justified in devoting a great deal of time to the sport. He was a man of feeling and of deep-seated principles; so much so, that early in life he adopted as his philosophy the credo that, in the realm of the intellect, leisure must be conquered. Therefore, though passionately fond of the outdoors and foxhunting, he had to make a choice of how to spend his hours. But his studiousness was not due to a frail constitution. Jefferson was every inch a man, physically as well as mentally, and was considered the most powerful individual in his county, being able to lift a thousand pounds without "undue" exertion. Six feet two and a half inches tall, he was "well proportioned and straight as a gunbarrel." In a day when rowing machines and artificial bicycles for exercise were unknown, Jefferson rigged up his own machine for measuring strength; and when, after a siege of studying, the machine registered a lower degree of muscular content than he approved of, he turned to field sports. It was during these periods that he permitted the recurring urge for riding and hunting to get out of control. Dipping into the pleasures these recreations afforded, he would then go back and work harder than ever at his studies.

After he had become the country's third President, he wrote a philosophical letter to his grandson, commenting on his life and the people with whom he had come in contact and saying that, of necessity, he had met in his time the extremes of human character: jockeys and moralists, racing men and philosophers, gamblers and statesmen. Often "in the enthusiastic moment of the death of a fox, the victory of a favorite horse and during a contest of mind in court of legislature,"[18] he asked himself which of these triumphs he should prefer. "When I recollect the various sorts of bad company with which I associated from time to time, I am astonished I did not turn off with some of them, and become as worthless to society as they were."

A chronicler of Jefferson's life said, "He was a keen hunter, as eager after a fox as Washington himself. . . ." He loved fine horses, and when studying at William and Mary College kept one or two in Williamsburg. At Monticello in later life he enjoyed riding—especially on a fiery and sure-footed animal "that could gallop down his mountain on a dark night and carry him through flood and mire safe to the next village. . . ." He wouldn't ride or drive any horses that were not "high-bred"; and when he traveled in his carriage, he always used five horses—"four for the carriage," and the other "for Burwell, who always rode behind him." The five favorites were *Diomede, Brimmer, Tecumseh, Wellington,* and *Eagle.* Bay was his preference in color—in fact, a horse of any other shade was never given stall space in his stables.

Reminiscing about Washington and Jefferson as patrons of field sports, a man wrote from Georgetown in 1830:

> About the year 1790, I was attending a jockey club at Alexandria; this was the first time I ever had seen the General. He was solicited to serve as one of the judges; he accepted and acted. Gen. Washington had a beautiful horse called *Magnolia,* that ran one of the days—he was not the winner. Mr. Jefferson had a fine young horse, called the *Roan Colt,* that ran one day, and I think won. This horse I have often heard spoken of as a superior horse. Gen. Washington sold *Magnolia* to Gen. H. Lee for $1500, after which he was sent to South Carolina, and there sold again for a much larger sum. Gen. Washington was fond of agricultural pursuits, of every kind of stock, and particularly the horse, of which he raised many. In his youthful days, he would (as I am well informed) play at many games that gentlemen played at for amusement, and for very small sums, but in no instance with a disposition to *gain,* and I think I may safely say never indulged even for amusement, beyond a reasonable hour.[20]

Alexander Hamilton (1757–1804), the man of action—the "evil genius of America," as Jefferson termed him—also foxhunted, but accounts of his activities in this direction are almost nonexistent. It is doubtful if he did much hunting in his teens before the Revolution. But later, in 1783, his name was listed among the active members of the St. George Hunt Club, with which he very likely hunted whenever possible.

Another foxhunter of this period was John Marshall, one of Virginia's most brilliant lawyers and Chief Justice of the United States for many years.[21] He probably learned the sport in his youth from Washington and Lord Fairfax, for at one time the former was Marshall's employer and friend and often took him with him on visits to Lord Fairfax's house, where life revolved around the chase.

Sportsmen were not limited to statesmen in Colonial times, reports show. During the 1760's in Virginia, the clergy added their names to the long list of those participating in the sports of the day. Bishop Meade of Virginia has left a most interesting account of their activities:

> It was not very uncommon for the clergyman of a parish to be president of its jockey club, and personally assist in the details of the race-course, such as weighing the men and timing the horses. It was common for clergymen to ride after the hounds in foxhunting; and they were as apt to nail the trophy of the day's chase to their stable door as any other men. The names of clergymen figured among the patrons of balls, and they were rather noted for their skill at cards. All of which was just as proper for clergymen as for planters, and more necessary. But in those days the bottle was the vitiating accompaniment of every innocent delight. The race must end in a dinner, and the dinner must end under the table. The day's hunt must be followed by a night's debauch.[22]

All of which reminds us that early English history is crowded with accounts of clergymen spending most of their time hunting. Tom Becket became the Archbishop of Canterbury under Henry II because of his interest in following buck-hounds. And the Bishop of Worcester (R. Brian) wrote to a distant clergyman, "Let them come, oh! reverend father! without delay; let my woods re-echo with the music of their cry and the cheerful notes of the horn, and let the walls of my palace be decorated with the trophies of the chase!"

In Leicestershire, the Abbot of St. Mary's (William de Clowne) was known far and wide for his skill in the field and his excellent hounds. They were so famous that the king granted him permission to become a professional hound dealer on the side. But when Henry VI came along, he thought the clergy were getting out of hand and neglecting their spiritual duties; so he issued a warning against "hawkynge, huntynge, and dawnsynge" among holders of church offices.

There was no such restraint in Colonial Virginia, however, and one parson of the period was "remembered as the jovial hunter who died cheering on the hounds to the chase."

> He mote go hunte with dogge and bich
> And blowen his horne and cryin Hey.[23]

So it is seen that through the penned and printed records of America which remain to tell us of older times, there runs the trail of the fleeing fox with hound and hunter at his heels. There were countless other sporting characters in Colonial days besides the few outstanding men mentioned here; and after the thirteen States united and legions more took up the chase, many of the names linked with history as having molded the course of this nation were also coupled with foxhunting. Not only the State and the Church, but business, the various professions and the land contributed sporting enthusiasts to swell the ranks of the foxhunting fraternity.

Notes

1. A Prayer and Sermon delivered at Charlestown (Mass.), December 31, 1799, on the death of George Washington, with an additional sketch of his life, by Jedidiah Morse, D.D.; printed by Samuel Etheridge, Charlestown, 1800 (rare).

2. George Washington, Woodrow Wilson; Harper and Brothers, N.Y., 1898, p. 49.

3. Life of Washington, Washington Irving; Peter Fenelon Collier, N.Y., 1897.

4. Washington's Diaries, John C. Fitzpatrick, editor; Houghton Mifflin Co., Boston and N.Y., 1925, Vol. I.

5. George Washington, Sportsman, from his Journals; 100 copies privately printed for John C. Phillips, Cosmos Press, Cambridge, Mass., 1928.

6. George Washington, Colonial Traveler, 1732–1775, J. C. Fitzpatrick; Bobbs-Merrill Co., Indianapolis, 1927.

7. Writings of Washington, edited by J.C. Fitzpatrick; U.S. Government Printing Office, Washignton, D.C., Vol. II.

8. Washington Speaks for Himself, Lucretia Perry Osborn, Charles Scribner's Sons, N.Y., 1927.

9. Works of John Adams, Charles Francis Adams; Charles C. Little and James Brown, Boston, 1850, Vol. II, p. 414.

10. Retrospections of America, John Bernard; Harper & Bros., 1887, p. 93.

11. Quoted from private letters in Colonial Virginia, Mary Newton Standard; J. B. Lippincott and Co., Philadelphia, 1917.

12. Extracts from the Diary of Jacob Hiltzheimer of Philadelphia, edited by his great-grandson, Jacob Cox Parson; Wm. F. Fell & Co., Philadelphia, 1893.

13. Recollections and Private Memoirs of Washington, G. W. Parke Custis; J. W. Bradly, Philadelphia, 1861, chap. 19, p. 384.

14. "Wolfe and Washington as Sportsmen," by A. G. Bradley, in *The Badminton Magazine of Sports and Pastimes,* edited by Alfred E. T. Watson; Longmans, Green and Co., London, New York and Bombay, Vol. IX (July to December 1899).

15. Washington Pre-eminent, Alice Hunt Bartlett; Brentano's, N.Y., 1931, Foreword, p. xvi.

16. George Washington, Sportsman, from his Journals; Cosmos Press, Cambridge, Mass., 1928.

17. Washington after the Revolution, William S. Baker; J. B. Lippincott Co., Philadelphia, 1898.

18. Life of Thomas Jefferson, James Parton; Riverside Press, Cambridge, Mass., 1882, p. 30.

19. Ibid.

20. *American Turf Register and Sporting Magazine,* March 1830, p. 353.

21. John Marshall (1755–1835), Chief Justice of the United States, 1801–1835.

22. Data furnished by Bishop Meade of Virginia to author of Life of Thomas Jefferson, James Parton; The Riverside Press, Cambridge, Mass., 1882, p. 56.

23. The Ploughman's Tale (about the sporting proclivities of the clergy), Geoffrey Chaucer.

TWENTY-SIX

THE FUTURE CHIEF JUSTICE'S OPINION

J. Blan van Urk

We have a description of a few months in the life of Roger Brooke Taney, Esq. (1777–1864), a descendant of Robert Brooke, Esq., just after his graduation from Dickinson College (Carlisle, Pa.):

I returned home [Calvert County, Md., on the Patuxent River] to my family. This was in the fall of 1795. I remained at home during the ensuing winter, which was idly spent in the amusements of the country. *My father kept a pack of hounds,* and was fond of fox-hunting. It was the custom to invite some other gentleman, who also kept fox-hounds, to come with his pack on a particular day, and they hunted with the two packs united. Other gentlemen, who were known to be fond of the sport, were also invited, so as to make a party of eight or ten persons, and sometimes more.

The *hunting usually lasted a week.* The party always rose before day, breakfasted by candle-light,—most commonly on spareribs (or bacon) and hominy,—drank pretty freely of eggnog, and then mounted and were in the cover, where they expected to find a fox, before sunrise. The foxes in the country were mostly the red; and, of course, there was much hard riding over rough ground, and the chase apt to be a long one. We rarely returned home until late in the day; and the evening was spent in a gay conversation on the events and mishaps of the day, and in arrangements for the hunt of the morrow, or in playing whist for moderate stakes. There was certainly nothing like drunkenness or gambling at these parties. I myself never played.

By the end of the week the hunters and dogs were pretty well tired, and the party separated. But before they parted, a time was always fixed when my father was to bring his dogs to his friend's house or they were to meet by invitation at the house of some other gentleman of the party where another week would be passed in like manner; and these meetings, with intervals of about a fortnight or three weeks, were kept up until the end of the season. I joined all of them; and when not so engaged, my father, with my elder brother and myself, hunted with his own dogs when the weather was fit . . . By the end of the winter I was a confirmed fox-hunter . . .[1]

Mr. Taney in addition to becoming a confirmed foxhunter managed to find time to work out a distinguished career as a jurist. From Attorney General under President Andrew Jackson, he went to the Supreme Court and subsequently succeeded John Marshall as Chief Justice.

Notes:

1. Memoir of Roger Brooke Taney, LL.D., Samuel Tyler, LL.D.; John Murphy & Co., Baltimore, 1872, p. 55.

TWENTY-SEVEN

THE FIRST ORGANIZED HUNT: THE GLOUCESTER FOX HUNTING CLUB

J. Blan van Urk

Before the Gloucester formation a great deal of hunting can be spotted in the private diary of Jacob Hiltzheimer of Philadelphia. That this man was one of parts can be recognized from the company he kept; moreover he owned a livery stable and thereby supposedly played an unheralded but important part in the history of this country. It would be well to narrate his indirect connection with immortality before disclosing the hunting extracts from his private papers.

It seems that when Thomas Jefferson came to Philadelphia as a delegate to the Continental Congress, he took lodgings near Independence Hall in a house on the southwest corner of Seventh and Market Streets. In this flat he wrote the rough drafts of the Declaration of Independence. Jefferson's own statement reads "At the time of writing that instrument . . . (I) lodged in the house of Mr. Graaf, a new brick house, three stories high, of which I rented the second floor, consisting of a parlor and bed-room, ready furnished. In that parlor I wrote habitually and in it wrote this paper particularly (The Declaration of Independence)."

Jacob Graaf's house, the one referred to by Jefferson, stood at the southwest corner of Seventh and Market Streets, directly opposite *Hiltzheimer's livery-stables.* Hiltzheimer purchased the property from Graaf in 1777. It seems probable also that Hiltzheimer's stables are referred to in the following anecdote. The stables were south of Seventh and Market Streets, probably near Chestnut Street, and therefore but a short distance from Independence Hall:

"A gentleman who had been a frequent visitor at Monticello during Mr. Jefferson's life gave Mr. Randall (Jefferson's biographer) the following amusing incident concerning this venerated body and the Declaration of Independence: 'While the question of Independence was before Congress it had its meeting near a livery-stable. The members wore short breeches and

Captain Samuel Morris (1734–1812). Community leader, spearhead, and President of the Gloucester Fox Hunting Club. *By Ralph L. Boyer, Courtesy The Derrydale Press.*

silk stocking, and with handkerchief in hand they were diligently employed in lashing the flies from their legs. So very vexatious was this annoyance, and to so great an impatience did it arouse the sufferers, that it hastened, if it did not aid, in inducing them to promptly affix their signatures to the great document which gave birth to an empire republic.' This anecdote I had from Mr. Jefferson at Monticello, who seemed to enjoy it very much, as well as to give great credit to the influence of the flies. He told it with much glee, and seemed to retain a vivid recollection of an attack from which the only relief was signing the paper and flying from the scene."[1]

Hiltzheimer's horseflies . . . launched the nation.

Notes

1. Some Colonial Mansions and those who lived in them, Thomas Allen Glenn; Henry T. Coates & Co., Philadelphia, 1900, second series, pp. 223–225.

TWENTY-EIGHT

BUFFALO BILL AND THE WEST CHESTER HUNT

J. Blan van Urk

Capitalizing on the theory that "a chosen few alone the sport enjoy," a group of Pennsylvanians informally established the West Chester Hunt a short time prior to 1872. Although this Hunt is not recognized by the M. F. H. Association of America, it nevertheless remains as one of the oldest in the United States, and a number of friends tell me that the sport shown by the present Master, Mr. J. C. Murtagh, and his American hounds is hard to beat anywhere.

Much could doubtless be written about the early days of the West Chester, but unfortunately only the barest details are available for telling here. It seems that right from the very start those who followed this pack, while enjoying an occasional visitor, preferred to keep quiet the fact that their line was the line of the fox and their pace the pace of the pack—perhaps lest too many people knowing of it might spoil the "go." And today Mr. Murtagh in sending me a skeleton résumé upholds the traditional West Chester modesty, for he writes, "Nothing spectacular has occurred in the last forty years, but we have managed to have our share of sport in that time and hope we will continue to do so for many years to come." To which all sportsmen will chant, "Hear! Hear!"

In 1874 the colorful Buffalo Bill was introduced to the ways of the chase behind the West Chester pack, which was owned and Mastered by Mr. Jefferson H. Shaner, a widely known foxhunter of his time. Later describing his visit to the town of West Chester, where his mother had been born and her sister had married Henry R. Guss, Colonel Cody, the Buffalo Bill, wrote in his autobiography:

When we reached West Chester, my uncle informed me that they had arranged a fox hunt for the next morning, and that all the people in the town and vicinity would be present. They wanted to see a real scout and plainsman in the saddle.

Early next morning many ladies and gentlemen, splendidly mounted, appeared in front of my uncle's residence. At that time West Chester possessed the best pack of fox hounds in America. Mr. Shaner, Master of the hounds, provided me with a spirited horse which had on a little sheepskin saddle of a kind on which I had never ridden. I was familiar neither with the horse, the saddle, the hounds, nor fox-hunting, and was extremely nervous. I would have backed out if I could, but I couldn't, so I mounted the horse and we all started on the chase.

We galloped easily along for perhaps a mile, and I was beginning to think fox-hunting a very tame sport indeed when suddenly the hounds started off on a trail, all barking at once. The Master of the hounds and several of the other riders struck off across country on the trail, taking fences and stone walls at full gallop.

I noticed that my uncle and several elderly gentlemen stuck to the road and kept at a more moderate gait. The eyes of the spectators were all on me. I don't know what they expected me to do, but at any rate they were disappointed. To their manifest disgust I stayed with the people on the road.

Shortly we came to a tavern and I went in and nerved myself with a stiff drink; also I had a bottle filled with liquid courage, which I took along with me. Just by way of making a second fiasco impossible I took three more drinks while I was in the bar, then I galloped away and soon overtook the hunters.

The first trail of the hounds proved false. Two miles farther on they struck a true trail and away they went at full cry. I had now got used to the saddle and the gait of my horse. I also had prepared myself in the tavern for any course of action that might offer.

The M. F. H. began taking stone walls and hedges and I took every one that he did. Across the country we went and nothing stopped or daunted me until the quarry was brought to earth. I was in at the death and was given the honor of keeping the brush.[1]

Notes

1. Buffalo Bill's Life Story, An Autobiography, by Colonel William F. Cody; Cosmopolitan Book Corporation, N.Y., pp. 245–247, 1924 edition.

TWENTY-NINE

THE FIRST FOXHOUND STUDBOOK

J. Blan van Urk

For the early foxhunting enjoyed in the Colonial and part of the pre-Civil War periods,[1] English hounds were generally preferred whenever they could be afforded by individual sportsmen or hunting organizations. Then, several years prior to the war between the States, a boom in American foxhound breeding swept certain sections of the country, and many Masters turned to the resultant cross-breds and to so-called American hounds.

It was at this juncture that the field-trial, fox-race, hill-topping foxhunters took the lead in furthering the native product, causing many Masters of packs to look to them for hounds. Private stud books were started; and, later, field-trial organizations systematized the keeping of records and standardized the requirements for pedigrees. Volume I of THE FOXHOUND STUD BOOK, official document of the National Foxhunters' Association (Roger D. Williams, Keeper of the Stud Book), was published in 1898.[2] (The National Foxhunters' Association had come into existence in 1893 as a result of a gathering of foxhunters at Waverly, Mississippi, as the guests of Captain Billy and Val Young.)

Next came a decided shift back to English hounds, as we shall note in future accountings. (Remember, in these particular phases we are dealing only with the tendencies of Masters and followers of the riding-to-hounds group.) This occurred a few years after the formation, through the initial efforts of an ardent American foxhound enthusiast (Harry Worcester Smith), of the vital and necessary Masters of Foxhounds Association of America.[3] While at first there was a division in hound allegiance among those in command of executive reins, by the time the first stud book was compiled for the Association, English hound advocates had swung the pendulum in their direction so that it appeared under title, THE ENGLISH FOXHOUND STUD BOOK OF AMERICA.[4] In this was "a list of eleven packs of foxhounds which can trace their entries direct to the English foxhound kennel stud book."

Three succeeding volumes,[5] brought out in 1915, 1922, and 1927, bore the same title and likewise contained only English hound entries. Despite the number of American foxhounds extant, clamor for their inclusion in the Masters of Foxhounds Association of America's Stud Book had not apparently reached a significant pitch during this time among riding to hounds foxhunters. And since stud books were already available to hound owners of the field-trial category, these foxhunters had little interest in what went on in the Masters of Foxhounds Association, which had been set up as a guide to so-called orthodox sport.

But with the publication (1930) of Volume V, the title was changed to THE FOXHOUND KENNEL STUD BOOK OF AMERICA. And this was the first stud book put out under the auspices of the Masters of Foxhounds Association of America which included American and crossbred hounds in addition to the already favored English. Covering the period between 1908 and 1931, this booklet listed forty-four packs of foxhounds owned or controlled by members of the Association. In 1937 the sixth volume of the series—second to list American and crossbreds with the English—was published with 134 packs (1931–1936) recorded. At the same time a new Keeper came on the scene in the person of Joseph J. Jones, Clerk of the Association.

And so we reach, in the above accounting of stud books, the fourth and last stage in the ebb and flow of the American foxhound's popularity. The trend swung back from the English to a general interest among followers of hounds in the American type; and with this shift or reversal, the American foxhound really, definitely and for all time came into its own as the supreme favorite in its native land.

Describing the great change that has been wrought in the American foxhound, Mr. O'Malley Knott said:

> The great difference between them [English and American hounds], that existed when Harry Worcester Smith, John R. Townsend and Joseph B. Thomas first started to kennel, breed, feed, exercise and train the American Hound to hunt as a pack, has gradually become less and less.
>
> Instead of a skulking, herring-gutted, weak, timid dog, that ran away yowling when you cracked a thong at him, some of the American packs today are under just as good control as the English Hounds, carry their sterns up and have courage both in and out of kennel, and as the result of proper feeding and regular exercise have furnished out and look more as the English did in the days of Peter Beckford. They are level and even enough to carry a long line packed up instead of being strung out as they used to be for the lack of condition and training.
>
> Everyone knows the wonderful cry and nose of American Hounds. There is danger, however, that our Hound Shows may become so competitive that

breeders will only breed for looks and lose some of that wonderful hunting spirit, as was the case at Peterborough.[6]

I have often been asked by American foxhunting tyros what is meant by such references to the Peterborough Show and its hound Standard in connection with inefficiency in the field. Without too much detail the situation can be explained in this manner. During the last half of the nineteenth century and the first part of the twentieth, the hound Standard set by the Masters of fashionable shire packs was predicated on requirements of their particular hunting countries. Despite the fact that the districts where the "fashionable" hound was (and is) suitable made up only a small proportion of England's hunting countries, Masters in other districts directed their breeding toward this same Standard regardless of what their own hunting situation called for. This meant that while these efforts produced winners at the various shows—with wins at the Peterborough the goal—aside from a certain number of packs, hounds were "absolutely unfitted for sport in hunting countries of a different nature." For example, to do the job in the grass country of Warwickshire the type of hound required is different in structure and conformation from that in Radnorshire and West Hereford; and a different type of hound is required for Fells of Cumberland and Westmorland, etc.

Elaborating on this theme, Richard Clapham, English authority, wrote:

> Granted that the shows at first tended to raise the standard of foxhound excellence, and have led to an all-around smartening up of provincial packs, they have at the same time tended toward breeding too much for points; the craze for bone, straightness, and the round cat-foot, has virtually made cripples of many hounds. A hound that stands over at the knees, and turns his toes in and his elbows out is not exactly the sort one would choose to hunt a rough country, especially if the said hound, in addition to having these faults in conformation, tipped the scales between seven stone and eight stone in weight. The rougher the country to be hunted, the more active and light-boned should be the hound, for weight tells a serious tale on the hills and jar and concussion play the very deuce with a heavy hound of "standard" conformation.[7]

So again the all-important and incontrovertible hound axiom pops up: each hunting country requires its particular type of hound; or, in other words, "upon his [the hound's] breeding depends the precise degree of usefulness which he is capable of contributing toward sport in the field. To man, with the assistance of nature, belongs the power and privilege of directing its course so as to produce the best results."[8]

Although in THE STORY OF AMERICAN FOXHUNTING there are no space limitations in dealing with the different Hunts, as all Masters have been advised—the publisher being a man of such rare timber and courage as to wish the author to go the limit on everything of a vital nature concerning present-day Hunts—a halt must be taken somewhere in the discourse about the American foxhound, lest this volume be devoted solely to that colossal and unending subject. Therefore, without further ado or too much dwelling, and with the possibility of a great deal more to be said about modern hounds as we come to them, we press on to events in historical sequence.

As a postscript I should like to urge—and this advice is as important as anything appearing in this series of books—that all youngsters learning the fine art of foxhunting *study hounds*. Pay attention to your Huntsman, his language, vocal and by horn, and the manner in which he handles the pack. Find out all you can about what hounds are doing at all times. Acquire an eye to hounds and an ear for their voice and cry. Be conscious of such things as the number of couples making up the pack and whether it is a bitch, dog or mixed pack. Note the direction of the wind on a hunting day, determining as far as possible what weather indicates good or bad scenting conditions, and then watch hound reactions and capabilities. Learn the major faults of hound character and constitution, but above all *respect hounds*. Remember that any hound can run a breast-high scent—excellence is determined in great measure by work on a cold trail. Furthermore, *enjoy hounds*—even if the horse is your primary joy, remember it takes all constituents to make up a well-rounded hunt.

You will never be entitled to the *true* label—foxhunter—until you know the real processes, technique and functions of the pack you follow. The jump, the burst, the color and companionship of hunting are only a part of the game. Once you know what is going on, and why, you will feel just a little bit richer and a little more satisfied with the world for having experienced and absorbed the magic of hound finesse. Behind a striving, earnest, well-planned and synchronized pack even the dismals of a blank day will thrill you. You will learn that hounds along with their courage and intelligence have a certain dignity, gentleness of manner, honesty, loyalty and spirit which compel respect and admiration. And so, think seriously of Hounds, Gentlemen (and Ladies)—*Please.*

> And remember this rule, if you want to be right,
> That the sport, not the riding, should be your delight;
> You are mounted to see it, so keep well in sight
> Of the hounds who are really the sportsmen.

N.B. These chapters on the American foxhound originally included full footnote references to the ground covered in Volume 1. There were so many of these notes, however, that it became necessary to eliminate all but the most vital in order not to break the continuity of the text. Consequently, it is important for the serious student of the foxhound to refer to the index of Volume 1 under *foxhound strains.*

Notes

1. See Volume 1.

2. Carrying on this work into the present, the Chase Publishing Company published Volume 1 of the International Fox Hunters' Stud Book in 1922, with S. L. Wooldridge, Keeper of Records.

3. Organization, development and importance to be accounted for in Volume III.

4. Volume 1 (1884–1908), compiled and edited for the M. F. H. Association of America by A. Henry Higginson, M. F. H., and printed by Frank L. Wiles, Boston, 1909.

5. Volume II (1909–1914) listed 14 English packs; Volume III (1915-1921) listed 16, and Volume IV (1922–1926) 18 English packs. These volumes and also Volume V were all compiled and edited by Mr. Higginson, and printed by A. T. Bliss and Company, Boston.

6. "The Spirit of the American Hound," in *The Chronicle,* November 24, 1939.

7. "The Similarity of American and Fell Foxhounds," by Richard Clapham; in *The Sportsman,* January 1932.

8. *The Foxhound,* London, November 1910, Vol. I, No. 1, p. 1.

THIRTY

GENERAL ROGER D. WILLIAMS , M.F.H. AND THE IROQUOIS HUNT AND POLO CLUB

J. Blan van Urk

The name and State of Kentucky suggest many things to many people: Churchill Downs on Derby Day with high-mettled racers—three-year-old *kings*—crossing the finish line; Lexington with its amazingly impressive breeding farms (Faraway, Greentree, Llangollen, Elmendorf, Idle Hour, Dixiana, Calumet, Duntreath and others); the far-reaching blue grass; the three- and five- gaited saddle-horses—trotting races and the great State Fair; white mustachioed Kentucky Colonels; mint juleps and bourbon; tobacco warehouses; yea, even beautiful women, and fair.

But there is more to Kentucky than all this—much more. Across my vision floats the long record of foxhunting of all types; the careful as well as casual hound breeding; the great hunter General George "Wash" Maupin; the Trigg and Walker hounds; "Big Chief" Samuel L. Wooldridge, one of the greatest of present-day hound breeders—"Walker Hounds with the Wooldridge Class"—Editor of *The Chase* and Keeper of Records of the International Foxhunters Stud Book; the late General Roger D. Williams, for many, many years "the most prominent hound breeder of the blue grass country"; and—the Iroquois Hunt.

When, from 1774 to 1810, settlers from Virginia "came swarming over that 'high-swung gateway of the Cumberlands' into Kentucky, they brought with them hounds and a love for hunting that has never wavered . . . they inherited [sic] the finest hunting grounds of the American Indians. . . . So the Kentuckian, . . . adapting himself to his new environment, continued to develop the best blood in fox hounds as well as in horseflesh."[1]

Probably the most famous and colorful of the early Kentucky foxhunters was old Uncle "Wash" Maupin, mentioned previously in connection with hounds and hound breeding. Maupin hunted as soon after his birth in 1807

Colonel Roger D. Williams, M.F.H. of the Iroquois Hunt for thirty-four years, on "Hickory Leaf."

as was practicable, and continued to do so until close to his death in 1868. Often referred to as the John Peel of America, the query "D'ye ken" Uncle "Wash" would have brought the reply "Yes I ken" him well:

> 'Twas the sound of his horn called me from my bed,
> And the cry of his hounds has me oft-times led,
> For Peel's view-hallo would awaken the dead,
> Or a fox from his lair in the morning.[2]

To Maupin foxhunting was more than just a sport; it was his life—"with his high peaked cap, flowered waistcoat, and garish scarf, he was conspicuous at every hunt."[3] When he wasn't hunting, he traded in negroes and mules.

The hunter-naturalist C. W. Webber, a Kentuckian, wrote in 1852, "I was enthusiastically addicted to fox hunting, and kept a fine pack of hounds. Several young men of the neighborhood [southern part of the State] kept packs of dogs also, and we used very frequently to meet, and join in the chase with all our forces." For a long time, it seems, a favorite but exasperating quarry was a certain grey fox thereabouts, who would run for an hour or so and then vanish apparently into thin air. This disappearing act so disrupted the entire community that superstition finally cropped up, some folk saying he must be a "weir-fox," and—far more serious—hounds not only lost their

A hunting morning in front of Historic Grimes Mill, on Boone Creek, which was remodeled into the Iroquois Hunt Clubhouse.

193

reputations but were acquiring inferiority complexes. Determined to solve the mystery, Mr. Webber hid himself one day near the point where scent had always failed, and, as he later described it, this is what he saw:

> In a little while the fox made his appearance, coming on at quite a leisurely pace, a little in advance of the pack. When he reached the corner, he climbed in a most unhurried and deliberate way to the top rail of the fence and then walked along it, balancing himself as carefully as a rope-dancer. He proceeded down the side of the fence next to the forest in which I was concealed.
>
> . . . more than two hundred yards [behind], the hounds came up to the corner, and the fox very deliberately paused and looked back for a moment, then hurried on along the fence some paces farther; and when he came opposite a dead but leaning tree, which stood inside the fence some twelve or sixteen feet distant, he stooped, made a high and long bound to a knot upon the side of its trunk, up which he ran, and entered a hollow in the top where it had been broken off, near thirty feet from the ground, in some storm.
>
> The tree stood at such a distance from the fence that no one of us who had examined the ground ever dreamed of the possibility that the fox would leap to it; it seemed a physical impossibility; but practice and the convenient knot had enabled cunning Reynard to overcome it with assured ease.[4]

Mr. Webber was filled with admiration at the stratagem and kept it secret, but someone else found it out anyway and "avenged himself by cutting down the tree and capturing the smart fox."

The Iroquois Hunt of Lexington, Kentucky, came into being in 1880, through the efforts of General Roger D. Williams. At this time the great American horse *Iroquois* was distinguishing himself at home and in England, and it was to honor him that the Hunt's title was selected.

Iroquois (by *Leamington* out of *Maggie* B.B. by *Australian*) was bred by Aristides Welch, and foaled at the Erdenheim Stud, Chestnut Hill, Philadelphia. Owned by Pierre Lorillard, he was the first American horse to win the English Derby, which he did in 1881 with Fred Archer up.

> The Yankee came down with long Fred on his back,
> And his colours were gleaming with cherry and black.[5]

When the news of *Iroquois'* winning this race was flashed to America, business was for a time "entirely suspended in Wall Street and the Stock Exchange rang with the cheering, again and again renewed."[6]

> Flashed red are American faces!
> Hurrah! for old *Leamington's* son.
> You'll show the pale Briton how races
> Across the Atlantic are won.

In addition to winning the Derby (and £12,000 for Mr. Lorillard) *Iroquois* also won the St. Leger.[7]

So the Iroquois Hunt chose a name to conjure with, and General Williams managed everything in keeping with it—good horses, and hounds with both blood and speed. It was not easy to stir up interest in this type of hunting organization when he first started. In a State where so many owners of private packs had already maintained hounds primarily for fox-racing and field trials, the General was compelled to go ahead cautiously.

> [This was] because of the rather provincial attitude which some friends and good sportsmen took toward the venture, on the supposition apparently that hunting in this way was un-American, or unmanly, or something of the kind; though their own forefathers in England and Virginia, and even in Kentucky followed the English methods in hunting so far as they could, and attempted to ride as close to the pack as it was physically possible in the new country of unfelled forests and unfordable streams. Certainly in the risks that are assumed and the ventures that are dared riding to hounds requires more nerve in the saddle and no less skill with hounds on the part of the Master and his staff.[8]

The General once said in concluding the write-up for a day's hunt, "When I state that on our fox hunt Judge Perry broke a leg, that Mr. Van Goode met with the same fate on the wolf chase, and that one of our members was killed a few years ago, you will agree with me that fox hunting in Kentucky is not without a spice of danger."[9]

In 1898 Teddy Roosevelt asked his friend, the then Colonel Roger D. Williams, to organize and captain a company of rough-riders from the blue-grass region. At the time a commentary expressed the opinion that "unquestionably his company will be the best-mounted one in the regiment, for it will be difficult to beat the Kentucky thoroughbreds these hundred men will have."[10]

General Williams was an organizer, Vice-President and then President of the National Foxhunters' Association, and also served as Master of Hounds at the annual meets held by this group. To him foxhunting was "not only a recreation and amusement, but a science and an art in which few ever attain proficiency." He wrote to his friend, Frank S. Peer, in 1906, "There are 100 counties in Kentucky and each has from two to twenty packs of hounds and two-thirds of the farmers without packs own two or more hounds." And the General and his Iroquois Hunt represented the most highly organized pack in the State.

For thirty-two years, from 1880 to 1914, this capable foxhunter and widely known hound man was M.F.H. of the Iroquois. It can be readily understood why he has been referred to as "gentleman, Kentuckian, soldier, author and *Sportsman*." The versatile Roger Williams was all this and more—musician, amateur actor, hound man and judge, expert horseman, athlete, explorer, big-game hunter and foxhunter. And his energy was boundless. An admirer wrote of this 1896, "There are moments when Roger D. Williams is not foxhunting, coursing coyotes, fooling with borzois, breeding bloodhounds, judging greyhounds, getting out studbooks or leading the Iroquois Hunt Club . . . he is just as apt to organize a coon hunt."

During a good part of his Iroquois Mastership, the General had as his Huntsman the competent Bonnie Stone. But when the great leader retired from regular hunting activities, the Iroquois Hunt followed suit.

It wasn't until the autumn of 1926 that increasing interest in foxhunting and a persistent demand by young Kentuckians caused the Iroquois to become active again. When fourteen sportsmen gathered at a dinner at the Ashland Club on November sixth of that year, the formal reorganization of the Hunt was carried through. "W. V. Thraves of the Deep Run near Richmond, Virginia, and Elliott S. Nichols, M.F.H. of the Bloomfield Open Hunt near Detroit were among the speakers." The following day twenty-three members of the new Iroquois tried a paper chase to determine how many of those who had expressed interest would show up.

By Thanksgiving Day ten couples of hounds trained by Bonnie Stone had been gathered together, and the Hunt held its first drag, preceded by a nine o'clock breakfast at the Chimney Corner. In spite of a torrent of rain forty-eight enthusiastic followers turned out for a six-mile run "with not one check."

Captains Frank Wright and Cabell Breckinridge of the Lexington Troop were helpful in reviving the Iroquois, and Captain William "Billy" Armstrong, a former instructor of equitation for the Black Horse Troop of Culver Military Academy, assisted members in learning the finer points of the art.[11] Stables and kennels for the Hunt were built on property adjoining the Lexington Troop's reservation.

But a large part of the enthusiasm which made possible the reëstablishment of the Iroquois can be credited to the young women of central Kentucky. It might be that they had read what General Roger Williams had penned at the time their mothers were in the saddle, for, under the heading "Women in the Field," he said among other things:

Elegance in riding is absolutely indispensable, or at least highly desirable. It is as easy to show gentle breeding in the field as in the drawing or ball room—probably easier; yet I have know women to give every evidence of it in the drawing room who seemed unable to show it in the field. . . . The rules, customs, and unwritten laws of the hunting field laid down for men, apply with equal force to women; they should bear in mind they have absolutely no privileges not accorded to men. This may sound harsh to the layman or novice (I hope this plain heart-to-heart talk with women will not be construed into a lack of gallantry upon my part), but I am sure will be fully understood and appreciated to the limit of any old hunter, either man or woman.[12]

And so, asking no quarter and giving none, the girls did all they could to revive the Hunt the General had worked so hard to create. The purposes of the newly organized group as set forth in the constitution and By-Laws at the time were (Article 2):

To encourage field sports, horseback riding and out-of-door life in Central Kentucky with particular regard to riding and fox hunting in the belief that the citizens of the Commonwealth of Kentucky will be benefited thereby, that indirectly the breeding of better horses and better foxhounds will be stimulated and the physical factor of health and the moral factor of sportsmanship will be fostered to the advantage of all.

It shall come within the province of the Hunt to encourage park riding, to aid in the building of an in-door riding ring near Lexington for use in the winter months, to help with the building of bridle paths near Lexington, to hold Hunter and Pony shows, to give barbecues to the farmers, to hold bench shows for foxhounds, to give drag hunts, paper chases and rabbit hunts, to hold an annual Hunt ball, to give private race meetings on the flat and over timber or brush informally as well as under the auspices of the National Steeplechase and Hunt Association, to hold polo tournaments, to give special attention to children and new recruits to the sport, and at all times to further the interests of horse and hound and good sportsmanship; but it is to be remembered that hunting the live red fox under the established and ancient laws of the sport is the chief purpose of a Hunt toward the improvement of which all other activities must tend and to the interests of which all other activities must be subservient.

Mr. L. B. Shouse and Mr. C. Kendall McDowell had been appointed Joint Masters of the Iroquois Hunt when it reorganized and proceeded to show good sport while they were in command. Mr. William Preston was President of the Hunt, Mr. J. Churchill Newcomb, Secretary, and Mr. Clarence Lebus, Jr., Treasurer. In addition, the Hunt had four Vice-Presidents, Messrs. S. L. Wooldridge, W. Arnold Hanger, Barry Shannon and Frank Vaughn, and a Board of Governors made up of Messrs. Shelby Harbison, Jr., William Woodward, William Armstrong, Frank S. Wright, John Gourlay and Robert Walker. Mrs. Lucas B. Combs,[13] daughter of General Roger D. Williams, was accorded the distinction of being elected Honorary President.

In 1928 the Hunt purchased Grimes Mill, located on Boone Creek just above where this tributary empties into the Kentucky River. This historic structure, built in 1803, was remodeled into a clubhouse, kennels and stables. In the same year the first annual Iroquois Horse Show was held.

Mr. W. Arnold Hanger, who has become such an ardent and successful racing man, and another McDowell (William C.) took over as Joint Masters in 1929, retaining their positions until 1931, when Mr. Edward F. Spears was elected M.F.H. It was in this year that the Iroquois Hunt adopted the "Blessing of the Hounds" custom, and each year the ceremony is performed by the Right Reverend H. P. Almon Abbot. The other event of that year was the merging of the Elkhorn Polo Club with the Iroquois Hunt and the subsequent changing of names to include both organizations—the Iroquois Hunt and Polo Club.

For nine years Mr. Spears has carried the horn for Iroquois. He still continues as both Master and Huntsman, but as an added supervisor of hunting affairs Mr. W. F. Pursley was persuaded in 1940 to accept a Joint Mastership, and he too hunts hounds.

The approximately twenty square miles of Iroquois country is bounded on the south by the Kentucky River with Boone Creek running through the middle. The territory near the river has heavily wooded, shallow ravines, but as a whole nine tenths of the country is rolling blue-grass turf and meadow land with "parked woodlands"—one tenth plough land. The many broad and deep creeks have firm banks for jumping, while the fences are of timber, chicken-coops and stone walls. Red foxes abound throughout the Hunt's country, and the pack of twenty-six couples of American (Walker) foxhounds goes out regularly from the first of October until the end of April, or until the hot weather starts.

Notes

1. "Fox Hunting in Old Kentucky," by Ida Earle Fowler, in *The Southern Magazine* (Kentucky Number), September 1935.

2. Chorus from "John Peel," by John Woodcock Graves.

3. Kentucky, A Guide to the Bluegrass State, sponsored by the University of Kentucky; Harcourt, Brace & Company, N. Y., 1939, p. 267.

4. The Hunter-Naturalist, Romance of Sporting; or, Wild Scenes and Wild Hunters, C. W. Webber; Lippincott, Grambo & Co., Philadelphia, 1852, pp. 270–272.

5. Extract from verse in *Punch*, June 11, 1881.

6. "The History and Romance of the Derby," Edward Moorhouse; The Biographical Press, London, Vol. II.

7. Race Horses and Racing, F. G. Griswold, privately printed in 1925.

8. *The Chase*, published at Lexington, Ky., February 1927.

9. *The American Field*, February 17, 1894.

10. "The Record of our Sportsmen in the Present War," by Henry Hauk Carruthers, in *Land and Water*, The Authority on American Amateur Sports, published in Boston, June 1898, p. 149.

11. I can testify to Captain Armstrong's great ability in and knowledge of horsemanship, having studied equitation under him and Colonel Robert Rossow, his superior. Both men were able to make their technique clear as instructors.

12. Horse and Hound, Roger D. Williams; published by the author in Lexington, Ky., 1905.

13. The author is indebted to Mrs. Combs for sending some of her father's (General Williams) private papers.

Horse and Hound assist in advertising sarsaparilla, furniture and carpets, family ointments, a Connecticut druggist, and a livery stable. Miss Annie Oakley (lower center), who used Kentucky Shaggies in her show, "Miss Rora," 1894. *From the collection of Harry T. Peters, M.F.H.*

THIRTY-ONE

THE FIRST LADY M.F.H.:
MRS. ALLEN POTTS

J. Blan van Urk

Among the many private packs maintained during pre-Revolutionary times, one of particular interest, on several counts, was the Castle Hill Hounds of Albemarle County, Virginia. This pack founded in 1742 by Dr. Thomas Walker, was the only one existing in the first era of American fox-hunting to span the years into the twentieth century with specific identification. Importing foxhounds from England, Dr. Walker, as Master of Hounds, named the pack after his estate Castle Hill. This man was a colorful, dyed-in-leather foxhunter, and his reputation as a sportsman was even greater than the one acquired because of his physical prowess. On this latter score, a by-phrase—"the Devil and Tom Walker"—was tossed about from one end of the Colonies to the other. Dr. Walker had other nicknames, and each and every one carried with it the affection and admiration of his legion of friends.

In modern times, the Castle Hill Hounds made foxhunting history when, upon being revived a long time after its original disbandment, it became the first pack *of record*[1] and *hunted* by an American woman—Mrs. Allen Potts, M.F.H. Here indeed is romance in sport! A lineal descendant of Dr. Walker, Mrs. Potts (née Gertrude Rives) exercised her prerogative and Mastered the pack which had been established well over a hundred years previously. The span of the Castle Hill's existence, without deduction for its period of non-hunting, was more than 170 years.

The Fields which followed this last of the Castle Hill Masters were small—perhaps a happy dozen—but they really knew how to cross country. Subscriptions were not required and everyone from miles around was invited to hunt—any time and all the time. When problems of the first World War became pressing, Mrs. Potts dispersed her hounds. But should the name Castle Hill ever be revived in connection with foxhunting—by authority—it would stand as the oldest pack in America. Even so, the record established, while of a distant day, is a remarkable and distinguished one.

Mrs. Potts rode to hounds for over forty-five years, and was prominent not only in the hunting field and show ring, but as a breeder of various types of horses. Because she can be classified as one of the greatest sportswomen and foxhunters this country has produced, with the added distinction of being the first woman Master of Fox Hounds, it is most important, historically, to quote her narrative directly. The following is taken from the original manuscript[2] written in longhand by Mrs. Potts in 1933, only a short time before her health broke. Don't shy like a frightened colt before a barrier at the size (length) of this—for it is as interesting and vital a chronicle of American sport as will be uncovered in many a day.

As to the oldest pack of Foxhounds in America—the Castle Hill Hounds, of which I am the hereditary Master—these hounds were brought to America during Colonial days by Dr. Thomas Walker, who was on the staff of General Washington and a member of the House of Burgesses. He brought about six or eight couple and built kennels for them at "Castle Hill," where the site can still be seen.

Dr. Walker was a great foxhunter, and in spite of all his other duties found time to indulge in his favorite sport and to build up a very fine pack of foxhounds. He was a brilliant man of great determination and fine character. He was very friendly with the Indians and due to his ability to make agreements with them was known as "Indian Tom Walker." He would take his horse and disappear, be gone for weeks and finally return having induced the Indians to agree to all his plans. It was after one of these successful and important trips that the "Crown" gave him as a reward for his services a grant of land. In this grant were included "Castle Hill," "Oak Ridge," the farm now known as "Happy Creek" and a part of Kentucky.

Soon after this Dr. Walker decided to go into Kentucky, so he set out on horseback with two of his followers, taking with him some of his foxhounds so that he could continue his favorite sport. In the pack was a big hound, a great favorite of Dr. Walker's and named after him, *Tom Walker.* On the trip one of the horses stepped on this hound's foot injuring him so that he could not travel. Dr. Walker had his men make a willow basket and strap it on the front of his saddle; and in this basket on a blanket he put *Tom Walker* and carried him all the way to Kentucky.

It is interesting to note that at this time all American hounds were black and tan, or tan, owing to their bloodhound blood. The English bred hounds of Dr. Walker were pied, white, with black and tan ears, saddle and half of their sterns' the upper half being white and slightly feathered. The Walker Foxhounds of today have the same body colors and the feathered stern.

After the death of Dr. Walker there was no foxhunting at "Castle Hill" and the pack gradually disappeared. It was not until many years later that I thought of reviving the Castle Hill Hounds and having them recognized. I always loved foxhunting and hunted whenever I could; but in those days there were no motors and in the winter the red clay roads in Virginia were bottomless, so I had to hack my hunters to all meets no matter how far, and hack home after the hunt was over, often not reaching home until late at night. I had at that time many good hunters that I had bred myself; and as I was still breeding a few colts each year, I felt that it would be a good thing if I could revive the old Castle Hill Foxhounds. Since I was hereditary Master I could hunt them myself and in this way make hunters of my colts without having to depend on other packs.

So I set out to get things in order preparatory to asking the National Steeplechase and Hunt Association for recognition. I rode day after day, seeing farmers and land owners about hunting over their land until I finally had *seventy-two names.* All of these men said that no hounds had ever hunted over their land and gave me permission to hunt regularly whenever I wished. This gave me a tract of about ten miles square. I then wrote to the National Steeplechase and Hunt Association and explained about the Castle Hill Hounds, told them what I wanted to do, and why, and asked that the Castle Hill Hounds be recognized. I wanted to hunt the hounds myself, but didn't know what the National Steeplechase and Hunt Association would do, particularly as up to that time there had never been a woman M.F.H. So I anxiously waited to hear.

I was in Charlottesville when the telegram came (I think Mr. Algernon Craven[3] was present, and a good many other hunting men). It was snowing and we were all around the fire in Johnson's Drug Store and I was anxiously wondering what the Hunt Committee would do about the Castle Hill Hounds, when Mr. Johnson came to the door of his office and said to me, "Mrs. Potts, I have a telegram here for you which has been sent from your home, and with your permission I will read it aloud as I think it will be of interest to all you hunting people. Here it is: 'To Mrs. Allen Potts, Castle Hill, Cobham, Albemarle County, Virginia. Committee met today. Castle Hill Hounds recognized unanimously and by acclamation. Many wishes for good sport. Signed, The Committee of the National Steeplechase and Hunt Association'."

Since I had to be hunting regularly before I could ask for recognition, I had built up a really good pack. American hounds at that time were very wild, resented handling of any sort and would often be off for days after hunting, so I had decided to try English bred hounds. I bought a few couple from Mr. A. Henry Higginson who owned and hunted the Middlesex Hounds. Major Wadsworth also gave me hounds, and finally I had ten couples of really good foxhounds.

It is very difficult to kill foxes in this part of Virginia as they breed in the mountains and have their dens under tons of rock. However, they come down into open country to hunt, and by starting out about daybreak they can be caught out on their way home and hounds can sometimes bring them to hand. I had a perfectly wonderful time. The farmers were delighted and always came out to wave to me as the hounds went by. I remember on one occasion, a very cold winter morning, we had picked up a fox on his way home and were "dusting his jacket" in great style when the fox crossed a wheat field. I was about to try to find a way around it when I saw the owner of the land watering his team. He hurriedly threw the harness off one of the horses and jumping on his back came up at a gallop, threw the gate open into the wheat field and yelled, "To hell with the wheat!"—and we all rode gaily over his crop. We succeeded in cutting the fox off from the mountains and ran into him actually in the open. This was one of the best runs I ever had, and the old farmer still talks of it when I see him.

My husband loved hunting as much as I did and used to hunt quite a lot with Colonel Dulany and Mr. Dick Dulany of Upperville. It was at Grafton, then known as No. 6, that the International Hound Trials were arranged. Mr. Harry Worcester Smith, M.F.H. of his pack of American foxhounds, and Mr. Henry Higginson, M.F.H. of his pack of English foxhounds, agreed to hunt their packs alternate days in the "Goose Creek" country and around Upperville, until the judges could decide which was the better pack.

My husband, Allen Potts, was made Clerk of the Match and had to hunt with the hounds every day. To mount him properly was a large order as he rode at about 200 pounds. However I got two horses ready for him. I could not leave home myself at that time, which nearly broke my heart; but I sent *Bachelor* and *Benedict,* two of my best hunters up to the trials in great condition.

The trials are history. The American Hounds won although neither pack killed a fox. There were full accounts printed each day of the runs. On one occasion when the whole hunt was stopped by a water gate across "Goose Creek," Allen jumped the water gate out of deep water—being the only one to get to the hounds. He was on my horse *Bachelor* who afterwards won the Deep Run Hunt Steeplechase in record time—running the race (a Point-to-Point of almost five miles over thirty-six jumps) in 11 min. 40 sec. with 180 pounds on his back, ridden by Dr. G. Harrison of Berryville, Va.

In those days before the World War, foxhunting was a great sport. Everyone was courteous to everyone else and good sport was the first thought of all. There was no wire and when the hounds were running, you crossed the country as best you could—if anyone got into trouble there was always someone to offer help. *The only thing was not to ride on the hounds.* It took a good horse and good jumper to follow the hounds then, as the distances were great and the fences timber. I have often gone out at four o'clock on a winter morning and taken hounds over the road ten or fifteen miles, then hunted and brought them back at night.

It has always been the fashion to say that English hounds are no good in this country—but my experience was the English hounds bred in this country are the best of all. On one occasion, at Christmas, we were having a combined hunt, and everyone was to bring hounds. When we finally got together that morning (near Barboursville, Va.) there were about *100 hounds* of every sort and size. And riders—hundreds of them, riding work horses, mules and ponies; also hundreds on foot! It was a great sight. Every hound shrieked in a different key and dragged on his rope—nearly all the hounds were led to the meet.

The crowd looked with interest at my three couples of hounds, who were around my horse with my two whips keeping them there. I heard people say, "You won't see them big, fat hounds no more today. They won't even see which way our hounds go." Well the word was given and the hounds were cast. It was stupendous!! Such shouts and yells and plunging horses and literally screaming hounds!! It was a great sight.

After about an hour the hounds settled down and about twenty (my three couple among them) really started a fox. He carried us many miles in a straight line and then doubled back to almost the point where we found him. By this time two of my hounds, *Garner* and *Despot,* were almost snapping at his brush, and they ran him to earth in a deep hole in the side of the mountain. My six hounds and four others were all that were left of the noble one hundred!!

I wanted to call it a day but the men who had followed wanted to dig him out—and as it was not my hunt and I was only a guest, I could say nothing. A pick and shovel were brought from a house close by and they started digging the fox out. *Garner* and *Despot* had other ideas—and before I could stop them they went into the hole and brought the digger out by the seat of his britches, much to his astonishment! I had to couple my hounds during the digging. When they finally reached the fox, he bit the men and made a break through horses and hounds (all the hounds were being held); but they were soon after him and picked him up in a few moments. I got the brush which hung on the kennel wall for years. The high light of the hunt was when one of the country men said to me, "The way them big, fat hounds could run!!"

The Castle Hill Hounds hunted regularly until the World War. Then all my "boys" (as I called them) offered their services to their country and I was left almost alone. My husband went overseas, as did all the men who had ridden with me. The hunting field is a great place to make real men—the foxhunters were among the very first to go to the aid of America and they made a splendid record.

Just before the War (in 1913) I went abroad for the first time. Allen asked me where I wanted to go, and I told him "to hunt with every big pack in Leicestershire and then to Venice." He said that was a big order but that we would try it. We reached England the end of October and stopped at Melton Mowbray, where we engaged hunters. My first experience was with the Cottesmore, Lord Lonsdale and General Brocklehurst, Joint Masters. They were cubbing, so we had to get out very early and go down to get our horses. I found my saddle on a beautiful chestnut mare (with a wild eye) and Allen's on a monstrous, ugly, lop-eared brown horse, fired all around. We had been told that the jobber was sending the best lady's hunter in England. By the time we got to the meet both the mare and I were in a lather.

I saw what I consider a wonderful thing at this first meet. The huntsman had out thirty couple of hounds and the whips were all around the covert except on one side. Rides were cut through the covert, and we stood at one end so that we could see what happened. *At least ten foxes crossed and recrossed that ride*—the hounds coming up and crossing their trails without a sound. At last the Huntsman galloped up and said, "Madam, have you seen the hunted fox?" In a few moments a fox crossed the ride—his mouth open and his brush dragging. *There was the hunted fox!* I was afraid to say a word. The pack came down the trail of this hunted fox; they stopped—and turned as one hound and boiled into the covert where they chopped the fox. I have never understood how that whole pack of hounds was kept on *one fox* with dozens on foot. It was wonderful.

But to get back to the hunt itself—my chestnut mare was by now almost pure white and had dug a large hole. My gloves were soaked with sweat and my reins slippery as grease. Allen was sitting, calmly smoking, on his large brown horse. At this moment I heard the horn and a faint "gone away" from the first Whip on the far side of the covert. With no word from me my chestnut mare leaped into action and swept around the covert and after the vanishing pack. The next twenty minutes was something to remember—but never to do again. I was carried at racing pace over huge places, through branches of trees, over ditches with guard rails, a hedge in the center and ditches on either side. It was impossible to stop the mare, but the pace finally held her; when the hounds ran into the fox and picked him up in the open field, I was there—but the mare was ready to stop. They gave me the brush, but everyone looked at me so queerly that I asked what was wrong. I was told that the mare was a great jumper but that no one had ever been able to hunt her—that they were surprised to see me on her—that I was lucky to be alive.

That hunt made many friends for me in England. English people are wonderful when they think that you really love sport. It turned out that Allen's big ugly horse was the great lady's hunter and that having heard that Allen was a fine rider and a strong man, the Jobber had sent the chestnut mare hoping that he could hold her!! Well, I had a wonderful time in England. I hunted with the Quorn, Pytchley, Warwick, Cottesmore, Mr. Fernie's Hounds and Belvoir. They found that I was an M.F.H. and every Hunt had the hounds "on the flags" for me. It is a great memory, for I am told that England is not the same now.

I have not hunted much since the War—I gave up the pack then—but I see a difference in the hunting and in the field. I send my hunters to hunt and watch them, but everyone motors now and the horses go in vans. The long hacks together and the long talks on sport and hunting are no longer

Mrs. Allen Potts, M.F.H. on her famous *Bachelor*, and her husband on *Brunette*.

indulged in. *Everyone seems in such a hurry*—as if they were anxious to get the hunting over and get back to the club house. The country is full of wire, and small panels are put in the fences so that it is impossible to ride your own line any more. I do not know very much about the actual condition of the hunting of today, but it seems to me that the warm personal interest and kindly words are missing, and the open house and warm welcome by the Master of the lovers of foxhunting are not as I remember them.

Notes

1. In author's possession.
2. At that time—by right of reestablishment.
3. Onetime Master of the Charlottesville Hunt—later, of the Albemarle County Hunt.

THIRTY-TWO

CUBHUNTING: 1935–1936

J. Stanley Reeve

If it is true, as some sporting sage once wrote—"Allah does not account to a man the years spent in the chase," then all is well. However, some of us have spent, or squandered, if you insist on it that way, a goodly number of our years in one form or another of the chase, and the number of bald heads, grey hairs, wrinkles, etc., one sees in the hunting field, don't altogether coincide with the old adage.—But, be all that as it may, another hunting season has rolled around, and let Allah be praised, that most of one's old friends are still with us, smiling as of yore, even if they have left their downy cots and connubial beds long before the first faint rays of an August sun have illumined the summer sky.

Cubs will be cubs, and as such must be scattered, be it in our own much beloved Chester County or the prickly gorse coverts of merrie England.

My first acquaintance with the dawn of an August day this season was on the sixteenth, under most delightful conditions, in the charming Tenth Century Stinsford House of my old friend, Alex Higginson, near Dorchester, England, when his valet knocked on our bedroom door, came in, and closing the window, said "It's four thirty, Sir, and a fine hunting morning. Tea and eggs in the library in half an hour, Sir." That was that, and another milestone in one's hunting career was passing.

Having motored from London the previous day with my good wife, after a couple of months of Europe with our family, visiting such places as Naples, Rome, Venice and its Lido, beautiful Lake Como, Zermatt and the Matterhorn, Paris, etc., it seemed quite like getting home, to once again be in the midst of an atmosphere of horse and hound, with such delightful companions as the Higginsons, Julian Chamberlain and Mrs. Valentine.

It's quite beyond my feeble efforts to adequately describe the old world charm of Stinsford House. Their Majesties King George and Queen Mary were this Summer celebrating the Silver Jubilee of their most gracious reign, while Stinsford House, with its beautiful walled gardens, which are under Mrs. Higginson's special care, is quietly celebrating its thousandth birthday, so while dressing that morning one could not help but wonder how many hundreds of sportsmen had been awakened in that same old high-ceilinged room, that same way, in years gone by, before and since the days when old James John Farquharson, of Langton, near Blandford, Dorset, hunted the whole of that lovely country at his own expense for fifty years, more than a century ago.

Stinsford House not only has atmosphere, but something else, and besides being a fitting abode for such a gallant gentleman as its present master, one feels a great sense of antiquity on entering its long oak paneled hall, hung with many of Julian Chamberlain's masterpieces and various trophies of the chase.

The tea and the eggs and the Master were already in the library when we arrived, so also was cold grouse shot in Scotland on the twelfth, and most delicious jam; and twenty minutes later we were rolling through the park gates in a Ford car on our way to meet hounds at Nether Cerne.

There was something pretty nice about all this. It may not sound so good, but it was. Personally, I was thrilled to the core, and, as old as I am, and as old as I hope to grow, I am sure I shall always be thrilled when going to a meet on a fine hunting morning. It must be in the blood.

The sun was just coming up in a huge red ball as we arrived at Nether Cerne Rough Corner, and as the car was being parked by the roadside the

The Cerne Giant

pack appeared over the hill. Eighteen and a half couples, dogs and bitches, locally known as the big pack, were having their turn this warm August morning. Dorset was dry as the proverbial bone, no rain for over six weeks and with great seams and cracks in the stubble fields, but, dry or wet, these good Cattistock hounds found a fox almost at once in some large patches of gorse on a steep hill overlooking the neighboring South Dorset country where the nude figure of the celebrated Cerne Giant, cut in the chalk of an adjoining hillside, rather distracts the visitor's attention from the work of hounds. No one seems to know who cut this colossal figure in the Dorset soil or for how many centuries it has been there, but tradition says that in the olden times, if the childless wives of the yeomen farmers desirous of sons and daughters would sleep at night in the trench forming part of the Giant's figure, their desires for offspring would be fulfilled. At any rate, the figure is three hundred feet high, and hounds, in crossing the hill, often run over the Giant.

Hounds didn't cross the Giant this morning, but the fox they found was no cub and straightened away for parts unknown to me, and hounds were stopped and put back into covert where they found several cubs and ran around the immediate neighborhood in a typical cubhunting fashion for over an hour, or until that particular covert was so foiled they could not do much more with it. Black Hill Withybed, just below us, was the next try and also produced cubs at once, hounds screaming to their line and rolling one over in about ten minutes of very nice work. The brush to Mrs. Reeve, then back at Stinsford House for a bath, a change of raiment and a snooze in the sun on the croquet lawn before luncheon.

At two o'clock that afternoon we left the hospitable Higginsons', as we were due at the Royal Clarence in Exeter at five, to meet our children who were coming down from London by train in order to hunt the next day with the Cheriton Otter Hounds. It was a lovely, leisurely journey from Dorchester to Exeter, across hill and dale through the country hunted by the Cattistock and East Devon packs. The children arrived in due time. We visited the Cathedral, had a chat with the gracious Bishop, dined and went early to bed, after making sure from the hall porter that our chauffeur knew the road to Torrington, where the Otter Hounds were to meet in the morning.

The Royal Clarence may have a royal suite tucked away among its long passageways and halls; if so, and wherever it may be, my family did not occupy it; probably the less said about our accommodations the better! However, we survived the night and eventually dawn arrived; August 17th breaking fine and clear.

It was market day, or something of the sort, in Exeter, and the city was crowded with people and all kinds of conveyances from donkey carts to wheelbarrows, as our big Daimler car nosed its way through the throng, and turning right-handed off the main street we were soon in the country once more, spinning along between high hedges and banks towards Torrington. Torrington may be historic and all that (it looks old enough at any rate) but to me it is famous as the birthplace of Will Leverton, our Huntsman at Radnor for many, many years, and I was only sorry I had not the time to make myself known to his family.

After about an hour we came to an old stone mill by a bridge and a quaint house, and a quick glance at the map told one it was the River Torridge, so putting two and two together we decided to stop and await developments. Pretty soon another car stopped and a genial soul leaned out and asked if this was where hounds were meeting, and quite before one could answer, the hound van arrived, so all was well.

It had been seven years since we had a day with the Cheriton Otter Hounds, but there were several familiar faces among those at the meet and all were most affable, indeed, and after collecting the cap, hounds moved off up the river. This Cheriton pack is a versatile lot of hounds as they hunt otter during the Summer and fox all Winter, but just what name they go by when hunting the fox, I failed to learn.

After walking up the river bank about half a mile a hound spoke; someone holloaed a bit further on, then there was a great burst of hound music and the hunt was on. Two otters were in front of hounds, the whole pack in the river swimming for dear life and simply screaming for all they were worth. It was a glorious sight, indeed, and well worth our long motor trip. Another view halloa from the opposite direction, then a short check; then another burst of music and a slow hunt up the river to the roots of an old tree where hounds were apparently marking their otter to ground; but after a bit of digging and much snarling the otter was viewed swimming downstream again. The pack was put on, hunted beautifully up and downstream for two hours and then ran quite out of scent, and as it was about lunch time, the Master, Mrs. Beaumont, said they would have a bite to eat and resume operations at two o'clock. A bite to eat sounded good to us, but the wherewithal to bite was in our car somewhere along the highway, about a mile up a long and terribly steep hill, and by the time we climbed the hill, found the car, ate our bite and returned, hounds were running again as strong as ever.

In the good old predepression days one was sometimes fortunate enough to drink champagne served from magnums, but champagne and nothing else did I ever see in magnums before. However, while climbing the aforementioned precipitous hill, endeavoring to find our meager luncheon, I was joined by the jovial soul who had arrived at the meet at the same time we did. He asked if we had plenty of lunch, and when informed that we had only a box of Huntley & Palmer's biscuits and a cake of chocolate, said he would give us some of his beer, whereupon we joined forces, found our wayward motors and sat down on the roadside to rest and eat. From under the seat of his car he produced the biggest bottle of beer one ever saw. It wasn't quite as big as those huge affairs in Italy that are surrounded by a birdcage of bamboo, but very nearly. Our friend must have had an awful thirst when he bought that big bottle, but it was fortunate for us, at any rate. He helped eat our biscuits and we helped drink his beer, and one hates to think what would have happened to him had we not come to his rescue. It was good beer, too; six of us drank all we could and there was about a quart left, which our friend said he would finish on his way home. The cry of hounds stopped the beer party; we hurried downhill to the river, caught up with the hunt and ran up and downstream for another hour and then decided to call it a day. On thanking the Master for a most pleasant hunt, she said, "Oh, don't go home now, we will kill this otter after a while, and anyhow, I never hunt after eight o'clock at night." However, as Exeter and the Royal Clarence were forty miles away and we were soaked to our middles, we apologized and climbed the long hill once more to our waiting car. Our wet clothes now began to feel cold and clammy, so on going through Torrington we stopped at a shop for dry woolies and bought the most wonderful long, very long and thick, grey stockings for two and six a pair. They were pretty snug, and I eventually arrived at the Royal Clarence in my stocking feet, much to the embarrassment of my daughters and the amusement of the assembled multitude.

THIRTY-THREE

A FIELD OF FIVE HUNDRED

J. Blan van Urk

The Bayard Taylor Memorial Hunt, the last one—the 144th Anniversary of the original—having been held on March 9, 1940. This was an amazing event, and, as far as my knowledge goes, established a record for the largest Field in the history of American foxhunting. Approximately 546 hunters met on Mr. Pierre S. du Pont's estate, Longwood Gardens, with about 140 hounds from seven neighborhood packs and at least 8,000 spectators.

The seven Hunts represented were: the Rose Tree Foxhunting Club, the West Chester Hunt, Foxcatcher Hounds, Mr. Stewart's Cheshire Foxhounds, Mr. Jeffords' Hounds, the Vicmead Hunt and Mr. Newbold Ely's Hounds. Mr. W. Plunket Stewart[1] was the Grand Master of Foxhounds and his Cheshire Huntsman, Charlie Smith, headed the six other Huntsmen.

When hounds moved off to draw Webb's woods, 357 of those who had mounted to attend the meet continued ready and eager for the chase. A forty-minute run ensued with many broken fences and quite a number of falls—expected, and resulting. But two amazing feats can be reported; first, for a Field of such size it was extraordinarily well mannered; and second, the combined pack of American, English and Welsh hounds owned the original line of their fox despite the crossing of two others during the chase. This must have made each Master and Huntsman proud of his particular hounds. Both foxhunters and hounds were apparently on their best behavior—and it was a wonderful thing! The first and most interesting fox managed to save his skin by scaling a chicken-house roof and taking refuge inside through a window on the far side. Mr. Mechior E. Becker, well-known character and foxhunter[2] of Kennett Square, caught him in time to prevent an avalanche of hounds from tearing the building apart—as well as the fox.

There were two who were active in the saddle on this, the 1940 Memorial, who had also ridden on the occasion of the Bayard Taylor Centennial Hunt in 1896. These were Mrs. Alexander Sellers and Mr. Moses Worth.

I made a special pilgrimage to Kennett Square for this event, in spite of the fact that no horse was available for a hundred miles around. The strange sensation of being grounded while the cry of hounds echoed across the fields was an experience which would have been terribly depressing to me had I not been consoled by Bill Swain, Managing Editor of the *Kennett News and Advertiser,* and Janet Owen, capable columnist of the *New York Herald Tribune's* "Saddle, Bridle and Spur." When the subjective ceased getting the better of the objective, I was aware that I had witnessed, even as a foot-slogger, an event of tremendous historical significance, as aptly stated in an editorial titled "Foxhunters' Day":

> Such a meeting as this does two things. First it gives farmers an opportunity to view a great and entertaining spectacle of the chase and partake in it as fellow sportsmen. Thousands of people viewed the Bayard Taylor Memorial Hunt. In this great day they saw an epic of the chase portrayed as it has been told often in song and story but seldom if ever in such proportions. The most hardened sceptic who came to criticize could not fail to have been impressed by the enthusiasm, the beauty, the strength of the sport as seen at "Longwood." Eight to ten thousand people were enabled to see a really great sporting show. They left the scene impressed with the fine spirit which was everywhere prevalent. They were given a good time and as a result, they went away with a little better knowledge of what foxhunting represents in America today. This country is such a melting pot, that the passion and understanding for the chase which is bred in the blood of all Englishmen has had many a diffusion in America. There is a tremendous task of education that lies ahead of those who wish to perpetuate foxhunting before the average American even begins to understand what Foxhunting means, or even considers it from a tolerant view. The Bayard Taylor Memorial Hunt was a great stride forward in this education process.
>
> Secondly, due to the foresight of the sportsmen in charge of this great affair, many gentlemen in positions of public responsibility were at the meet. Welcome and greetings were made to the State Senator from Pennsylvania, to the Governor of Pennsylvania, to the Lieutenant Governor, to the Secretary of Agriculture, to the Secretary of Welfare, to the Republican State chairman and it is interesting to note the remark of the Lieutenant Governor, the Hon. Samuel S. Lewis on viewing the Bayard Taylor Memorial Hunt. "I never saw anything like this in my life," said he. "If any adverse legislation appears in Harrisburg, the governor will know how to decide it."[3]

Notes

1. President of the M.F H. Association of America (1939–).
2. M.F.H. of his own pack.
3. *The Chronicle,* March 15, 1940; published at Middleburg, Va., by Stacy B. Lloyd, Jr.

SOURCES AND CREDITS

"Dedication"
Joseph B. Thomas, M.F.H.
From *Hounds and Hunting Through the Ages* (1928)

"No Fleas on This Fox"
J. Blan van Urk
From *The Story of American Foxhunting, Volume I* (1940), pp. 5, 6

"The Hunters"
Samuel J. Henry
From *Foxhunting Is Different* (1938), pp. 111–116

"The Hounds"
Frederick Watson
From *Hunting Pie* (1931), p. 34

"Some Things Are Too Serious for Joking"
J. Blan van Urk
From *The Story of American Foxhunting, Volume II* (1941), pp. 18–21

"The Irish Hounds: Mountain and Muse"
J. Blan van Urk
From *The Story of American Foxhunting, Volume I* (1940), pp. 133–135

"Attributes of a Good Hound"
Joseph B. Thomas, M.F.H.
From *Hounds and Hunting Through the Ages* (1928), pp. 74–76

"Legend of the Hounds"
J. Blan van Urk
From *The Story of American Foxhunting, Volume II* (1941), pp. 392–396

"Martha Doyle"
Richard E. Danielson
From *Martha Doyle* (1938)

"The Epping Hunt"
Thomas Hood, Esq.
From *The Epping Hunt* (1930, originally published 1829)

"Mr. Carteret and his Fellow Americans Abroad"
David Gray
From *Mr. Carteret* (1929)

"Young Entry"
Gordon Grand
From *Colonel Weatherford's Young Entry* (1935), pp. 2, 7, 10, 13, 30

"Ting-a-Ling"
David Gray
From *Gallops II* (1929)

"Philippa's Fox-Hunt"
Somerville and Ross
From *Some Experiences of an Irish R.M.* (1927, originally published 1899)

"A Nineteenth-Century Miracle"
Somerville and Ross
From *All on the Irish Shore* (1927, originally published 1903)

"The Brooke Hound"
Gordon Grand
From *The Southborough Fox* (1939), p. 51

"The Hunting If"
Angela Shortt (1932)

"Trying"
Gordon Grand
From *Colonel Weatherford and His Friends* (1933)

"The Silver Horn"
Gordon Grand
From *The Silver Horn* (1932)

"Colonel Weatherford's Brush"
Gordon Grand
From *The Silver Horn* (1932)

"Old Man"
Gordon Grand
From *Old Man and Other Colonel Weatherford Stories* (1934)

"And the Second Is Like Unto It"
Gordon Grand
From *Old Man and Other Colonel Weatherford Stories* (1934)

"Loss of a Friend"
Tad Shepperd
From *Pack and Paddock* (1938)

"The First M.F.H.: Robert Brooke, 1650," (pp. 28, 29)
"Prominent Foxhunters of an Early Day," (pp. 55–63)
"The Future Chief Justice's Opinion," (pp. 110, 111)
"The First Organized Hunt: The Gloucester Foxhunting Club," (pp. 66, 67)
J. Blan van Urk
From *The Story of American Foxhunting, Volume I* (1940)

"Buffalo Bill and the West Chester Hunt," (pp. 79, 80)
"The First Foxhound Studbook," (pp. 60–64)
"General Roger D. Williams, M.F.H. and the Iroquois Hunt and Polo Club,"
(pp. 279–285)
J. Blan van Urk
From *The Story of American Foxhunting, Volume II* (1941)

"The First Lady M.F.H.: Mrs. Allen Potts"
J. Blan van Urk
From *The Story of American Foxhunting, Volume I* (1940), pp. 45–50

"Cubhunting: 1935–1936"
J. Stanley Reeve
From *Red Coats in Chester County* (1940), p. 93

"A Field of Five Hundred"
J. Blan van Urk
From *The Story of American Foxhunting, Volume I* (1940), pp. 113, 114